Tragedy and Af...
Euripides, Shakespeare

It has become commonplace to speak of the "death of tragedy" in recent literature and to link this demise to modern thought. Both these assumptions, Ekbert Faas argues, are misleading. Though many modern writers refute the tragic as a limiting, if not inappropriate vision of life, such rejection is not new. It can be traced throughout literary history to the very origins of the genre.

Only a few decades after tragedy was born, Euripides parodied and repudiated it through structure and characterization in such plays as *Heracles* and *Orestes*, here termed anti-tragedies. Shakespeare used similar strategies in *Troilus*, *Hamlet*, and *Lear*. In the late plays, he also evolved a new genre, here called post-tragedy, in which the tragic sense of something conclusively accomplished through suffering is replaced by a more open-ended and cyclical view of life. Another instance of post-tragedy is found in Goethe. Dissatisfied with the tragic ending of *Faust I*, the German poet drew on Kālidāsa's *Sacontalá* as a model for his expanding vision of life beyond the tragic presented in *Faust II*. Goethe's Sanskrit source here also reminds us that tragedy, while central to Western culture, is more or less unknown elsewhere.

In our tradition, tragedy is far from defunct even today, as Faas shows in his final chapter. Despite the recent manifestations of anti- and post-tragedy in the theatre of cruelty and of the absurd, it survives in such psychoanalytic variants as Pirandello's *Six Characters* and Arthur Miller's *Death of a Salesman*.

EKBERT FAAS is Professor of Humanities and English at York University in Toronto.

Tragedy and After:
Euripides, Shakespeare, Goethe

EKBERT FAAS

McGill-Queen's University Press
Kingston and Montreal

©McGill-Queen's University Press 1984
ISBN 0-7735-0416-8 (cloth)
ISBN 0-7735-0605-5 (pbk)
Legal deposit 2nd quarter 1984
Bibliothèque nationale du Québec
Printed in Canada
Reprinted 1986
First paperback edition 1986

Canadian Cataloguing in publication Data

Faas, Ekbert, 1938–
Tragedy and after
Includes bibliographical references and index.
ISBN 0-7735-0416-8 (cloth)
ISBN 0-7735-0605-5 (pbk)
1. Tragedy – History and criticism. 2. Drama –
History and criticism. I. Title.
PN1892.F32 1984   801'.952   c83-0099165-4

Parts of two chapters, "Goethe's Transcendence of Tragedy" and "Hamlet, or the
Slave-Moralist Turned Ascetic Priest," have appeared in a slightly different form in,
respectively, *Comparative Literature* 31, no 4 (fall 1979), and *Process Studies* 13, no 1
(spring 1983). The author wishes to thank the editors of these journals for permission
to reprint this material.

This book has been published with the help of a grant from the Canadian
Federation for the Humanities, using funds provided by the Social Sciences and
Humanities Research Council of Canada.

For my mother

Contents

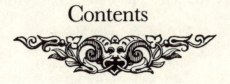

Tragedy and Psychology 176

Conclusion 189

Tragedy and After

Introduction

"THE DISINTEGRATION OF Form in the Arts." "The Death of Tragedy." In our apocalyptic age we seem to crave visions of surcease in all areas of traditional value. Deprived of real hope by the threat of nuclear war, we at least like to glory in the unprecedented specialness of our situation. We have seen it all, reached the apogee of hubris in our power to annihilate the human race, and have learned to question all the values which have brought us this far. It's as if we were lost in a vortex of somehow heroic negation which scholars hasten to honour with the appropriate pedigrees. As far as tragedy is concerned, there have been at least two major attempts of this kind.

One, by George Steiner, links the demise of the genre to the death of God. "In the nineteenth century," we read in *The Death of Tragedy*, "Laplace announced that God was a hypothesis of which the rational mind had no further need; God took the great astronomer at his word. But tragedy is that form of art which requires the intolerable burden of God's presence. It is now dead because His shadow no longer falls upon us as it fell on Agamemnon or Macbeth or Athalie."[1] Morse Peckham's *Beyond the Tragic Vision*, another study along the same lines, associates the death of tragedy with the kind of thought first advocated by Friedrich Nietzsche. Peckham admits that this philosopher spoke of a rebirth rather than the death of tragedy in his time. But Nietzsche, in the critic's view, used the term "in such a profoundly new way that no connection between the old meaning and the new survives... We are aware of this when we see our critics fumble with the best of modern drama, Shaw's *Heartbreak House*, for example, Samuel Beckett, or Ionesco. In truth, no truly twentieth-century man can write a tragedy."[2]

Such attempts to explain the death of tragedy according to some evolutionary model *à rebours* are not without their proselytizing zeal and naïveté. What is more, they represent a distortingly one-sided account of the actual facts and issues. Is tragedy really as extinct as these studies make us believe? What precisely, if anything, suffered extinction when tragedy died – merely a literary genre or an entire vision of life? Finally, is modern man really the first to witness such a decease? The whole matter, it would seem, needs reconsidering from a new angle.

Argument and Approach

First, how final and universal is the alleged death of tragedy in our time? Scarcely anyone would deny that it is a fact for many authors. Ionesco, for instance, denies the "sometimes incomprehensible but objective laws"[3] governing the universe which tragedy, for all its portrayals of human suffering, seems to uphold. Roland Barthes, for similar reasons, denounces the tragic as a "falsification of life."[4] For tragedy, in Barthes's view, "is nothing but a means to absorb the human dilemma, to subsume and hence to justify it under some form of necessity, wisdom or purification." On the other hand, there are authors like Arthur Miller, who, in "Tragedy and the Common Man," reaffirms some of tragedy's oldest values – "the indestructible will of man to achieve this destiny"[5] – for the modern theatre. Who, then, in some twenty or thirty years from now, will be remembered as the more "truly twentieth-century man," Ionesco or Arthur Miller? Whatever the answer, we already know that *Death of a Salesman* has affected our modern sensibility as much as any play by Ionesco or even Beckett.

Second, there is the question of perspective. Before talking about tragedy, let alone its demise, we should realize that the genre so designated may, after all, be a specifically Western phenomenon. To all evidence, there are no tragedies in classical Indian, Chinese, or Japanese literature. Contrary to the quietly universalist assumptions of many critics, the tragic seems to be a strictly Western phenomenon. Seen from a global perspective, it is at once more than a mere literary genre and less than a world-view of universal validity. In dealing with man's most urgent problems, death and suffering, it brings to a focus the teleological bias of mainstream Western thought. For tragedy, as Barthes recognizes, is Western man's most daring effort to justify the human dilemma under the guise of some metaphysical scheme.

Without doubt our understanding of tragedy and particularly of its alleged demise can only benefit if we look at the genre from this multicultural perspective. What if the nihilism we tend to associate with the death of tragedy or of God turns out to be what Hindus or Buddhists have been taking for granted ever since a time before the first tragedies were written? We still might not want to exchange our disillusionment for their fatalism, but an attempt to understand the latter might temper our all-too-fashionable despair.

Third and last, there is the question of history. Were the writers of our time really the first whom the tragic understanding of suffering struck as limited or erroneous? The answer offered by the following study is that at least three major playwrights of the past – Euripides, Shakespeare, and Goethe – came to much the same conclusion. If we want to date such matters, then the first death of tragedy, as far as we know, occurred in the works of Euripides less than half a century after the genre was created by Aeschylus. It happened again in the dramas of Shakespeare as well as in the second part of Goethe's *Faust*. And undoubtedly there are other authors – Büchner and Strindberg are only two of the more obvious – who fit into the same context. But my attempt in the following pages is to give examples of the repeated "death" of tragedy throughout Western literature, not to write a complete history of such events.

In turn, "repudiation" rather than "death" is clearly the more appropriate term for describing these occurrences. Wherever we observe them, as in Ionesco's *The Chairs*, Shakespeare's *King Lear*, or Euripides' *Orestes*, they seem to result from carefully worked out dramaturgical strategies. What is more, neither Shakespeare nor Goethe remained content with such "anti-tragic" denials. Works like *The Winter's Tale* and *Faust II* show, in one way or another, how the playwrights reached out beyond the tragic towards an independent, "post-tragic" understanding of human suffering. Not surprisingly, non-Western sources reinforced these endeavours (as in the case of Kālidāsa's *Sacontalá* and Goethe's *Faust*) as soon as such works became available towards the end of the eighteenth century. On the other hand, Shakespeare's romances, though often compared with Sanskrit drama, show how the same impulse could realize itself without such outside influence.

All this calls for some terminological clarification, however tentative. For reasons to be spelled out in more detail later, "tragic" as used in the following pages denotes a purposive rather than a pessimistic vision of life. Even suffering and death, in the tragic perspective, are shown somehow to serve a meaningful purpose. In some cases, as in Aeschylus's *Oresteia*, they are seen to serve the progress of civilization directly. In others, as in Sophocles' *Ajax*, they are shown to help man achieve his ultimate dignity. In turn, human suffering can be presented in ways that, at the least, exert a beneficent influence on the spectator or reader. The fear and pity aroused when we first witness the chaotic immediacy of suffering may be purged through hindsight. For as long as the play's plot is properly unified, we may learn to understand in its proper context of cause and effect what at first surprised us. As a result we may become more dispassionate when confronted with similar matters in real life. Finally, in Judaeo-Christian tragedy human suffering is shown to test the righteous, as in the Book of Job, to punish the wicked, as in Marlowe's *Doctor Faustus*, or, more generally, to help unfold the dark paths of divine providence.

Most central, then, to all these cases, at least for the purpose of this study, is the assumption that suffering and death, however terrifying, have a function in an ultimately purposive scheme of things. Only detailed interpretation can show which specific dramaturgical techniques communicate this tragic vision in each particular play – quite apart from the fact that drama is by no means the only art form capable of doing so.

The same applies to works here designated as "anti-" or "post-tragic." The dramaturgical strategies found in so-called anti-tragedies, for instance, are multiple and various. Anti-tragedy tends to misguide spectators, where tragedy guides them towards a recognition of things set in their teleological order. It confuses and shocks, where its counterpart provides us with cathartic or otherwise meaningful effects. It tends to portray life in its situational and psychological singularity rather than to subsume it under all-encompassing schemes, packaged in consistent plots. At the same time, specific anti-tragedies may share few of these or of the other dramaturgical strategies we shall discuss in the following pages. What they have in common, however, is a basic denial – or at least questioning – of the tragic vision of death and suffering as somehow meaningful in the general order of things.

The anti-tragic is thus close to what has come to be called the absurd, at least in Ionesco's sense of what is "devoid of purpose" and cut off from all "religious, metaphysical, and transcendental roots."[6] But there is good reason for using a neutral term like anti-tragic instead of one as heavily charged with other connotations as absurd. My intention is neither to make Euripides, Shakespeare, and Goethe our contemporaries nor, worse, to derive the theatre of the absurd from their influence. Thought-provoking as attempts to compare, say, *King Lear* with Beckett's *Endgame* or Chekhov's *The Seagull*[7] may be in general, they tend to break down in trying to establish similarities in detail. For what can be demonstrated as shared – the awareness, for instance, that the tragic is a falsification of life – will be differently expressed by each author and period. Edgar and the blind Gloucester in *King Lear* have little in common with Lucky and the blind Pozzo in *Waiting for Godot*, however hard we may try to find similarities. But Gloucester's "As flies to wanton boys, are we to th' gods, / They kill us for their sport" (IV.i) may well remind us of Godot in Beckett's play or of Apollo in Euripides' *Orestes*. For the affinity here stems not from an accidentally shared oddity of incident or characterization. Instead, it forms part of the way in which the two plays, though separated by many centuries, call into question the same tragic understanding of suffering, however diverse its Graeco-Roman or Judaeo-Christian variants.

What, finally, is the post-tragic, particularly as distinct from the anti-tragic vision of life? Here again we are primarily concerned with the authors' post-tragic attitude towards human suffering and only by extension with the dramaturgical techniques that help to communicate this vision. While post-tragedy has shed most traces of its origins, anti-tragedy either repudiates or questions the tragic vision of suffering as meaningful. Unlike post-tragedy, then, anti-tragedy still depends upon the traditions which it denies. The Old

Man in Ionesco's *The Chairs*, for instance, reduces to an absurdity an established element of tragedy known at least since Aeschylus's *pathei mathos*, or "Through suffering, learning" (*Agamemnon* 176–8)[8]: before jumping to his death in the sea, he claims to have "Suffered much, learned much."[9] The anti-tragic is simply the under-side of the tragic: it lives by its denials.

By contrast, post-tragedy affirms an independent vision. Here suffering is neither meaningful nor absurd in an ultimate metaphysical sense. It simply and unavoidably exists. Like the world in Robbe-Grillet's view, it is "ni signifiant, ni absurde. Il *est*, tout simplement."[10] In Shakespeare's romances, for instance, individuals either literally or metaphorically are often reborn to each other towards the end. But we are always reminded that such rebirth is simply towards another death. Similarly, the heroes in these plays may occasionally learn from their ordeals. Yet there is nothing to give such developments the sense of grandeur and finality we associate with tragedy. In turn, suffering and death are not shown to serve a teleological purpose in an historical or cosmic sense. Nor are they made to appear absurd. At best, the "decay of one life," as Shakespeare's contemporary Montaigne put it, "is the passage to a thousand other lives," or inversely, "*The birth, encrease, and augumentation of every thing, is the alteration and corruption of another.*"[11] Hence, post-tragedy moves in cycles, where tragedy progresses towards goals. Even where it builds upon tragic elements, as in *The Winter's Tale*, post-tragedy does not negate them as anti-tragedy does. Instead, it tends to transform and integrate them. The teleological thrust of Leontes' tragedy is caught up in the cyclical birth-death-rebirth symbolism of *The Winter's Tale* as a whole. The first, closed part, which at first seems to climax in the tragic wisdom Leontes has acquired through suffering, dissolves into the open-ended second part; and though the play comes to an end, its cyclical patterns point beyond it.

To be sure, anti- and post-tragedy, despite the radically different visions of life they project, tend to share several characteristics that defy or ignore specific aspects of tragedy that we may describe as Aristotelian. Central to that philosopher's concept of mimesis is the belief that the poet, unlike the historian, should present things not as they are but as they ought to be.[12] The poet, in other words, should in some way or other interpret, make sense of things. While tragedy, then, is basically explanatory, anti- and post-tragedy are exploratory. Instead of arranging events in a progressively conceived unity, with beginning, middle, and end, initial complication, climax, and resolution, they show that things are basically unpredictable, repetitive, unfathomable – in short, independent of human meaning. Their forms abound with loose ends, digressions, broken-backed structures, and fake solutions.

We find similar contrasts regarding character portrayal. As Aristotle sees the matter, men are first of all moral agents of either good or bad quality. Secondly, they are, or at least ought to be, consistent, even to the degree of being at least consistently inconsistent. In other words, the logical coherence to be observed in a plot, in which every event must be properly motivated, applies equally to the portrayal of character. Characterization in tragedy thus serves the same explanatory purpose as tragedy's vision of life in general. In the characters, just as in the incidents of the play, the right thing is "to endeavour always after the necessary or the probable; so that whenever such-and-such a personage says or does such-and-such a thing, it shall be the necessary or probable outcome of his character; and whenever this incident follows on that, it shall be either the necessary or the probable consequence of it."[13] From this vantage point, Aristotle finds fault with Euripides' portrayal of some of his characters precisely where such characterization is most typically anti- or post-tragic.

But why introduce two new terms, anti- and post-tragedy, where two old ones – "drama of the absurd" and "romance," for instance – might have been used to similar purpose? The answer is by no means found in a predilection for neologisms or terminological controversy. Instead, I tend to share the view of an old Chinese sage, Chuang Tzu, that words are a means for catching ideas the way we catch fish with a net: when we have caught the fish, let us throw away the net.[14] Readers who may be puzzled to see well-known classics like *King Lear* renamed anti-tragedies and Shakespeare's romances post-tragedies are welcome to treat the new terms in the spirit of Chuang Tzu's anecdote. My aim is not to impose a new terminological dogmatism but to throw fresh light on some of the classics of our literary heritage. On the other hand, no established terms such as romance and drama of the absurd, each with its multiple other connotations, would have served the present purpose. For my aim was not to argue that Goethe, like Shakespeare, wrote a romance, or Shakespeare and Euripides, like Beckett or Ionesco, dramas of the absurd, but to demonstrate the recurrent negation and / or transcendence of the tragic vision of human suffering.

The Tragic

According to Aristotle, the first to define the term, the tragic arouses not only horror but also pity. No situation, in the philosopher's view, strikes us as more horrifying and pitiful than murder or the like "done or meditated by brother on brother, by son on father, by mother on son, or son on mother."[15] The *Oresteia* is one of Aristotle's examples. Here Clytaemnestra, together with her lover Aegisthus, has murdered her husband Agamemnon upon his return from Troy. Now Apollo, god of Delphi, orders Orestes to kill his mother in retribution:

> He said that else I must myself pay penalty
> with my own life, and suffer much sad punishment. (*Libation Bearers* 276–7)

Orestes, despite some hesitation, fulfils Apollo's command.

There is a comparable situation in what T.S. Eliot called "the next greatest philosophical poem to the *Divine Comedy*."[16] The *Bhagavad Gītā*, centre-piece of India's national epic, the *Mahābhārata*, is by no means a tragedy. But the protagonist's situation at its beginning is as potentially tragic as that of Orestes. Arjuna, head of the army of the Pandavas, does not face an anonymous enemy. There, amidst the opponents he is about to kill in battle, he sees his own party's "fathers and grandfathers, brothers, sons, grandsons [and] friends." Overwhelmed with grief, he casts aside bow and arrows and staunchly refuses to fight. "I do not see how any good can come from killing my own kinsmen in this battle ... Alas, how strange it is that we are preparing ourselves to commit great sinful acts, driven by the desire to enjoy royal happiness. I would consider it better if the sons of Dhritarashtra killed me unarmed and unresisting, rather than fight with them." But here, too, there is a god who will persuade the hero to do otherwise. The command of Vishnu, supreme Hindu divinity, who has taken human shape as Arjuna's charioteer, is as unequivocal and insistent as Apollo's: Arise, fight, and kill.

The Supreme Personality of Godhead said: time I am, the Destroyer of the worlds, and I am come to engage all people. Except for you [the Pandavas], all soldiers on both sides here will be slain. Therefore, get up and prepare to fight.[17]

So Arjuna will finally kill his kindred, just as Orestes murders his mother and uncle. But the mere murder of relatives does not turn the *Bhagavad Gītā* into a tragedy.[18] Suffering alone, even if perpetrated in the most potentially tragic of situations, is not enough to warrant the designation. What does warrant it – and the *Oresteia* gives us one of the earliest examples – is the way in which such suffering is seen to be meaningful. In the *Bhagavad Gītā* there is no such meaningful context – only *samsara*, or the eternal rounds of suffering. Suffering is a mere fact of life and no progress will, in an ultimate sense, ever eliminate it or make it easier for us. It does not even ennoble us, make us wiser, or appear justified as some divine retribution or test.

Nor does the *Bhagavad Gītā* attribute the existence of suffering to the Devil or man's sinfulness. Vishnu himself takes the blame for it all when, in the celebrated eleventh chapter, he suddenly reveals himself as a cosmic monster "eating this entire universe" with his "blazing death-like faces and awful teeth."[19] For Vishnu, like most other Hindu divinities, is the creator and destroyer combined. What he tells Arjuna about suffering has little bearing on its possible origin, meaning, or justification. Since there is no theodicy, man's attitude towards suffering is all that matters. Vishnu's advice is not "Be good and you will prosper," "Try to resolve the problem by following some metaphysical scheme of progress," or "Withdraw yourself from action altogether." Action and, finally, even murder are inescapable facts of life. Whatever suffering we may have to inflict or undergo should therefore be approached with the same self-detachment. "Kill with respect for the victim." "Act without acting." "Detach yourself from the fruits of your actions in pursuing them." This is ultimately a world of paradoxes, and the only access to it is one of elaborate psychophysiological rituals no Westerner perhaps has ever penetrated or accurately described. But whatever it is, we would be wrong to label it tragic.

Turning to the *Oresteia*, we find an almost diametrically opposed attitude towards suffering. Aeschylus seems to have little interest in man's subjective response to suffering or in psychology generally. What concerns him are all-encompassing questions such as those that the Hebrew prophets, at roughly the same time, tried to resolve in Genesis or Job. Here as in the Old Testament we witness the beginnings of Western man's rage for universal order and meaning, which has lasted to this very day. "Let Force, and Right, / and Zeus almighty, third with them, be on your side" (*Libation Bearers* 244–5), exclaims Electra when Orestes is about to kill his mother. "Where / is the end?" asks the Chorus, recalling after the deed has been done the endless "chain of bloodlettings" (933) that led to this murder. "Where shall the fury of fate / be stilled to sleep, be done with?" (1074–6). The playwright's answer, to be studied in the following pages, unfolds a dialectic of progress, achieved through the very suffering we have witnessed.

Aeschylus's solution to the problem of human suffering, of course, is only one of many that have been found within the wider radius of the tragic. Critics, for good reason, have stressed the parallels between, for example, *Prometheus Bound* and the Book of Job, some of them concluding that the Old Testament prophet may even have drawn his inspiration from the Greek playwright.[20] However much they may differ, the two texts share a similar attitude towards the suffering undergone by the protagonist. Prometheus's agonies benefit mankind, while Job's benefit the sufferer himself. For the test imposed upon Job by God's wager with Satan gives him the chance to prove himself righteous. The negative counterpart of this divine justice is shown in most of the *de casibus* tradition[21] or in a tragedy like Marlowe's *Doctor Faustus*, the damnation of whose protagonist, though horrifying and pitiful, can nevertheless be seen as justified and "meaningful" within the general Christian framework. How then shall we define – or, rather, circumscribe – the tragic?

All of us should be entitled to our own tragic sense of life. But there is, or ought to be, a difference between subjective apprehensions of the tragic and what the term can be said to reflect in a historical sense from our present-day perspective. Any such reassessment, however, must start with an important caveat. Among the questions pondered by philosophers and theologians throughout world history, none may be more crucial than the question raised by human suffering. But it is in our Western – that is, Graeco-Roman-Judaeo-Christian – culture alone that most of the answers tend to converge upon a central concept: the tragic.

Sanskrit and Nō drama, for instance, completely lack a comparable concept, and there is little in the actual plays that might call for it.[22] But more importantly, the Buddhist and Hindu response to suffering differs from the traditionally Western one to the degree of calling for a term more in opposition to than in agreement with the tragic. Whereas Western civilizations tend to contain the fact of human suffering within their all-encompassing moral or purposive schemes, Hindu and Buddhist cultures view it as an unalterable condition of life. They simply leave it to the individual to face up to suffering by means of subtle psychophysiological techniques. There is nothing here to allow for a tragic – that is, meaningful, ennobling, teleological, or enlightening – presentation of suffering. Open or tacit assumptions of most critics to the contrary, tragedy is not a universal phenomenon. To pretend that it is, particularly at a time when most of world drama can be read in translation, is at best an ill-mannered habit from the days of Western cultural imperialism.

What has been said implies a second point. We know that the tragic is open to multiple definitions.[23] But most of the more recent ones tend to fall into two often diametrically opposed categories. One type of definition regards the tragic as negative, nihilistic; the other treats it as a medium which ultimately makes us realize that suffering, in one way or another, can be meaningful. I.A. Richards and Karl Jaspers remain two of our most prominent advocates of the former. Tragedy, as Richards defines it, "is only possible to a mind which is for the moment agnostic or Manichean. The least touch of any theology which has a compensating Heaven to offer the tragic hero is fatal."[24] Not surprisingly, critics of similar persuasion tend to conclude that Christian tragedy is a contradiction in terms. Karl Jaspers, in so concluding, ironically ends up including Sanskrit drama in the category of tragedy.

> The whole world seems a carrion-ground,
> A plain of corpses slain by Siva's servant, Time.
> The firmament at dusk seems red
> With blood of victims executed.

Such lines from *Kausika's Wrath* lead Jaspers to claim that the tragic mood "assumes the many shapes of so-called pessimism ... whether in Buddhism or in Christianity, in Schopenhauer or in Nietzsche, in the *Edda* or in the *Nibelungenlied*."[25]

It is typical of such radically negative definitions of the tragic that their adherents have to conclude that very few "real" tragedies, especially among the best-known contenders, can be said to exist. To I.A. Richards there is barely a handful of them, and all of these are Shakespearian. The rest, including the greater part of Greek drama, should be renamed "pseudo-tragedy."[26] It is characteristic also that negative definitions of the tragic are for the most part twentieth-century products. As such they probably reflect the general mood of a period in which the more traditional understanding of the concept, as found, for instance, in Aristotle and Hegel, has been questioned or refuted as a falsification of life. As its most obvious connotation is suffering, the word "tragic," by way of serving to express the critic's own modernistically disillusioned view of life, simply had to change its former connotation of "meaningful" into "meaningless."

Perhaps the most forceful protest against such negative definitions of the tragic comes, not surprisingly, from a major contemporary playwright. Arthur Miller's "Tragedy and the Common Man" of 1949 is well known, but its central comment on the genre warrants full quotation in this context. In numerous reviews and conversations, Miller had been struck by a "misconception of tragedy":

It is the idea that tragedy is of necessity allied to pessimism. Even the dictionary says nothing more about the word than that it means a story with a sad or unhappy ending. This impression is so firmly fixed that I almost hesitate to claim that in truth tragedy implies more optimism in its authors than does comedy, and that its final result ought to be the reinforcement of the onlooker's brightest opinions of the human animal. For, if it is true to say that in essence the tragic hero is intent upon claiming his whole due as a personality, and if this struggle must be total and without reservation, then it automatically demonstrates the indestructible will of man to achieve his humanity.[27]

Among twentieth-century theoreticians defining the tragic in similarly positive terms, A.C. Bradley is probably the most influential. Equipped with the awareness of a Western critical tradition that some of his colleagues seem to lack, Bradley sets out by acknowledging Hegel as the only major philosopher besides Aristotle who treated tragedy "in a manner both original and searching." The Shakespeare critic may find fault with Hegel's emphasis on how the tragic hero's suffering serves the self-realization of Eternal Justice. But Hegel's "insistence on the need for some element of reconciliation in a tragic catastrophe" seems to him of the highest value.[28]

In a similar way, Walter Kerr agrees with John Jones that tragic events mark a point of something "decisively accomplished."[29] Just as Bradley returns to Hegel, so Kerr invokes Aristotle who, in discussing various ways of perpetrating the deed of horror, finds the best in something close to a happy ending – "what we have in *Cresphontes*, for example, where Merope, on the point of slaying her son, recognizes him in time." This, of course, seems to contradict Aristotle's defence of Euripides for giving his plays unhappy rather than conciliatory endings.[30] But Aristotle, in calling him "the most tragic certainly of the dramatists," so Kerr argues, simply overstated his case in trying to clear Euripides from the charge of actually violating the tragic norm by his unhappy endings.[31] It is worth recalling, in this context, that the philosopher otherwise tends to use the word *tragikos* in the sense of "solemn" or even "exalted," a usage which seems to have been the linguistic norm of his day.[32]

Repudiations of the Tragic

It is precisely this something "decisively accomplished" which comes under attack wherever nineteenth- and twentieth-century writers refute the tragic. What Aristotle, Hegel, or Miller saw as cathartic, as pointing towards dialectical progress, or as asserting the indestructible will of man to achieve his humanity, now is frequently viewed as a distorting, limiting, or falsifying interpretation of reality by writers such as Huxley, Ionesco, and Robbe-Grillet. One, rather self-contradictory, refutation of this kind stems from Marx. On the one hand, Marxists tend to criticize the tragic as an obsolete mode of perception, superseded by their own inexorably scientific analysis of reality. On the other, they remain indebted to a teleological view of history as well as a rationalist understanding of life, themselves both crucial to tragedy.

An essay like Ludwig Marcuse's "The Marxist Interpretation of the Tragic" illustrates the more strictly critical aspect here. Marxism, in Marcuse's view, marks the "end of Christian idealistic tragedy." Bogus expectations about the salvation of mankind in this world or a beyond have kept the genre alive for two thousand years. Despite its celebrations of decline, tragedy always pointed upwards ("Immer ging es im Unter-Gang aufwärts").[33] But how after Auschwitz and Hiroshima can we continue to talk about a tragic dialectic or, worse, divine providence?

A different aspect of the tragic comes under attack by Bertolt Brecht. Tragedy, he argues, presents the hero's suffering as inescapable. Yet in most cases this inescapability, if properly analysed, could easily be traced to certain social conditions amenable to revolutionary change:

To arouse tragic emotions in the spectator would be permissible only if the hero is locked in a truly inescapable situation. For we can only share his grief with impunity, when no practical advice can be given him. The inescapability, in other words, must by no means be social, that is, dependent on our present order of society, which after all is certainly not an eternal category one couldn't escape from.[34]

The Marxists here are often more rigorous than Marx himself, who, after all, thought the decline of the *ancien régime*, for instance, was tragic up to a certain point. As long as this régime believed in its self-justification, Marx argued, "the error on its side was not personal but historical [weltgeschichtlich]. Its decline was therefore tragic."[35] The statement serves to remind us that dialectical materialism, the by-now most powerful ideological creed on earth, stems from an inversion of Hegel's idealistic dialectic in which the tragic pinpoints the prime event in the recurrent step-by-step unfolding of progress. This occurs when one form of civic order (thesis) comes into conflict with its successor (antithesis). Taken individually, each side may be totally justified. But such partial justice means little to the inexorable march of the World Spirit. This, as it leads thesis and antithesis to their ultimate reconciliation in a higher synthesis, may often realize itself through the suffering of either party. To Hegel, Sophocles' *Antigone*, "that supreme and absolute example of tragedy," offers a perfect illustration of this dialectic:

The public law of the State and the instinctive family-love and duty towards a brother are here set in conflict ... Polynices, in war with his own father-city, had fallen before the gates of Thebes, and Creon, the lord thereof, had by means of a public proclamation threatened everyone with death who should give this enemy of the city the right of burial. Antigone, however, refused to accept this command, which merely concerned the public weal, and, constrained by her pious devotion for her brother, carried out as sister the sacred duty of interment ... Each of these two sides realizes only one of the moral powers, and has only one of these as its content ... and the meaning of eternal justice is shown in this, that both end in injustice just because they are one-sided.[36]

In the gradual evolution of his dialectical and tragic vision, Hegel's sympathies shifted from the principle of love towards that of legality, or from Antigone's perspective towards Creon's.[37] In Marx, a similar change becomes strong enough to turn the conflict between two more or less equally justified positions into something closer to an ascendance of a new, desirable order of society over one which, now obsolete, has lost its justification before its disappearance. Even if, following Georg Lukács, we rephrase Marx's characterization of the tragic as expressing "the heroic decline of a class" or the "moment in which an existing social order is dialectically dissolved,"[38] the question remains as to when exactly this tragic dissolution of, for instance, the *ancien régime* had ceased to be tragic by becoming a mere obstacle to revolutionary progress. Is ignorance of one's obsolescence sufficient reason for being labelled tragic? Or had not the Marxists better abandon all attempts to make the tragic one of their terms?

Bertolt Brecht reached that very conclusion, but not before falling victim to some of the contradictions discussed above. *The Measures Taken* (1929), which marks his entry into a lifelong career as a Marxist playwright, is *prima facie* perhaps his most propagandistic play. A revolutionary willingly has himself executed for failing in his mission, while a Control Chorus praises the four agitators for taking the right measures in killing their comrade. "Only if instructed by reality can we / Alter reality." The Moscow Central Organ of the International Union of Revolutionary Writers nevertheless found serious fault with the play. Its reviewer, Alfred Kurella, argued that Brecht, in depicting his protagonist's failure as the result of a conflict between reason (the Communist Party's long-term planning of the revolution) and emotion (his recurrent urge to help the afflicted spontaneously rather than programmatically), had slipped back into idealist thinking. Another review even calls the play tragic and, as Reinhold Grimm shows, does so for good reason. For *The Measures Taken*, perhaps against its author's intent, dramatizes a conflict which the arch-idealist Schiller had described as the tragic conflict *par excellence*: "when one moral duty has to be infringed, so that one can act according to a higher and more general one." Schiller himself had dealt with it in his *Don Carlos*, a play which Brecht admired greatly. Upon realizing what he had produced, Brecht tried to do his best to camouflage the "tragic" elements in his play, but to neither his nor the critics' full satisfaction. From *Mother Courage* to *Galileo*, tragic conflicts kept emerging in his plays, frequently forcing the playwright to apply the revision process he had already practised on *The Measures Taken*.[39]

As my final chapter will argue, Freudian psychoanalysis outdoes Marxism in attempting to refute the tragic while remaining forever unable to emancipate itself from its influence. Here we shall simply recall Freud's version of the birth of tragedy as outlined in *Totem and Taboo*. Tragedy to Freud, as to Marx, is the product of a hopelessly atavistic age, to be analysed from our psychoanalytically scientific vantage point. Morality, religion, society, we remember, all stem from the murder of the primal father, the historical analogue and source of the Oedipus complex. And so does tragedy. After the band of brothers kills and devours the father for keeping all the women to himself, their contradictory feelings of hatred and admiration for the deceased first engender remorse. In order to allay this burning sense of guilt, they institute the totemic system, whereby the totem or father-substitute comes under special protection against repetitions of the original crime.

Remembrance of the triumph over the primal father, however, leads to regularly celebrated rituals in which the crime, symbolically perpetrated by killing and devouring the totem animal or father-substitute, may be repeated with impunity. These totem feasts, so Freud suggests in the final pages of *Totem and Taboo*, are at the root of both Christian communion and Greek tragedy. Devouring the flesh and blood of Christ, just as more indirectly the crucifixion itself, "is essentially a fresh elimination of the father, a repetition of the guilty deed," Freud writes. Analogously, the tragic hero "had to suffer because he was the primal father":

In the remote reality it had actually been the members of the Chorus who caused the Hero's suffering; now, however, they exhausted themselves with sympathy and regret and it was the Hero himself who was responsible for his own sufferings. The crime which was thrown on to his shoulders, presumptuousness and rebelliousness against a great authority, was precisely the crime for which the members of the Chorus, the company of brothers, were responsible. Thus the tragic Hero became, though it might be against his will, the redeemer of the Chorus.[40]

Prometheus, the redeemer of mankind! However one might object to the Freudian theory in detail, his insight into the deeper affinities between Christianity and Greek tragedy is startling enough to survive the contortions of his argument.

In any case, both tragedy and Christianity, to Freud, are primitive illusions from the infancy of mankind analogous to the fantasies of the neurotic and as such should come under similar psychoanalytic surveillance. Little did Freud realize that, thus deflated, the tragic would yet remain one of the major influences on his theories. The basic psychoanalytic method of converting the random babblings of a neurotic patient into an "intelligible, consistent, and unbroken case history"[41] may, in Freud's view, stem from a universal human demand for "unity, connection, and intelligibility from any material, whether of perception or thought, that comes within its grasp."[42] Yet, more specifically, it derives from a distinct tradition in Western rationalism for which Aristotle's demand that a tragedy should have a causally consistent unity of action – "with its several incidents so closely connected that the transposal or withdrawal of any one of them will disjoin and dislocate the whole"[43] – set the all-powerful precedent. Similar precedents can be shown to exist for Freud's therapeutic method.

The Twentieth Century

Besides these half-hearted refutations of the tragic found in Marxism and psychoanalysis, there are numerous twentieth-century attempts to make a more radical break with tragedy. Here again the strongest impulse comes from the playwrights. In 1949 the author of *Death of a Salesman* proclaimed the possibility of a twentieth-century tragedy based on some of its oldest conventions. Three years later Eugène Ionesco had one of the characters in his *The Victims of Duty* make the exactly opposite claim. Nicolas, a bearded poet, propounds a new anti-Aristotelian theatre of the irrational and absurd which, along with the identity of character, plot, and motivation, would abandon the notion of tragedy – "the tragic's turning comic, the comic is tragic, and life's getting more cheerful." Earlier in the play, the protagonist, Choubert, gives some of the reasons for this break with the Aristotelian tragic matrix. As Choubert suggests, Aristotle's demand for a surprising but logically consistent dénouement so perfectly achieved in the combined reversal (*peripeteia*) and last-minute recognition (*anagnorisis*) of Sophocles' *Oedipus Rex* has dominated Western drama ever since:

All the plays that have ever been written, from Ancient Greece to the present day, have never really been anything but thrillers. Drama's always been realistic and there's always been a detective about. Every play's an investigation brought to a successful conclusion. There's a riddle, and it's solved in the final scene.[44]

Ionesco's parody of Aristotelian poetics turns into a caricature of Freudian psychoanalysis when all this theorizing suddenly becomes brutal reality. The detective, said to be typical of Aristotelian tragedy, makes his appearance as an actual policeman who subjects Choubert to a gruelling psychoanalytic interrogation. As a result, the hero completely regresses into infancy until his wife becomes his mother and the pychoanalyst–policeman his father. To make the parody complete, the detective advocates strict Aristotelian (alias Freudian) standards of plot (alias case history) consistency. "As for me I remain Aristotelically logical ... I don't believe in the absurd, everything hangs together, everything can be comprehended in time."[45]

As suggested by *The Victims of Duty*, the theatre of the absurd most clearly defines itself by its negation and inversion of the traditional tragic vision. Although more radical in its anti-tragic stance than Marxism and Freudian psychoanalysis, it still, for the very fact of being *anti*-tragic, depends almost entirely upon what it rejects. Absurd, as Ionesco wrote in an essay on Kafka, "is that which is devoid of purpose ... Cut off from his religious, metaphysical, and transcendental roots, man is lost; all his actions become senseless, absurd, useless." The absurd, then, is the opposite of the tragic, short of the fact that both are primarily concerned with the miseries of human existence. For "in trying to express the helplessness of a beaten man, one broken by fate for example, tragedy [still] admits the reality of fate and destiny, of sometimes incomprehensible but objective laws that govern the universe."[46] But Ionesco, like other modern playwrights, refuses to acknowledge such laws. His own plays, however comic, go beyond that. For as "the 'comic' is an intuitive perception of the absurd, it seems to me more hopeless than the 'tragic.'"[47] Similarly, tragedy to Dürrenmatt presupposes values like guilt, measure, and responsibility. But in the helter-skelter (*Wurstelei*) of our century,

there are no longer guilty men, and no responsible ones either. Everybody cannot help it and nobody wanted it to happen ... We are nothing but children's children. That is our bad luck, not our guilt: guilt is only possible as a personal achievement, as a religious deed.[48]

Yet the full theory of the anti-tragic theatre of the absurd can only be deduced from the plays themselves. No complete account of their implied poetics has been attempted to date, so a few examples will have to suffice within this context. Kafka's *The Trial*, in a dramatic adaptation by André Gide and Jean-Louis Barrault of 1947, was probably the prototype of the theatre of the absurd. This, as Martin Esslin suggests, was mainly due to a radical new fusion of clowning with nonsense poetry and hallucination, the techniques of film montage with those of pantomime and ballet.[49] But more important still was the fact that Kafka's novel, in truly exemplary fashion, describes a world turned absurd. For *The Trial*, instead of simply negating traditional values, at first sets them up and then inverts them. The technique, of course, is not a new one.

Some of the greatest works of Western literature derive part of their impact from simultaneously assuming and transmogrifying major patterns, themes, or figures of our cultural heritage. King Lear, for instance, plays the role of a Job abandoned by God. Goethe has Faust pursue his Promethean urges in a cosmological framework set by God's biblical wager with Satan before he saves him under conditions largely borrowed from Sanskrit drama. Kafka, in portraying the absurd world of *The Trial*, sets his story in contrast to the biblical paradigm it alludes to. The man from the country begging admittance to the law, for instance, at first resembles Job in "curs[ing] his evil fate aloud" when denied entrance. But he gradually turns into a pitiful caricature of his self-righteous biblical predecessor. As he grows old, "he only mutters to himself. He grows childish, and since in his prolonged study of the doorkeeper he has learned to know even the fleas in his fur collar, he begs the very fleas to help him and to persuade the doorkeeper to change his mind."[50]

It is the same with K. himself. "Oh that I knew where I might find him!" clamours Job, "that I might come even to his seat! I would order my cause before him, and fill my mouth with arguments."[51] K. also wants to confront his judges and the law. But whereas God appears to Job through the whirlwind vindicating his righteousness, the Law under which K. is arrested, put on trial, and executed without conviction remains forever elusive. "The ranks of officials in this judiciary system mounted endlessly, so that not even the initiated could survey the hierarchy as a whole."[52] In fact, nobody is sure if the Law exists at all. K. and the other accused find out only that this judiciary system is like a machine blindly grinding away as if it had long been abandoned by the engineer who designed it. *The Trial*, in short, seems to portray the moralistic cosmos of *Job* deprived of its God and guarantor.

The fact that K., upon his arrest, lives in a country with regular jurisdiction underscores the strangeness of the Law that victimizes him. Even when he is finally hauled off to execution, the protagonist and his murderers make an ironic escape from a policeman who tries to stop them. There is a similar contrast in Beckett's *Waiting for Godot*. Here the dramatis personae occasionally invoke God and Christ. But the Godot they are waiting for, though he is frequently associated with hell or salvation, at best resembles a god out of one of Kafka's "sordid nightmares."[53] Before making decisions, so Vladimir and Estragon speculate, he has to consult his agents, his correspondents, his books, his bank account. And whatever actions result from all this reveal little concern for justice. For unknown reasons he beats one boy, who minds the sheep, but is good to the other, who minds the goats.

Like tragedy, *Waiting for Godot* deals with human suffering and misery. But here even the ultimate gesture of despair turns into a farce. "ESTRAGON What about hanging ourselves? VLADIMIR Hmm. It'd give us an erection." Instead of ennobling the protagonists, suffering simply brutalizes them. Their own misery has only made the two tramps more callous concerning that of others. Like so much else, humanitarianism is at best a role one might act for one's amusement. When the blind Pozzo cries for help, Vladimir self-consciously exclaims: "To all mankind they were addressed, those cries for help still ringing in our ears! ... Let us represent worthily for once the foul brood to which a cruel fate consigned us!" But instead of helping Pozzo, Vladimir ends up striking him. Nor does suffering serve the self-realization of some higher purpose. "The tears of the world are a constant quantity... They give birth astride of a grave ... Down in the hole, lingeringly, the grave-digger puts on the forceps." Far from serving the self-realization of dialectical progress, suffering is the only sign of a life that is decaying. Though the play arouses fear and pity, these do not reinforce each other to produce the cathartic effect Aristotle speaks of. Instead, they are either separate or tend to cancel each other out. When the blind and helpless Pozzo is beaten by Vladimir, we feel genuine pity for him. But this feeling yields to one of plain horror when Pozzo, minutes later, tells the tramps to strike his dumb servant Lucky: "Give him a taste of his boot, in the face and the privates as far as possible."[54]

Here as elsewhere, the theatre of the absurd frustrates our traditional tragic expectations at every turn. Claiming to have "Suffered much, learned much," the Old Man in Ionesco's *The Chairs*[55] seems to parody the classical *pathei mathos* ("Through suffering, learning").[56] He even has a Promethean message that could "save humanity" if only there were someone to reveal it to the world. Since all his guests are purely imaginary creatures sitting on empty chairs, the arrival of an actual Orator looking like "a typical painter or poet of the nineteenth century" is a surprise in itself. But an even greater one is in store for us when the Orator sets about to deliver the message after the old couple have jumped into the sea in order to "die in full glory [and] become a legend."[57] Deaf and dumb, he can only stammer inarticulate sounds, and when he finally writes the message on a blackboard, the results are an equal disappointment.

Euripides, Shakespeare, Goethe

Anyone familiar with Shakespeare or Euripides should be surprised not so much by the novelty of such techniques as by their slapstick crudeness. To take one example from Shakespeare's *Troilus and Cressida*, Ulysses, provoked by Achilles' refusal to fight against Troy, pleads for hierarchic subordination on the human as much as on the cosmic level. The speech, some forty lines long, is a *locus classicus* for the Renaissance concept of a God-ordained natural order. In the play itself it is the motive force for whatever happens in the Greek camp from then on.

> The heavens themselves, the planets, and this center
> Observe degree, priority, and place,
> Insisture, course, proportion, season, form,
> Office, and custom, in all line of order.
> ...
> But when the planets
> In evil mixture to disorder wander,
> What plagues, and what portents, what mutiny,
> What raging of the sea, shaking of earth,
> Commotion in the winds, frights, changes, horrors,
> Divert and crack, rend and deracinate
> The unity and married calm of states
> Quite from their fixure? O, when degree is shaked,
> Which is the ladder of all high designs,
> The enterprise is sick.   (I.iii)

Ulysses and his friends lay elaborate plans for snubbing Achilles in order to make him rejoin the battle, and at some point their championing of order and degree is about to carry the day. After Hector's challenge of Achilles has, by a piece of astute diplomatic manoeuvring, been answered by Ajax instead, Achilles feels piqued enough to vow to fight Hector the following day. But a message from Queen Hecuba and her daughter, his "fair love," reminding him of some oath sworn to them, is all that is needed to thwart his "great purpose":

> Fall Greeks, fail fame, honor or go or stay,
> My major vow lies here; this I'll obey.   (V.i)

His oath is quickly forgotten, however, when news arrives that Hector has killed Achilles' bosom friend Patroclus. This leads to another anticlimactic surprise. Hector as we know is to be killed by Achilles. But just as expectations concerning a restoration of order among the Greeks are violated by the actual events, so the chivalric "theme of honor and renown" (II.ii) which, with Hector's own consent, prevails over the political decisions of the Trojans is brutally cut short by the manner of Hector's death. Ruthless treachery replaces the courtly code of honour when a defeated and cowardly Achilles has his Myrmidons murder the unarmed Trojan hero. Where we expected a tragic death, there is no more than a brutally mangled corpse. Nothing here makes us feel elated, let alone reconciled with what we have witnessed: "Hector is dead," as Troilus remarks; "there is no more to say" (V.x).

Or take an example from Euripides. Hecuba, despite her unparalleled suffering – she recently had her daughter, Polyxena, sacrificed by the Greeks, and Polydorus, son and last heir of Troy, murdered by a friend, Polymestor

- has not lost her belief in divine justice. The gods are strong, she tells Agamemnon,

> and over them
> there stands some absolute, some moral order
> of principle of law more final still.
> Upon this moral law the world depends;
> through it the gods exist; by it we live,
> defining good and evil. Apply that law
> to me.   (*Hecuba* 799–803)

Remembering Aeschylus, Hecuba at this point appears like a living embodiment of *pathei mathos*. But to our surprise, this *mater dolorosa*, made so wise by all her tragic suffering, turns into a vengeful fury as soon as she gets her way. Suffering has not made her more human but simply more brutal. With the help of her women she plucks out Polymestor's eyes and kills his sons, fully rejoicing, as she protests herself, in this revenge (1258).

The anti-tragic bias of twentieth-century playwrights, then, is by no means an innovation of our time. Nor am I the first to take note of it. Hegel observed it in Shakespeare as well as in some of the literary productions of his own time. Claiming that art should, if true to its essential notion, "reflect on us the vision of a harmony," he found *King Lear* sorely deficient even as a tragedy. What it presents is not tragic but a "vision of absolute evil and depravity." To Hegel's dismay, "this unstable dissolution of everything spiritual, which forces its way through every dissonance, however repulsive," had become the fashion of his time:

moreover, it has even given us what we may describe as the humour of the abominable thing, a kind of burlesque simulation of irony, an atmosphere in which a Theodor Hoffmann, for example, has found himself so much at home.[58]

To many of Hegel's Romantic contemporaries, such negative categories had already turned into positive affirmations of a new poetics. To Victor Hugo, Shakespeare was the model for a new kind of drama "which, in the same breath, molds the grotesque and the sublime, the terrible and the absurd, tragedy and comedy." To A.W. Schlegel, similarly contradictory modes yoked by violence together adequately expressed the spirit of an age which, like his own, was no longer ruled by harmony and hope but, on the contrary, by tensions and disharmonies of every kind. His brother Friedrich Schlegel announced a post-classical period under similar premises, while Schelling, in his *Philosophy of Art*, declared "the mingling of opposites, that is, above all of the tragic and the comic," to be "the basic principle of modern drama." To Hegel's *bête noir*, E.T.A. Hoffmann, there was a new, Romantic way of "moving the feelings of the spectator in a uniquely strange manner,"[59] derived from a radical fusion of the comic with the tragic.

Even Goethe, although generally averse to such Romantic speculations, came to acknowledge that the mingling of tragedy and comedy might be used for its "barbaric advantages."[60] What else, after all, was tragedy than "a psycho-ethical phenomenon presented in form of a readily understandable paradigm"? But whatever it may be, it was far too narrow for his expansive temperament. Tragedies, he noted in another of his *Maximen und Reflexionen*, are nothing else but versified passions of people, who turn objective facts into God knows what. Fascinating to him, by contrast, was the possibility of viewing a case of tragic guilt in such a way that no tragedy would have to follow it. This, of course, is what the poet, much to the indignation of some critics, has done in his *Faust*. For all that, Goethe was too radical a thinker to be caught in a one-sided rejection of the tragic or a mere mingling of the tragic with the grotesque. The second part of *Faust*, as we shall see, fully bears out the author's claim that his nature was far too conciliatory for a tragic poet and that the irreconcilable was quite absurd in this so utterly trivial world.[61]

Regarding Shakespeare, we lack comparable pronouncements by either the poet or his contemporaries. Granted, there is the occasional complaint (as in Sidney's *Defence of Poesie*) that English plays, in their mingling of clowns and kings, were neither "right tragedies nor right comedies" but "mungrell Tragy-comedie[s]."[62] Yet in general we find little to show that Shakespeare's transcendence of tragedy, as evident in the plays themselves, was then discussed within the conceptual framework used in this study. The same is true of Euripides' plays and whatever scanty comments on them have come down to us. Nevertheless, both playwrights were well aware of the visions of life here characterized as anti- or post-tragic. A disbelief in the meaningfulness of suffering, a radical questioning of all values, a cyclical rather than a teleological view of life – such attitudes were current in both classical Greece and Renaissance Europe. In turn, Euripides is known to have been as familiar with the philosophy of his age as Shakespeare seems to have been with the philosophy of Montaigne. The French essayist's doctrine of suspending judgment, for instance, may well have reinforced Shakespeare in a stance which Euripides derived from Heraclitus, Anaxagoras, and Protagoras.

Shakespeare had only scanty knowledge of Euripides, but what he could read of him in Montaigne must have confirmed his tendencies both to negate and to transcend tragedy. Tragedies affirm a certain order in the universe, whereas Euripides' plays taught the philosopher the "volubilitie and incomprehensiblenesse of all matters." "What meaneth this burden? *In a slippery and gliding place let vs suspend our beliefe*," Montaigne asks. A couplet by Euripides is made to spell out the answer:

> Gods workes doe travers our imaginations,
> And crosse our workes in divers different fashions.

The tragic imposes meaning and order on life, where, after all, there may be none. It postulates a divine world as the guarantor of that order where God may not exist or may be indifferent to our wishful thinking. Montaigne's own attitude to these matters again is summed up in a couplet by the Greek playwright:

> O *Iupiter*, for vnto me
> Onely the name is knowne of thee.[63]

In a certain sense the tragic, in surrounding suffering with meaningfulness and nobility, implies an ultimately escapist attitude. It avoids rather than confronts the destructive side of nature. To go according to nature, Montaigne writes, "is but to follow according to our understanding." What goes beyond we call "monstrous and disordered." Yet those precisely are the aspects of life which Euripides and Shakespeare retrieved: all the irrational, absurd, and "cruel" forces of nature which the tragic tends to subsume under its anthropomorphic orders. To Montaigne, these orders were as questionable as they were to certain Greek philosophers who refused to decide "whether there be any thing or nothing." Another of Euripides' couplets which rounds out this argument clearly prefigures one of Shakespeare's most central concerns:

> Who knowes if thus to live, be called death,
> And if it be to dy, thus to draw breath?[64]

Finally, turning to Euripides himself, we have Aristotle's negative assessment of his tragedies, which our first section will try to translate into the more neutral terminology used here. As noted before, the philosopher, in discussing tragedy, advocated a strict consistency of both plot and character portrayal. Everything had to be either necessary or probable, so that whenever a dramatic character does or says something, it should be the necessary or probable outcome of his character, just as any incident should be the logical consequence of those preceding it. "From this one sees ... that the Dénouement also should arise out of the plot itself."[65]

Not surprisingly, Aristotle finds fault with Euripides on every one of these points. *Medea*, in which the dénouement depends upon a stage artifice, serves him as an example of the kind of fake solution so frequent in Euripides' plays. Moreover, Euripides, unlike Sophocles, is found deficient in making the chorus an "integral part of the whole"[66] and in letting it take a share in the action.[67] Hegel, we remember, criticized *King Lear* for transgressing beyond the limits of the tragic with its uncompromising "vision of absolute evil and depravity."[68] Aristotle found similar fault with the characterization of Menelaus in Euripides' *Orestes*. For in the philosopher's view, "there is no possible apology for improbability of Plot and depravity of character, when they are not necessary and no use is made of them, like the improbability in the appearance of

Aegeus in *Medea* and the baseness of Menelaus in *Orestes*." Euripides, to Aristotle's disapproval, painted men as they are, not, like his fellow playwright Sophocles, as they ought to be.[69]

To sum up, then, tragedy, from its very beginnings, found both writers who practised the genre and others who rebelled against and transcended it. Western literary culture has been remarkably consistent in imposing the tragic vision on authors from Sophocles to Arthur Miller; but not all of them conformed to the pressure, and it is no surprise that three of the greatest playwrights in the tradition were also the greatest iconoclasts. Euripides, Shakespeare, and Goethe thus anticipated the anti- and post-tragic theatre of our time. But unlike a Ionesco or Beckett, they were also writers of traditional tragedy – Euripides in, for instance, *Iphigenia at Aulis*, Shakespeare most clearly in *Romeo and Juliet*, and Goethe in the first part of *Faust*. In each case, then, we can trace the transition from tragedy via anti- towards post-tragedy. But before turning to the earliest of the three authors, it is appropriate that we look into the origins of tragedy proper.

The Birth of Tragedy

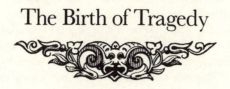

ONCE THE EVIDENCE concerning the origins of tragedy is examined, little else emerges other than that "Aeschylus created tragedy as we understand it."[1] In turn, there is little in the playwright's development, as far as we know, that calls for such concepts of the Dionysiac or mythopoeic as Nietzsche, in *The Birth of Tragedy*, associated with these beginnings.[2] The sequence of Aeschylus's works (after the redating of *The Suppliants*[3]) – with *The Persians* produced in 472, *The Seven against Thebes* fixed in 467, *The Suppliants* itself dated after 468, the *Oresteia* produced in 458, and *Prometheus Bound* as a possibly non-Aeschylean play[4] probably written after 458 – suggests the very opposite. To begin with, there are few later tragedies more unmythological than Aeschylus's first.

Aeschylus's Early Tragedies

The ghost of Darius, the Persian Queen, the Chorus, as well as Xerxes himself, in bewailing their nation's defeat at Salamis, may frequently invoke the Greek gods and especially Zeus. But here already Zeus has been reduced to a moralistic cipher for which Solon's didactic religiosity rather than the colourful mythographies of Hesiod or Homer provides the precedent. "For no man who has an evil heart," we read in Solon's "Prayer to the Muses," "ever escapes [Zeus's] watchful eye, and one way or another in the end his justice is made manifest."[5] Equally reminiscent of the Old Testament Yahweh is Aeschylus's Zeus, who, in Darius's words, has punished Xerxes for his "pride and godless arrogance." For

> Zeus is the chastener of overboastful
> Minds, a grievous corrector.   (*The Persians* 828–9)

Aeschylus was not to rest content with this simplistically moralistic use of myth. But even where myth and morality, in the subsequent plays, are made to fuse in more complex ways, he does not lose sight of his initial concern. Thus, Zeus, Apollo, Hera, and other divinities, as invoked by the Chorus of Theban virgins, seem to preside over the beginning of *The Seven against Thebes* only to be questioned later. "That our bulwarks stand fast against the onset of the foe," Eteocles tells the Chorus, "be that your prayer" (216–17). Aware that a "hateful black curse" (696–7) is infecting his family like an incurable disease, he feels that the gods have already abandoned him. "For them our death," he exclaims, "is the admirable offering" (703). Yet despite all this, Eteocles neither denies the gods nor accepts his fate like a mere fatalist.

Against the simplistic propitiatory worship of the Chorus, the hero hints at a dialectic involving destiny and the gods. His *amor fati* obedience to fate finds its counterpart in a teleological interpretation of traditional myth. Eteocles' responses to the messenger's description of the Seven against Thebes to a large extent read like Hesiod's account of the Olympians' ascendance over their more primitive forebears turned theodicy. Of giantlike stature, most of the warriors are characterized by their overweening pride and defiant attitude towards the Olympians or, in the case of Hippomedon and Parthenopaeus, are linked with Zeus's monstrous opponent Typho and his daughter, the Sphinx, through their heraldic devices. By contrast, the Theban defenders described by Eteocles are marked by their modest trustworthiness or, more specifically, by their claims to be champions of the Olympians. Where Eteocles describes the opponent of the Typho-warrior Hippomedon, this opposition of devices is developed in enough detail to give the oncoming battle some of the dimension of a war in heaven:

> for man with man they shall engage as foes
> and on their shields shall carry enemy Gods.
> The one has Typho breathing fire, the other,
> Hyperbius, has father Zeus in station
> sitting upon his shield, and in his hand
> a burning bolt.
> No one has yet seen Zeus defeated anywhere.
> Such on each side are the favors of the Gods;
> we are on the winning side, they with the vanquished
> if Zeus than Typho mightier prove in battle.   (509–20)[6]

While Eteocles is simply made to repeat Hesiod's well-known account of Zeus's victory over Typho here, he is given more specifically prophetic insights later. His father's hateful black curse tells him "first of gain and then of death" (698), a formula which anticipates the Chorus's response after the messenger has reported the mutual slaughter of Eteocles and Polyneices. There is "sorrow and joy at once" (817), rejoicing because Thebes has been saved and lamenting because of the human sacrifice the gods had to claim in achieving their purpose. But the play's conclusion, initiating the conflict dealt with in Sophocles' *Antigone*, deprives this theodicy of its future-oriented component.[7] As yet a real solution to the problems of evil and suffering is out of sight. The curse at the end of *The Seven against Thebes* is only handed down to the next generation, and "the chain of blood-lettings," as a later play was to call it (*Libation Bearers* 933), will continue uninterrupted. In *The Suppliant Maidens* we see Aeschylus groping his way towards solving this problem.

Whereas *The Seven against Thebes* presumably concluded the trilogy to which it belonged, *The Suppliant Maidens* is thought to have been an opening play. Hence we ignore the outcome of the story in which, reminiscent of the earlier play, a group of fifty maidens seeks help and refuge at an altar dedicated to several gods. No less desperate than the Theban women, they threaten to hang themselves from the statues of the gods unless the king of Argos protects them from their hated Egyptian cousins who want to marry them. Nevertheless, their whole attitude is more hopeful throughout. While acknowledging that Zeus's dark plans cannot be traced easily (86), they somehow trust in these plans even though they may cause them a good deal of suffering (1070-1):

> All providence
> Is effortless; throned,
> Holy and motionless,
> His will is accomplished.   (97-100)

This belief that Zeus, guiding by ancient law, holds the beam of balance (672, 822-3) and provides a perfect end for all things (629) is frequently reiterated throughout the play (see also, 139-40, 624). We know from the original story that at the end of *The Suppliant Maidens* these expectations are still remote from their fulfilment. The Greek maidens are to marry their cousins but, forced to do so, will murder them during the wedding night. The only exception is Hypermestra, who, to save the life of her husband Lynceus, is prepared to break the vow she made to her forty-nine sisters and her father. But put on trial, she is vindicated by Aphrodite, who, as a fragment of the third play seems to tell us, justifies Hypermestra's love-inspired treachery in the name of the life-forces ruling the universe:

> Holy heaven yearns to violate earth,
> And desire seizes earth to share in marriage;
> And rain, fallen from streaming heaven,
> Impregnates earth; and she brings forth for mortals
> The food of herds and Demeter's grain.
> And by watery union the season for trees
> is perfected. Of these things I am cause.[8]

The function of Aphrodite in this final scene of the trilogy seems to anticipate that of Athena in the trial scene of *The Eumenides*. *The Suppliant Maidens* also presages the later play in frequently invoking Apollo, whose son is said to have cleansed Argos "of deadly, monstrous / Serpents, that the earth, soaked in old / Curses of blood, had sprung and smeared in wrath" (263–5). Although we cannot be sure if the actual Apollo enacted a similarly expiatory role in the lost parts of the trilogy, we know that Aeschylus made him perform it in the *Oresteia*.

As patron of agriculture, legislation, prophecy, the arts, medicine, divination, and many other activities, Apollo was the most popular and influential divinity in ancient Greece.[9] Granted, the country had neither a Bible nor a Church, but Apollo, "vicar on earth of the heavenly Father," as E.R. Dodds puts it, "came to fill the gap."[10] Resembling ecclesiastical law as it united the various medieval states, the worship of Apollo and his consultation at the oracles, above all in Delos and Delphi, linked the otherwise separate and often fiercely antagonistic city-states. Both Athens and Sparta placed themselves under his protection. No wonder that Apollo plays the crucial role in Aeschylus's most complex dramatic statement about the interrelationship of a divinely ordained fate with human suffering and evil.

Aeschylus, Hegel, Nietzsche

Hegel, as we recall, was fond of pointing to Sophocles' *Antigone* as "the most excellent and satisfying work of art" among "all the fine creations of the ancient and the modern world." This was, no doubt, because it provided him with a perfect illustration of his understanding of history, the dialectical self-revelation of the World Spirit towards its own perfection. But the philosopher was well aware that Sophocles, in thus exploring "the opposition ... between ethical life in its social universality and the family as the natural ground of moral relations," had only followed the lead of Aeschylus. In his extensive discussion of *The Eumenides*, Hegel praises Aeschylus's "sterling imagination" for providing him with what he describes as a mythical precedent to his philosophy. The Furies, he writes,

pursue Orestes on account of the murder of his mother, a murder which Apollo, the younger god, had directed, in order that Agamemnon, the slaughtered spouse and king, should not remain unavenged. The entire drama consequently is concentrated in a conflict between these divine Powers, which confront each other in person. The right [which the Furies] enforce as against Orestes is only the family-right in so far as this is rooted in the blood relation. Apollo opposes to this natural ethical relation ... the right of the spouse and the chieftain who has been violated in respect to the highest right he can claim.[11]

Hegel may have taken the *Oresteia* as a mere confirmation of his theories. But taking a hint from Ernst Topitsch's investigations into the mythical preformations of Western philosophy,[12] one might well turn the argument around or ask if Hegel's dialectic would ever have come into being without the dramatic model first provided him by Aeschylus. For where indeed before Hegel do we find a more perfect demonstration of the triadic sequence of thesis, antithesis, and synthesis which forms the nucleus of the philosopher's dialectic? Although it is not revealed to us before we reach the end of the trilogy, this threefold step, from one murder leading to a second and from there towards a reconciliation, is laid out with almost mathematical precision. Whatever else may have motivated them in murdering Agamemnon, Clytaemnestra and Aegisthus justify their deed as revenge for other murders involving blood relationships. Agamemnon's father Atreus butchered his brother's children and fed them to their father Thyestes. Agamemnon himself sacrificed his and Clytaemnestra's daughter Iphigenia so that his fleet might sail to Troy. Clytaemnestra's plea here is forceful enough to influence the Chorus of the elders of Argos, who at first are fiercely antagonistic to her:

> Here is anger for anger. Between them
> who shall judge lightly?
> The spoiler is robbed; he killed, he has paid.
> The truth stands ever beside God's throne
> eternal: he who has wrought shall pay; that is law.
> Then who shall tear the curse from their blood? (1560–5)

The notion that "he who has wrought shall pay," while running like a guiding thread through the first two plays of the trilogy (*Agamemnon* 532–3, 1527; *Libation Bearers* 313–14, 1009), involves the even more central concept of inherited guilt. Though confined to the curse laid upon a specific family, this miasma comes close to the Judaeo-Christian notion of hereditary sin.[13] As many lines in the *Oresteia* try to convince us, there seems to be no escape from its force, which frequently assumes the shape of evil spirits or demons. Almost as if he were trying to mislead us, Aeschylus even makes the prophetic Cassandra say that, lurking about the house of Atreus, there is "a drunken rout / of ingrown vengeful spirits never to be cast forth" (*Agamemnon* 1189–90). The resultant chain of blood-lettings seems to be endless.

> All the world's waters running in a single drift
> may try to wash blood from the hand
> of the stained man; they only bring new blood guilt on. (*Libation Bearers* 72–5)

The truth of this seems to be borne out in the second part of the trilogy. Just as Clytaemnestra avenged the murder of her daughter on her husband, so her son avenges the murder of his father on Clytaemnestra. But there is a difference, to be spelled out in the last play. The Chorus concluding *The Libation Bearers* raises the obvious question: "Where / is the end? Where shall the fury of fate / be stilled to sleep, be done with?" The answer is that, considered dialectically, Orestes' murder of his mother had a motivation diametrically opposed to that which prompted Clytaemnestra to murder her husband. It was in the working out of this distinction that Hegel saw Aeschylus's "sterling imagination"[14] at its most insightful. Orestes' revenge was better justified than Clytaemnestra's because "the knowledge of the substantiality of marital life is something later and more profound than the purely natural connection between mother and son, and constitutes the beginning of the State as the realization of the free and rational will." Aeschylus may in fact state it somewhat differently. But in working out the antithetical positions of *Agamemnon* versus *The Libation Bearers* and finally resolving this conflict in *The Eumenides*, he is no less explicit than Hegel. Apollo, testifying on behalf of Orestes, whom he compelled to do the murder, in fact sounds more Hegelian than the philosopher himself. The murder of a woman, he argues, is not comparable to that of a king:

> It is not the same thing for a man of blood to die
> honored with the king's staff given by the hand of god.   (625–6)

Of course, there is more at stake here than a simple Homeric quarrel between two rival factions among the gods. Even before the jury acquits Orestes following Athena's intervention, the Furies or prosecutors complain that "Zeus has ruled [their] blood dripping company / outcast, nor will deal with [them]" (365–6). Hesiod's story of the Olympian male ascendance over the previous dynasties of the gods is still in progress, and as the *Oresteia* draws to a close, the younger gods are about to win another round. Athena may attribute this victory to the powers of Persuasion (971), but the Furies, before they yield to a combination of blackmail and bribery (826, 893), know otherwise. Just as Apollo assures them that neither the elder nor the younger gods have any consideration left for them (721–2), so they themselves have no illusions about the fact that "the orders of an elder time" have been destroyed (728 and passim) –

> the hard hands of the gods
> and their treacheries have taken [their] old rights away.   (879–80)

In turn, the younger gods never question their basic anti-female attitude. Athena, the goddess born solely of a man, declares that she is "always for the male" (737). Apollo points to her as proof for his rather specious argument that "There can / be a father without any mother" and that "The parent is he who mounts" (660, 662–3). What will bring the seemingly endless chain of blood-lettings to a resolution, then, is a dialectic involving the conflicting rights both of the humans and of the gods.

How do the two interrelate? The Chorus at the end of *The Suppliant Maidens* declared itself content "if ill / Is one-third of its lot." Its counterpart in *Agamemnon* adds a more meaningful dimension to this stoical attitude. Suffering may after all have a god-given purpose:

> Zeus: whatever he may be, if this name
> pleases him in invocation,
> thus I call upon him.
> I have pondered everything
> yet I cannot find a way,
> only Zeus, to cast this dead weight of ignorance
> finally from out my brain.
> ...
> Zeus, who guided men to think,
> who has laid it down that wisdom
> comes alone through suffering.   (160–6, 176–8)

Several recent critics have treated this "Through suffering, learning" as the final message of the play. But like the phrase itself, these interpretations beg the further question of what such wisdom might consist of. Dodds's attempt to show that it evolves through the three protagonists – "from Agamemnon, the blind instrument of justice, who never learns, through Clytaemnestra, the half-blind instrument, who learns too late and incompletely, to Orestes, the conscious instrument, whose insight comes before the deed and achieves contact with the divine will"[15] – remains unconvincing. Unsure to the very last as to whether his case be "right or wrong" (468, 612), Orestes completely entrusts its justification to Apollo. After his acquittal, he has learned no more wisdom than to assure his judges that if ever a future prince of Argos should plan to attack their country, he would haunt them even after his death. His language here recalls the justice of curses and revenge from the trilogy's beginning rather than the striving for compromise that marks its end:

> but though I lie then in my grave, I still shall wreak
> helpless bad luck and misadventure upon all
> who stride across the oath that I have sworn: their ways
> disconsolate make, their crossings full of evil
> augury, so they shall be sorry that they moved.   (767–71)

Immediately after taking this vow, Orestes, along with Apollo, leaves the stage. The final scene, in which the Furies are changed into the beneficent Eumenides by Athena's persuasive force, is witnessed by no one except the attendants at the trial, who remain silent throughout. Even the Chorus, which might sum up the meaning of what we have seen, is absent; its role is played by the Furies, while the "Chorus" of women for the final procession articulates little more than its ritual function. The only party left which might fathom the oracular *pathei mathos* is the audience. This becomes all the more apparent when both Athena and the Eumenides, in "asides" which are as obvious as they are unusual in Greek tragedy, address the Athenian citizens sitting in the audience. By turning into Eumenides, the former Furies, of course, have just given these spectators an example of the wisdom they themselves are invited to practise after the play is over:

> CHORUS
> Farewell, farewell. High destiny shall be yours
> by right. Farewell, citizens
> seated near the throne of Zeus,
> beloved by the maiden he loves,
> civilized as years go by,
> sheltered under Athene's wings,
> grand even in her father's sight.   (996–1002)

It might be said that, in a certain sense, the spectator is the most important dramatis persona in the *Oresteia*. Aeschylus, especially at the beginning of the trilogy, misses no opportunity of raising questions and expectations, of guiding and even misguiding his audience. There are few other plays introduced by a comparable abundance of comments on destiny, the gods, their grace and retributive justice, of how good will win out in the end, how suffering brings wisdom, how the future will be known only once it has come, or how

> From the gods who sit in grandeur
> grace comes somehow violent.   (182–3)

It is easy enough, upon rereading the play, to pick out a phrase like the last one, link it with similar notions elsewhere, and conclude that the poet from the beginning guided our attention in a specific direction. But the opposite is nearer the truth. The spectator, rather than being directed in this way, is drawn into the welter of conflicting opinions that confuse and tantalize the dramatis personae. Yet unlike these, he gradually is allowed to rise to a position from which Time "in his forward flood" (*Eumenides* 853) begins to reveal its dialectical patterns in advancing Greece to higher and higher glory.

He also learns that such progress, which Zeus, the once colourfully anthropo-morphic God in Homer, has come to represent as an almost abstract teleologi-cal principle, can only be realized through the often innocent suffering of both humans and the other gods. We are sufficiently aware of what calamities Agamemnon, Clytaemnestra, and Orestes had to go through. But even the once-powerful Furies are made to feel "disinherited, suffering, heavy with anger" because the younger gods "have ridden down / the laws of the elder time, torn them out of [their] hands" (778–9).

As we watch Zeus's plans unfold through the agonies of mortals and immortals,[16] we even notice changes about the god himself. In *Agamemnon* he is the "great guest god" (60) who destroyed Troy because Paris violated the law of hospitality. In *The Libation Bearers* he becomes the guarantor of an Old Testament–like justice proclaimed by Orestes, Electra, and the Chorus alike. The vengeful forces of the nether world, which Zeus will reject later (*Eumenides* 365–6), are still called upon to fulfil his behests (380f). Orestes' exclamation, "Warstrength shall collide with warstrength; right with right" (461), aptly characterizes this dialectic without progress, a further dimension that Zeus, the supreme embodiment of the teleological thrust of the entire trilogy, assumes in *The Eumenides*. Although Orestes has abused the law of hospitality in order to murder his hosts, Zeus, the former "guest-god" who avenged Paris's lesser crime by destroying Troy, now becomes a mother-murderer's "Savior" (760). Such contradictions, serving the ulterior purpose of political progress, however, are perfectly in tune with the dialectical unfoldings of what Zeus stands for. The god's ultimate appellation – before he is said, in the final lines of the trilogy, to have met with Destiny to confirm eternal peace between Pallas and her guests – is the God of the Political Assembly (973). Long before Aristotle told his fellow citizens that they were "city-state animals,"[17] Aeschy-lus gave them the appropriate god.

Hegel's philosophy, in I. Knox's view, simply consolidates "the socio-political and historico-cultural *status quo*," while his theory of tragedy justifies "the human sacrifice upon the altar of some Moloch principle."[18] Similar accusations could be levelled at Aeschylus when he makes Athena, the main executor of Zeus's political theodicy, pronounce herself in favour of Athenian imperialism (*Eumenides* 864–5) or brag about similar exploits accom-plished just before Apollo called upon her to review the pleadings of Orestes' case:

> I was beside Scamandrus. I was taking seisin
> of land, for there the Achaean lords of war and first
> fighters gave me large portion of all their spears
> had won, the land root and stock to be mine for all
> eternity, for the sons of Theseus a choice gift. (397–402)

Today's audiences, aware of more recent imperialism, would not be the first to view such lines with scepticism. No doubt there were several among Aeschylus's spectators in 458 who already felt similar misgivings. Ever since Salamis and Plataea, the Athenians had waged a merciless expansionist war, forcing some countries into submission, enslaving or annihilating others. Thucydides, an Athenian himself, reports how his fellow citizens, at about the time of the *Oresteia*, had all but lost the popularity they once enjoyed as rulers. "For the Athenians insisted on obligations being exactly met, and made themselves unpopular by bringing the severest pressure to bear on allies who were not used to making sacrifices and did not want to make them."[19]

Besides its implicit imperialism there were other aspects of Aeschylus's trilogy which might well have aroused scepticism when it was first performed. Euripides in 458 was in his twenties, and it is tantalizing to imagine how the young poet either then or at a later point reacted to the famous trilogy. *The Eumenides*, in particular, however grandiose in attempt, could so easily be seen as a self-parody. Apollo, the most mysterious divine power among the Homeric Olympians,[20] is made to argue in Orestes' defence like a somewhat blundering, easily angered, and bullying lawyer; the Furies, while losing the argument, have the upper hand in casuistry. Their exchange, after Apollo has recalled the horror of Agamemnon's murder and minimized that of Clytaemnestra, is worthy of an Aristophanes:

CHORUS
Zeus, by your story, gives first place to the father's death.
Yet Zeus himself shackled elder Cronus, his own
father. Is this not contradiction? I testify,
judges, that this is being said in your hearing.
APOLLO
You foul animals, from whom the gods turn in disgust,
Zeus could undo shackles, such hurt can be made good,
and there is every kind of way to get out.   (640–5)

None of this supports Nietzsche's claim in *The Birth of Tragedy* that Aeschylean tragedy for a brief period revived Greek myth before both fell victim to the anti-mythic and anti-Dionysiac trends in Sophocles and Euripides.[21] The philosopher is right about the early disintegration of myth, which began at about the time when tragedy came into its own. Even before Xenophanes criticized Hesiod and Homer for making their gods commit adultery and deceive each other, Hecataeus had found Greek mythology "funny."[22] But otherwise Nietzsche's argument is true only in reverse. The philosopher rarely mentions, let alone discusses, individual plays, and where he does, the results are somehow incongruous with his primary categories of the Apollonian and Dionysiac. These, we recall, translate Schopenhauer's notion of the Will, the source of eternal life and suffering, into more affirmative terms, the Apollonian being the impulse towards creation, the Dionysiac the counter-current towards destruction and death. Dionysiac art, of which tragedy is the perfect manifestation, Nietzsche writes,

makes us realize that everything that is generated must be prepared to face its painful dissolution. It forces us to gaze into the horror of individual existence, yet without being turned to stone by the vision ... Pity and terror notwithstanding, we realize our great good fortune in having life – not as individuals, but as part of the life force with whose procreative lust we have become one.[23]

Such an art, much as Nietzsche's philosophy in general, makes a mockery of all theodicy and teleology. Nevertheless, it was the author of the *Oresteia* – a "grand parable of progress"[24] rather than of the "natural cruelty of things" – who, along with Sophocles, became Nietzsche's major champion for this Dionysiac theatre. In fact, Nietzsche misreads Greek drama much as he did Wagner's operas, in which the Dionysiac, he thought, had been reborn. *The Birth of Tragedy*, as its author admitted in "A Critical Backward Glance" of 1886, was an "arrogant and extravagant book" which "addressed itself to artists" – and, one might add, to the artists of the future. There is little in either Wagner or Greek tragedy that seems to reflect "God as the supreme artist, amoral, recklessly creating and destroying."[25] Not until Artaud's *théâtre de la cruauté* and its followers in the twentieth century did this notion become central to Western theatrical history.

Nietzsche's book, then, seems to describe the death rather than the birth of tragedy. This is especially true of what Nietzsche says about *The Bacchae* and of what he misjudged as a rebirth of tragedy in his own time. Euripides' *The Bacchae*, apart from being perhaps the only Greek play to fit Nietzsche's Dionysiac ideal, was also perhaps the last play by the youngest of the three major Greek tragedians. To Nietzsche, this is proof that an ancient popular tradition like the worship of Dionysus cannot be totally suppressed, even by the most extreme rationalism.[26] In fact, *The Bacchae* and its genuinely Dionysiac spirit mark the end point in a gradual transcendence of the tragic which, if we choose to retain the Nietzschean terms, is essentially Apollonian rather than Dionysian. Here, as well as in plays like *Heracles*, Euripides retrieved some of the dimensions of myth which Aeschylus, in trying to express his teleological view of life, had turned into something closer to allegory. Aeschylus, not Euripides, systematized myth by way of dramatizing a new philosophy of life which Nietzsche sums up in a quotation from Anaxagoras: "In the beginning all things were mixed together; then reason came and introduced order."[27]

Thus Zeus, in the *Oresteia*, is little more than a philosophical abstraction, whereas the other gods are made to perform an all-too-human charade in which the lapse into the farcical remains a constant, though hardly intended possibility. In light of the Athenians' penchant for legal debate, the pettifogging divinities in *The Eumenides* provide yet another example of Xenophanes' famous dictum that the "Ethiopians say that their gods are snub-nosed and black, the Thracians that theirs have light blue eyes and red hair."[28] Or so at least it might appear to someone like Euripides, who, though a close associate of the Sophists of his day, was equally familiar with pre-Socratic philosophers, to the point of echoing their dicta in his plays.

The pre-Socratic echoes are even stronger when Euripides, in his repeated controversy with Aeschylus, alludes to the *Oresteia* in several of his plays. But along with the Aeschylean theodicy, there were two further aspects of classical tragedy, found in Sophocles rather than Aeschylus, which turned into central targets for the anti-tragic parodies of Euripides. One, heroic humanism, has a twentieth-century advocate in Arthur Miller, to whom the tragic hero in his very destruction "demonstrates the indestructible will of man to achieve his humanity."[29] The other, placing primary emphasis on the causal consistency of the story, is caricatured by one of Ionesco's characters, who claims that plays, from ancient Greece to the present, have been nothing more than thrillers.[30]

Sophocles and Aristotle

Exaggerated as this comment may be, it is not inappropriate with regard to either *Oedipus Rex* or the influence that Sophocles' play was to exert through Aristotle's *Poetics*: at least among the plays that have survived, *Oedipus Rex* presents a *tour de force* in detective-story suspense without equal in Greek drama. Its *in medias res* technique, of course, is all too common in the works of the three great tragedians. But nowhere else (except in Euripides' *Ion*, which in parts can be read as an ironical commentary on the *Tyrannus*) is this gradual revelation of the past achieved through an investigative process of comparably labyrinthine complexity, following leads and false leads, turns and counterturns.

As in a detective story, the spectator views this process through the consciousness of the prime investigator. Of course the Greek audience, so familiar with its myths, would probably have known in advance the solution to the story so doggedly pursued by the protagonist.[31] But even a good detective novel loses little of its first attraction upon a second reading. Once we know, we have all the more leisure to study the author's ingenuity in bringing about his solution in such intricate yet none the less inescapable ways. And where else do we find greater ingenuity of this kind in a drama not directly or indirectly influenced by *Oedipus Rex* itself? The play is a unique achievement, and as such its impact on Western literature and on tragedy in particular, thanks mainly to Aristotle's *Poetics*, is without parallel.

The story of Oedipus, who, as predicted by the oracle, kills his father Laius and marries his mother Jocasta, is too familiar to need repeating except for some of its more intricate details. Jocasta hands her ill-omened child to a herdsman to be killed (1173). But out of pity this Theban gives young Oedipus to a Corinthian fellow shepherd (1133ff) who passes him on to King Polybus (1022). Oedipus grows up at the court of Corinth; then somebody at a dinner calls him a bastard. He goes to Delphi to consult Apollo about the charge and instead is told that he will kill his father and marry his mother. Fleeing his doom, he leaves Corinth, only to encounter and kill his true father Laius at a crossroads (771ff). There is one survivor among Laius's servants (756), who later, when he sees Oedipus become the husband of the widow queen, asks to be let go as far away from Thebes as possible (761-3).

The play opens several years after these incidents, when Thebes is suddenly stricken by the plague. Oedipus is told by the Delphic oracle that the plague will disappear only when the murderer of Laius has been found and punished. The action of the play from then on consists of little else than Oedipus's search for the culprit, whom he eventually finds to be himself. By line 860, Oedipus has found out about and sent for the single survivor at the crossroads who, when he appears at line 1109, turns out to be the Theban shepherd who saved young Oedipus's life. Similarly, the messenger from Corinth who arrives at line 924 with the news of Polybus's death is found to be the Corinthian shepherd who years earlier received young Oedipus from his Theban colleague and passed him on to Polybus.

Others of Sophocles' detective-story techniques can best be described by referring to Aristotle, to whom *Oedipus Rex* was the most perfect work of literature and whose *Poetics* is to a large extent modelled upon the play. Even critics and scholars today show little awareness of the extent to which Aristotle, in thus making *Oedipus Rex* the centre-piece of his aesthetics, relied on an oddity even within the Sophoclean *oeuvre*. Had he lived more recently, Aristotle would probably have been a passionate reader of crime fiction; as it was, he found in *Oedipus Rex* some of the detective-story–like criteria to which, he felt, literature should conform in general. Here, for instance, was a story clearly more important than characters, thought, diction, melody, or spectacle, which the philosopher ranks in that order. It is the very opposite of the episodic – that is, worst – kind of plot, in which "there is neither probability nor necessity in the sequence of its episodes." It represents one action, "a complete whole, with its several incidents so closely connected that the transposal or withdrawal of any one of them will disjoin and dislocate the whole."[32]

More specifically, Aristotle discusses the two devices of reversal and discovery and stresses the adroitness with which Sophocles made them arise out of the causal consistency of the story. Oedipus, when the messenger from Corinth reports to him Polybus's death, for a moment believes he has escaped the prophecy that he would murder his father. But before long he learns that he was not related to Polybus, a reversal confirmed by the arriving Theban shepherd, who is forced to testify to Oedipus's identity with the murderer of

Laius. This is what Aristotle with his customary precision describes as the perfect case of peripeteia and anagnorisis combined, a fusion made even more powerful by the fact that the discovery arises "from the incidents themselves, when the great surprise comes about through a probable incident, like that in the *Oedipus* of Sophocles."[33]

To Aristotle the combination of reversal and discovery found in *Oedipus Rex* is a powerful means of arousing pity and fear. This fact, in turn, sheds some light on the much-disputed concept of catharsis. Aristotle defines tragedy as

the imitation of an action that is serious and also, as having magnitude, complete in itself... in a dramatic, not in a narrative form; with incidents arousing pity and fear, wherewith to accomplish its catharsis of such emotions.[34]

Prima facie, the concept seems to involve a contradiction. For "what is done by violence," to Aristotle, "is contrary to Nature."[35] How can tragedy, imitating the worst aspects of life, be the greatest form of poetry when poetry itself is supposed to imitate things, not as they are but as they ought to be? In the general hierarchy of entelechies all driving towards their own perfection, poetry, in this sense, speaks in the universals of that potential perfection rather than in the particulars of imperfect reality. We take pleasure in artistic mimesis primarily because in seeing things imitated we are "gathering the meaning of things."[36] While nature "always strives after 'the better,' "[37] art anticipates this process of teleological self-improvement and aims at filling out "the deficiencies of Nature."[38] Art "partly completes what nature cannot bring to a finish, and partly imitates her."[39] How then can tragedy, with its display of violence arousing fear and pity, lead us towards such perfection?

Aristotle's answer is contained in the very notion of catharsis. And since catharsis results most effectively from a combination of peripeteia and discovery when arising from the very structure and incidents of the play,[40] it also involves his concept of plot unity. To the philosopher, pity and fear are irrational emotions, and their purging, brought about by presenting the irrational in an ordered context, can only have the aim of making man more rational. For to Aristotle,

rational principle and mind are the end towards which nature strives, so that the birth and moral discipline of the citizens ought to be ordered with a view of them ... And as the body is prior in order of generation to the soul, so the irrational is prior to the rational.[41]

However, no catharsis is possible without some form of violence, whether displayed *coram publico*, narrated, or only anticipated. Of all these possibilities, the theatre-of-cruelty effect demanded by Antonin Artaud would have been the least desirable to Aristotle. Those, he writes, "who make use of the

Spectacle to put before us that which is merely monstrous ... are wholly out of touch with Tragedy." And here again Sophocles provided him with the perfect solution. "The Plot in fact should be so framed that, even without seeing the things take place, he who simply hears the account of them shall be filled with horror and pity at the incidents; which is just the effect that the mere recital of the story of *Oedipus* would have on one." Rather than perpetrate the deed of horror knowingly and consciously, like Euripides' Medea, the protagonist should do it "in ignorance of his relationship, and discover that afterwards," like Oedipus. Or even better, he should not do it at all, like Merope in *Cresphontes*, who, "on the point of slaying her son, recognizes him in time."[42] Thus, after fear and pity have been aroused, all can still end happily. More important, in other words, than the actual presentation of suffering and violence is the device of peripeteia, which causes surprise while also letting us recognize what surprised us as an ordered sequence of cause and effect. The pity and fear aroused will be purged by such hindsight.

Sophocles also gave Aristotle a model for his second-most important constituent of tragedy, which is "character." Just as the good portrait painter, without losing his subject's likeness, should make him more handsome than he is, so the tragedian should imitate personages better than the ordinary man. If painters such as Zeuxis "depicted the impossible, the answer is that it is better they should be like that, as the artist ought to improve on his model." Analogously, Aristotle reports Sophocles as having said "that he drew men as they ought to be, and Euripides as they were."[43] Of course, the tragic hero must not be entirely faultless, for then his passing from happiness to misery would cause our moral outrage. He ought to have a flaw, even if only a small one. Whether "a moral fault or failing of some kind,"[44] this *hamartia*, it seems, is basically meant to serve the function of making the hero's superior greatness acceptable to an audience of ordinary mortals. In illustrating this point, Aristotle adduces Homer and Agathon instead of Sophocles, but only perhaps because *Oedipus Rex* had just been invoked in the preceding passage:

As Tragedy is an imitation of personages better than the ordinary man ... [the poet] in portraying men quick or slow to anger, or with similar infirmities of character, must know how to represent them as such, and at the same time as good men, as Agathon and Homer have represented Achilles.[45]

In discussing how Sophocles drew men as they ought to be rather than as they are, Aristotle also touches upon how tragedy should use myth. The tales about the gods, he suggests, may be as false as Xenophanes thinks they are. But even if they conform neither to fact nor to the philosophical sense of how things ought to be, they could still be sanctioned by opinion and tradition.[46] This also, though less dispassionately stated, seems to be Sophocles' basic attitude towards the Olympians. Though less frequently than in Aeschylus or Euripides, we find them everywhere in his plays, either appearing *in propria persona* or at least being talked about by the mortals. But somehow Sophocles seems to be looking the other way. *Ajax*, probably his earliest surviving play, has a truly Homeric opening.[47] Athena allows her protégé Odysseus to watch the discomfiture of his opponent. To laugh at your enemies: "What sweeter laughter can there be than that?" she exclaims (78–9). But all she receives in return is a lesson in human compassion. The noble Odysseus, who will later overturn his chief commanders' verdict against Ajax's burial, is far from exultant:

> ... I pity
> His wretchedness, though he is my enemy,
> For the terrible yoke of blindness that is on him.
> I think of him, yet also of myself;
> For I see the true state of all of us that live.   (121–5)

Another lesson in human greatness is given by the protagonist himself. Despite his destruction and others' claim that the gods destroyed him, the story of his suicide is, in C.H. Whitman's phrase, "one long paean of triumphant individualism."[48] Ajax's death has regained him his honour and restored the social balance disturbed by his madness.

To retrace the evolution of this heroic humanism through Sophocles' individual works, a task carried out by Whitman and others, could add little that is new. It is enough to recall the darkening of the poet's vision in the middle period of the *Trachiniae* and *Oedipus Rex*, with their near-existentialist depiction of innocent suffering in a gratuitously cruel universe, and the deepening of his earlier optimism in *Philoctetes* and *Oedipus at Colonnus*, those final links "in the chain of Sophoclean humanism which sees godhead operative in the moral being of man"[49] rather than in the gods of traditional mythology. Just as Athena in the first play is taught a lesson in humane behavior, so Oedipus in Sophocles' final work, after a life of *pathei mathos*, is himself apotheosized to the level of the divine, while Neoptolemus in *Philoctetes* gives us another, though more complex demonstration in compassion. Persuaded by Odysseus to rob the illness-stricken protagonist of his powerful bow, he eventually, after seeing Philoctetes in his agony, proves to us that "Justice is sometimes better than wisdom" (1244)[50] and hands the bow back to its owner. We know from a lecture by Dio Chrysostom that Neoptolemus, who more and more turns into the play's protagonist, was largely Sophocles' addition to the earlier versions by Aeschylus and Euripides.[51] While Philoctetes persists in his hateful refusal to rejoin the Greeks at Troy, Neoptolemus extends his compassion even further. He promises to take Philoctetes to his homeland even though this may mean a total break with the Greek army. Heracles' *deus ex machina* intervention at this point clearly vindicates Neoptolemus's spirit of compromise as against Philoctetes' stubbornness. For now Philoctetes has to yield to what he refused at Neoptolemus's behest.

Jan Kott recently questioned the nobleness of Philoctetes, reminding us that in all other versions of his story since *The Little Iliad* he is the one to murder old Priam after dragging him by the hair from Zeus's altar.[52] Such an argument, of course, raises the by-now proverbial question as to the number of Lady Macbeth's children. But it is easy enough to see Sophocles' protagonists generally in a more questionable light than that spread by the hero worship of other scholars. What, for instance, are we to think of blind old Oedipus at Colonnus, reputed to have "learned in time" by one critic[53] and to have "gained wisdom through suffering" by another.[54] Oedipus's favourite activity remains to invoke curses on those he believes guilty, and there is none of the ironic poetic justice with which, in the earlier play, he unwittingly called these maledictions upon his own head. Now his curses, for which he vociferously invokes divine justice (1382), have become deadly weapons which will strike the guilty and the innocent, like his beloved Antigone, alike. If these are the results of Oedipus's association with the kindly Eumenides (90, 486f), what do we have here but an almost polemical inversion of Aeschylus's "grand parable of progress" in the *Oresteia*? And if Greek tragedy, as Albin Lesky says so rightly, "was a product of the Greek way of thinking, and one of its components ... the 'need to explain,'"[55] how possibly could the play's episodic plot satisfy this criterion? There is little in the successive appearances of several characters that explains to us Oedipus's final apotheosis.

This is not to suggest that Sophocles either asked himself such questions or deliberately tried to invert tragedy's three major patterns of teleology, heroic humanism, and mimesis. But the possibilities of such parody lay at hand, and by the time *Oedipus at Colonnus* was written, the youngest of the three major tragedians had already explored them to their limits.

Euripides:
Towards Anti-tragedy

IS "BEING" GROUNDED in human language or simply a nonsense word leading to fake problems? Modern as they may sound, questions such as this one, raised in a well-known controversy between Heidegger and Carnap,[1] are not new. Over two millennia ago, Western philosophers were already divided over similar disputes. "That which can be spoken and thought needs must be," wrote Parmenides,

for it is possible for it, but not for nothing, to be ... One way only is left to be spoken of, that it *is*; and on this way are full many signs that what *is* is uncreated and imperishable, for it is entire, immovable and without end.[2]

The Sophist Gorgias probably aimed his *On the Nonexistent or On Nature* directly at Parmenides, arguing that "first and foremost ... nothing exists; second ... even if it exists it is inapprehensible to man; third ... even if it is apprehensible, still it is without a doubt incapable of being expressed or explained to the next man."[3] In other words, there is no such thing as Being. And even if there were, our intellect would be incapable of grasping it, our means of communication unable to articulate it. Title and style of the treatise clearly show Gorgias's parodic intent; but as W.K.C. Guthrie points out,[4] it would be wrong to assume that the philosopher therefore lacked seriousness.

Euripides, Traditionalist and Innovator

The same applies to Euripides, who echoes the Sophists in many of his sayings and rhetorical experiments.[5] Statements of his which now strike us as mere truisms or *jeux d'esprit* could entail the most serious consequences. Euripides' "Zeus, whoever Zeus may be for I know not save by hearsay,"[6] for instance, sounds ordinary enough to a twentieth-century agnostic. However, as the opening line of a lost play entitled *Melanippe*, so Plutarch reports, that parenthesis caused such uproar that the playwright saw himself forced to change it into "Zeus, as truth itself has said." Equally apocryphal, perhaps, but no less revealing is a second anecdote about Socrates, who always used to watch the first productions of Euripides' new plays. This time he was attending *Electra* but left the theatre in disgust at the point where Orestes, trying to ascertain the nature of goodness, concludes: "We can only toss our judgements random on the wind" (379).[7]

A little later, Plato would decide in his *Laws* that blasphemies like Orestes' "O Phoebus, your holy word was brute and ignorant" (*Electra* 971) deserved severest punishment. To Plato, it was a proven fact that the gods existed and were concerned with the fate of mankind but could not be bribed. Offenders against these beliefs were to be sentenced to a minimum of five years' solitary confinement in a reform centre where "members of the Nocturnal Council" would try to "ensure their spiritual salvation." If the culprit suffered a relapse after that, he was to be executed. Not all blasphemers or heretics, of course, were to enjoy the privilege of this *Nineteen Eighty-four*-style mental-rehabilitation program. A punishment worse than death, lifelong and total solitary confinement in a special prison in the country, was held in store for those found "subhuman" in their stubbornness.[8] No doubt a man like Euripides would have found himself among the condemned of one kind or another; the mere fact of being a poet would have been enough in itself to incur the philosopher's disapproval. While forbidding tragedians to enter his Republic, Plato allowed for one kind of tragedy only, the one which is enacted on a regular basis by the model community of his brainwashed citizens. Our entire state, he writes, "has been constructed so as to be a 'representation' of the finest and noblest life – the very thing we maintain is most genuinely a tragedy."[9]

If we abstract it from its polemical bias, that statement no more than articulates in particularly pointed form the mainstream philosophical and / or political implications of tragedy in both theory and practice from its beginnings. For Aeschylus the emphasis may lie on a combination of theodicy and political progress, while Sophocles simply stresses the nobility of man in the face of a hostile universe. To Aristotle, who mainly follows the lead of Sophocles, tragedy may serve the function of purging an audience of fear and pity by tracing the logical chain of cause and effect leading to the events that produce such emotions. To Hegel, who in this stems from Aeschylus, it embodies the dialectical unfoldings of the World Spirit at the points where thesis and antithesis come into conflict. In each case, and Plato's fanciful proposition is no exception, tragedy amounts to the implicit demonstration of a metaphysical and / or ethical theorem in the wider sense.

When this theorem was first questioned by Euripides, of course, none of Plato's and Aristotle's discussions of it, let alone those of Hegel, yet existed. But as we have seen, the roots of its three major components – teleology, mimesis, heroic humanism – were clearly prefigured in the works of Aeschylus and Sophocles. Euripides, in fact, was familiar with the traditional tragic mode to the point of writing "tragedies" of both Sophoclean and Aeschylean orientation throughout his life. Whatever un-Sophoclean elements it may contain in the portrayal of Phaedra, *Hippolytus*, one of Euripides' earliest plays, gives us a lesson in human nobility no less explicit than those contained in either *Ajax* or *Philoctetes*. The protagonist, an innocent victim of his father's curse, dies with true forgiveness on his lips:

> HIPPOLYTUS
> ... I free you from all guilt in this.
> THESEUS
> You will acquit me of blood guiltiness?
> HIPPOLYTUS
> So help me Artemis of the conquering bow!
> THESEUS
> Dear son, how noble you have proved to me!   (1449-52)

Another play, which may well be his last, proved Aeschylean enough to Hegel to be singled out, along with the *Oresteia* and others, as embodying the conflict between the "ethical life in its social universality and the family as the natural ground of moral relations."[10] *Iphigenia in Aulis* may be un-Aeschylean in showing how the true motive force behind the sacrifice of the heroine is not so much an offended divinity but the "terrible passion [that] has seized all Greece" (809). But the words with which Iphigenia embraces her sacrifice, suggesting that the gods have a right to demand it since it will lead to the triumph of her people, are spoken in the true spirit of Aeschylean theodicy.

> Because of me, never more will
> Barbarians wrong and ravish Greek women.
> ...
>   O Mother, if Artemis
> Wishes to take the life of my body,
> Shall I, who am mortal, oppose
> The divine will? No – that is unthinkable!
> To Greece I give this body of mine.
> Slay it in sacrifice and conquer Troy.   (1379-80, 1394-7)

The dates of *Hippolytus* and *Iphigenia at Aulis* warn us against describing Euripides' anti-tragic vision as one that gradually evolved as he grew older. Whether or not there was a development along these lines remains an open question. At the same time, many of Euripides' surviving plays reveal distinct techniques which seem to question, invert, or transcend the tragic patterns he inherited from his predecessors. Such patterns are Sophocles' heroic humanism, the unified plot structure which Aristotle found in his model tragedy *Oedipus Rex*, and Aeschylus's teleological dialectic, which was to find its systematizer in Hegel. Most of the techniques can, for clarity's sake, be described as either anticlimactic or projective audience manipulation – two of anti-tragedy's most powerful means of questioning, negating, and inverting the tragic vision. Anticlimactic audience manipulation arouses certain expectations in order to frustrate them. This happens in, for instance, *Orestes*, whose entire plot is a series of such anticlimactic strategies. We are led to expect, one after another, the traditional outcome of a "suppliant" action, a "rescue" piece, and a "vengeance tragedy." But each of these "tragic" actions, as Anne P. Burnett has shown, ends "in conglomerate failure."[11] Projective audience manipulation is at work when the audience is given certain information that permits it to recognize the dramatis personae's ignorance or self-delusion. Euripides' *Ion* offers us an example.

Hermes, in a typically Euripidean prologue, tells us that Ion, now temple servant at Delphi, was born of Apollo's union with Creusa. Now Creusa has come to consult the oracle because her more recent marriage with Xuthus has remained childless. So neither Ion nor Creusa realizes, as we do, that a son is talking to his mother when they first encounter each other. Ion's and Creusa's blind dilemmas, the mother trying to murder her son and he attempting to have her executed, are revealed to us from a truly Olympian perspective. We turn fellow voyeurs of Hermes when the god, after delivering his prologue, decides to watch the spectacle from a hiding place in a laurel grove. It is the detective-story pattern of *Oedipus Rex* all over again, but with a difference. In Sophocles' play, the truth so doggedly pursued by the protagonist finally stands revealed to us as a causally consistent chain of events. The truth uncovered in *Ion*, by contrast, is how much humans are puppets in the hands of gods who seem as confused as the mortals themselves. What Hermes predicts at the end of the prologue – Xuthus will be made to believe that Ion is his son and Apollo's union with Creusa remain a secret – comes true only in part. The god's sexual escapade is made known at least to Ion, Creusa, and the Chorus of her attendants, and that by Athena who was sent by Apollo because, had he come himself, he might have been "blamed for what / Has happened in the past" (1556–7). Here projective audience manipulation has joined forces with its anticlimactic counterpart, which, generally speaking, is the more versatile and frequent of the two.

Euripides and the Sophists

When Euripides, in *The Bacchae*, made his final, though half-hearted foray into the world of the post-tragic, Heraclitus may well have been his mental guide. Before that, the playwright without doubt drew inspiration from the Sophists in evolving the anti-tragic techniques observable in other of his plays. Particularly relevant here must have been the Sophistic *dissoi logoi*, a genre Protagoras initiated with his two books of "antilogies." A surviving treatise entitled "Concerning Just and Unjust" provides us with an example; although later than Euripides' *Electra*, it shows the kind of Sophistic argument that may have influenced the poet in writing his play. As against those who hold that "the just is one thing and the unjust another," the anonymous author argues "that the just and the unjust are the same." Given specific circumstances, it is just to tell lies, to break an oath, or even to murder one's nearest and dearest. Here Aeschylus's *Eumenides* seems to provide one of the examples: "In the case of Orestes and of Alcmaeon, even the god answered that they were right to have done as they did."[12] The same argument is central to Euripides' *Electra* and, in fact, is presented in a *dissoi logoi* dispute between the protagonist and her brother. Orestes, after the murder of Aegisthus, suddenly suffers pangs of conscience about killing his mother. But Electra, whose attitude carries the day, is as adamant as the unknown Sophist:

ORESTES
O god!
How can I kill her when she brought me up and bore me?
ELECTRA
Kill her just the way she killed my father. And yours.
ORESTES
O Phoebus, your holy word was brute and ignorant.
ELECTRA
Where Apollo is ignorant shall men be wise?
...
ORESTES
As matricide I shall stand trial. I was clean before.
ELECTRA
Not clean before the gods, if you neglect your father.
ORESTES
I know – but will I not be judged for killing Mother?
ELECTRA
And will you not be judged for quitting Father's service?
ORESTES
A polluted demon spoke it in the shape of god –
ELECTRA
Throned on the holy tripod? I shall not believe you.
ORESTES
And I shall not believe those oracles were pure.
ELECTRA
You may not play the coward now and fall to weakness.
Go in. I will bait her a trap as she once baited one
which sprang at Aegisthus' touch and killed her lawful husband.
ORESTES
I am going in. I walk a cliff-edge in a sea
of evil, and evil I will do. If the gods approve,
let it be so. This game of death is bitter, and sweet.   (968-87)

Electra

This is not to say that the play as a whole simply dramatizes the dislogistic relativism of the Sophists. Euripides' probing scepticism goes far deeper than that, deep enough, in fact, to encompass such relativism itself. This is most obvious when we look at the play's protagonist in comparison with her counterparts in Aeschylus's *The Libation Bearers* and Sophocles' *Electra*.[13] Speaking in the most general terms, Euripides puts his audience into a quandary about Electra and her cause, whereas neither Sophocles nor Aeschylus leaves us in doubt as to how to judge the heroine. In this, Euripides more or less retains the characterization of Electra found in Sophocles and Aeschylus but drastically changes the circumstances and repercussions of the murder she helps to perform.

Surprisingly, the heroine is a *bête noire* to many critics who denounce her as a "self-pitying slattern" (M. Hadas),[14] "a condescending psychopathic shrew" (G.S. Kirk),[15] or an "obsessive neurotic ... more concerned with [her] standard of living than with morality" (E.T. Vermeule).[16] In fact, there is hardly a character trait even among her more unappealing ones which cannot be found in her more heroic namesakes. Euripides' Electra may be full not only of self-pity but of self-destruction and suicidal "hatred of living" (121; see also 688, 757). But in this she merely follows the model pattern of the Sophoclean tragic heroine like Antigone or Electra herself, who, when threatened with being buried alive, finds that the sooner this will happen, the better (387). She may be "wild and stubborn" (1117), but hardly more so than her Sophoclean counterpart, whose rebelliousness (as in the contrast between Antigone and Ismene) is thrown into striking relief by her sister Chrysothemis's "prudence and caution" (1015).[17] In justifying the imminent murder of Clytaemnestra she may argue a justice of primitive retaliation – "If the first death was just, the second too is just" (1096). But here again she simply picks up on Electra's arguments in Sophocles:

> If life for life be the rule,
> Justice demands your life before all others. (581–2)[18]

For all that, Euripides' Electra may be more gratuitously self-righteous than Sophocles'. But she is less so than Aeschylus's. The Electra of *The Libation Bearers*, in fact, is characterized by little else. "Let Force, and Right, / and Zeus almighty, third with them, be on your side" (244–5), she tells Orestes. "There has been wrong done. I ask for right. / Hear me, Earth. Hear me, grandeurs of Darkness" (398–9). Here as elsewhere she is associated with the chthonic forces and their simple eye-for-an-eye justice. In praying for evil (146) and in invoking

Earth, conquering Justice, and all the gods besides (147–8), she knows that her thirst for revenge is as implacable as that of the Furies themselves:

> For we are bloody like the wolf
> and savage born from the savage mother. (421–2)

Euripides' Electra exclaims how gladly she would die in Mother's blood (281), eagerly takes on the planning of Clytaemnestra's death (647), and actually guides Orestes' sword during the murder (1225). In all this, she only acts out in psychologically realistic detail what her Aeschylean counterpart represents in the abstract.

The same is true of her obsessive involvement with her father, her loathing for the mother, and her puritanical attitude in general. All of these traits are to be found in either Aeschylus or Sophocles. If they are more pronounced in Euripides, it is not because he has turned his heroine into an obsessive neurotic but simply because he has the deeper psychological insight. It is all very well to claim that Electra is more concerned with her standard of living than her morality because she happens, once too often, to reflect on Clytaemnestra's sumptuous clothes or to complain about not having the right husband. But her mother's most outstanding attribute when she appears on stage *is* her luxuriousness. Electra, when all the great princes of Greece came to ask for her hand, *was* forced to marry a peasant (21f). There is a tendency among critics to mention Electra and Orestes in one breath as if the heroine shared her brother's arrogance and blasé intellectualism. But it is Orestes, not Electra, who refers to the Old Man who saved his life as "this human antique" (553). It is he, not she, who calls Electra's husband "one of nature's gentlemen" (262) and concludes that, looking for the good, "We can only toss our judgements random on the wind" (379). If this speech, as Diogenes Laertius reports, made Socrates leave the theatre, it may well have been because of its silliness rather than its Sophistic subtlety. By contrast, Electra has several qualities which make her, in many ways, a more human figure than her namesakes in either Aeschylus or Sophocles. Acknowledging that her farmer husband is "equal to the gods in kindliness" (67), she addresses him as "My dearest husband" (345) and, quite against his wishes, insists on toiling to keep his house in order (75). She also clearly loves her brother, and in a deeper way than the Electra of either Sophocles or Aeschylus.

What, then, makes us feel ambivalent about Euripides' heroine and her cause? In principle, her cause is no less just than in the other plays. In practice it is sanctioned by the good Old Man, saviour of Orestes, who, after shedding some tears in the presence of the protagonist (501f), is Electra's staunchest supporter in advising Orestes to kill both Aegisthus and Clytaemnestra (613). "I will escort you on your way with greatest joy" (670), he tells him. Even the Chorus, after Orestes has killed Aegisthus, talks of "high justice routing the unjust" (878), while Electra, not surprisingly, gains more and more confidence in the gods as the guarantors of the justice she enacts. Her initial complaint, that no god ever heard her helpless cry (199–200), yields to a more aggressive scepticism after she is reunited with her brother. Never, she exclaims, "believe in god / again if evil can still triumph over good" (583–4), and as if to fulfil her side of the bargain she quickly falls to invoking Zeus, Hera, and Earth (671ff). Her confidence after the death of Aegisthus will be strong enough to sway the reluctant Orestes into murdering their mother: "O gods! O Justice watching the world, you have come at last" (771).

But it all collapses like a house of cards. Even Electra, let alone her weaker brother, is overwhelmed by guilt and horror when faced with the actual crime, and the word justice, which had anaesthetized her imagination against the crude facts of actual experience, never again crosses her lips:

> ELECTRA
> Weep greatly for me, my brother, I am guilty.
> A girl flaming in hurt I marched against
> the mother who bore me.
>
> ...
>
> ORESTES
> You saw her agony, how she threw aside her dress,
> how she was showing her breast there in the midst of death?
> My god, how she bent to earth
> the legs which I was born through? and her hair – I touched it –
>
> ...
>
> She cracked into a scream then, she stretched up her hand
> toward my face: "My son! Oh, be pitiful my son!"
> She clung to my face,
> suspended, hanging; my arm dropped with the sword –
>
> ...
>
> I snatched a fold of my cloak to hood my eyes, and, blind,
> took the sword and sacrificed
> my mother – sank steel to her neck.
>
> ELECTRA
> I urged you on, I urged you on,
> I touched the sword beside your hand
>
> ...
>
> ORESTES
> Take it! shroud my mother's dead flesh in my cloak
> clean and close the sucking wounds
> You carried your own death in your womb.
>
> ELECTRA
> Behold! I wrap her close in the robe,
> the one I loved and could not love.   (1183–1231)

This heart-rending epilogue to the murders cuts across all the previous resemblances between Euripides' play and its Aeschylean or Sophoclean counterparts. Aeschylus's Electra may be close to Euripides' in self-righteously vengeful ferocity and determination, but in the *Oresteia*'s dialectical movement towards a higher form of justice she is no more than the almost allegorical representative of a strictly retributive justice which is left behind in *The Eumenides*. After fulfilling this function, she makes her last speech, which she explicitly announces as such, well before the actual murders of Aegisthus and Clytaemnestra, and never reappears in the final part of the trilogy. Sophocles' Electra may closely resemble Euripides' in some of her psychological characteristics, such as the one that inspired Freud to label the female counterpart of the Oedipus complex after her. But however much her sister and others criticize her, the play as a whole seems to throw such reproaches back into the teeth of her detractors. Especially towards its end, Sophocles' *Electra* builds up towards a veritable crescendo in praise of the heroine's "true nobility" (1080).[19] Having "lived faithfully / In duty to God / And to the great eternal laws, and found / In these [her] victory" (1096-9), Electra has won the "twofold crown, / Wisdom and piety" (1088-9). "And who / Condemns?" asks the Chorus after Clytaemnestra has been murdered. Its answer, "Not I" (1424-5),[20] clearly is the one the audience is invited to give, too. It is easy enough to disagree, as many critics (including the present one) do – but only by overriding the implied interpretation which Sophocles, even more explicitly than Aeschylus, tends to build into his plays.

Euripides, then, for large parts of his *Electra*, seems to follow either Aeschylus or Sophocles. But he only does so in order to crush the expectations such parallels have aroused. For all that, the play is far from being structured around a single feat of anticlimactic audience manipulation. *Electra* is not confined to a mere debunking of values. Instead, it gives them credit and criticism to an equal degree, thus disarming their detractors and supporters alike. Whatever techniques of audience manipulation are used in the process are a mere means to the end of this reductive process.

Even before the play begins, we are told that Clytaemnestra is not the monster who in Sophocles' version seems ready to see her daughter Electra buried alive unless she ceases to bemoan her father (374ff). When Aegisthus laid plans to kill Orestes, it was the mother who saved her son's life (27f). Whatever Electra may subsequently have to say about "Tyndareus' hellish daughter" (117), who "rolls in her bloody bed / and plays at love with a stranger" (211-12), Clytaemnestra's actual appearance as a vain but insightful woman who is forgiving rather than vindictive and half-remorseful instead of self-righteous does not come as a total surprise. In both Sophocles and Euripides, Electra secures her impunity before she proceeds to accuse and insult her mother. But in Sophocles, Clytaemnestra breaks her promise, threatening that Electra will be punished as soon as Aegisthus comes back (626-7). In

Euripides, her response after having been (worse than in Sophocles) called a murderess, whore, and hypocrite is one of psychoanalytic sophistication which totally disregards the insult. This woman, it seems, has done too much protesting, arguing, and insulting herself but has learned that words, especially with puritanically idealistic natures like her daughter's, more often than not are prompted by psychological impulses totally alien to the arguments at hand.

Already Electra's language, which so frequently circles around her love for the father, her wish to murder the mother, and an almost voyeuristic concern with Clytaemnestra's sexuality, has shown us that there are other motives than Agamemnon's death which sharpen her urge to kill her mother or, worse, die herself "in Mother's blood" (281). In an ironic twist of audience manipulation, it is Clytaemnestra who is made to confirm this impression in her laconic reply to Electra's impassioned harangue:

> My child, from birth you always have adored your father.
> This is part of life. Some children always love
> the male, some turn more closely to their mother than him.
> I know you and forgive you. I am not so happy
> either, child, with what I have done or with myself.
>
> ...
>
> O god, how miserably my plans have all turned out.
> Perhaps I drove my hate too hard against my husband.   (1102–10)

Anticlimactic audience manipulation, which further detracts from Electra's cause, occurs in the portrayal of Aegisthus. The same technique is already found in the early *Heracleidae* (circa 429 BC). Here Eurystheus, would-be executioner of Heracles' children, is introduced as the "king, whose record is as black / As sin" (17–18). But his personal appearance after he has been defeated completely contradicts this description. He openly confesses his misdeeds and faces death with dignified courage, while Alcmene, Heracles' mother, turns into a vengeful fury insisting that his body be thrown to the dogs. In *Electra* the reversal is less theatrical but equally effective. In the protagonist's memories, Aegisthus pelts Agamemnon's stone memorial with rocks or in his drunken fits leaps and dances on the burial mound. But in fact he turns out to be a man worshipful of the gods and generously attentive towards his unknown guest, Orestes, who abuses this hospitality in order to murder him.

As much as such techniques deflect our sympathies from the murderers towards their victims, however, they never invalidate the avengers' justification completely. There is enough left to see Electra's cause as properly motivated and ethically justified. Our doubts, in other words, are not focused on a specific case but on the validity of such motivation and justification in general. The spectator, "Hypocrite ... mon semblable – mon frère," is not allowed the escape into self-righteousness himself. D.H. Lawrence once observed that from its very beginnings, Greek drama, by contrast to some of its non-Western counterparts, was presented to be judged at first by some god, later by an Olympian audience which replaces him. "The spectacle is offered to us. And we sit aloft, enthroned in the Mind, dominated by some one exclusive idea, and we judge the show."[21] Euripides' *Electra* is an exception only in the proverbial sense of confirming the rule. For in the labyrinth of the playwright's manipulative strategies, the spectator never gets a chance to complete his judgment. The techniques which in Aeschylean and Sophoclean tragedy invite us to make such judgments are countered by others which cancel them out. The metastructures of meaning typical of Western drama are reduced to a degree zero.

On these grounds, Emily T. Vermeule is right in saying that critics like Rose and Hadas have fallen into Euripides' trap when they denounce Orestes and Electra as two "fanatical monomaniacs" committing a crime "as dastardly as conceivable."[22] But she falls into a worse trap herself in deciding that the play, instead of indicting human beings, is "another phase in [the playwright's] campaign against Apollo, [and] the morality of the gods."[23] This is a view shared by other critics, and on the face of it there would seem to be good support for it. For what else could be meant when the *deus ex machina* Dioscuri, appearing just after Electra has wrapped Clytaemnestra's corpse in Orestes' cloak, are made to declare, "On Phoebus I place all / guilt for this death" (1296–7)? Are they not acquitting Electra of her share in such guilt? But what the Dioscuri blame on the god in his absence is little else than what Apollo in *The Eumenides* takes upon himself, declaring that he bears responsibility for Clytaemnestra's murder (579–80). In their prediction of the events told in *The Eumenides*, the Dioscuri reiterate the same thought: "Loxias will take / all blame on himself for having asked your mother's death" (1266–7). Moreover, blaming Apollo for the murder is not their only comment on the matter. Justice has claimed Clytaemnestra, they argue a little earlier, but Orestes has "not worked in justice" (1244). In their divine verdicts such paradoxes seem to be of the very essence:

> As for Phoebus, Phoebus – yet he is my lord,
> silence. He knows the truth but his oracles were lies.   (1246–7)

As if trying to enhance our general sense of life's paradoxical illusoriness, the Dioscuri even recall the story of *Helen*, an earlier play by Euripides in which they put in a similar last-minute *deus ex machina* appearance. Helen never went to Troy. "Zeus fashioned and dispatched a Helen-image there / to Ilium so men might die in hate and blood" (1281–3). In an ultimate sense, this seemingly gratuitous feat of divine cruelty remains as unjustified as Apollo's role in making Orestes murder his mother. There is no theodicy or teleology to vindicate the cruelty of existence; fate, as embodied by Zeus and Apollo, makes a mockery of such wishful thinking. All we can do is accept the "ghastly absurdity of existence" which Nietzsche associated with the Dionysiac, erroneously blaming Euripides for its destruction.[24]

> Compulsion is on us to accept this scene, on you
> to go complete the doom which fate and Zeus decreed.
>
> ...
>
> Doom is compelling, it leads and we follow –
> doom and the brutal song of Apollo.   (1247-8,1301-2)

To put it somewhat differently, Euripides retrieved myth from the moralistic and teleological encrustations imposed upon it by Aeschylus. This is particularly noticeable with regard to Apollo, the most Olympian god of the Zeus dynasty.

Without wanting to enter the debate over the primordial nature of Greek myth,[25] there is good reason to assume that Apollo, before he became the god of reason, patriarchy, and progress, had a more demonic, amoral, and destructive nature. The entire *Iliad* begins when the god, angered at Agamemnon's discourtesy to one of his priests, sends a deadly plague among the king's soldiers and kills off their cattle and dogs with his arrows. Unlike Hesiod, Homer is known to have purged his gods of such primitive behaviour as castration, child-swallowing, and incest, making them almost totally human in both their virtues and their vices. It is all the more surprising therefore that Apollo emerges as the most mysterious and least anthropomorphized divine power in the *Iliad*.[26] At one point, we even see him in the shape of a vulture enjoying the view of the battle from the top of an oak tree (VII.65ff).

In the *Theogony* the god is conspicuous mainly for his absence, but his transformation into the main representative of the Olympian spirit, which Hesiod celebrates in Zeus himself, must have occurred shortly thereafter. Like Zeus, victor over Typhoeus, the monstrous progeny of Earth and Tartarus who is hurled down into the underworld, Apollo, in the third Homeric hymn, kills the great she-dragon Python,[27] like Typhoeus a child of Gaia. Aeschylus, in the *Oresteia*, finally turns Apollo into what a recent critic, following Bachofen, calls the "arch-opponent of matriarchy." By now, the god had become "all sunlight, Olympian, manifest, rational."[28] Or, as Jane Harrison writes: "Orthodoxy demanded that about Apollo there should be nothing 'earthy' and no deed or dream of darkness."[29] If an orthodoxy, it must have been a recent one, and Euripides' "brutal song of Apollo" in the *Electra* was not the only charge which the playwright brought against it.

Euripides:
Towards Post-tragedy

THE PLAYWRIGHT'S RADICAL retransformation of this orthodoxy into something more primitive, amoral, fatalistic is in many ways typical of his anti-tragic dramaturgy in general. For if Aeschylus, in creating tragedy, turned myth into a near-allegorical abstract, Euripides, in questioning the tragic vision, had to dismantle this ideological metastructure imposed on myth. In this, *Heracles*, probably written a little over a decade before *Electra* (circa 413 BC), is his most stunning achievement. Recent critics of the play have tried to do justice to what their predecessors denounced as a "broken-backed," "grotesque abortion" falling so "clearly into two parts that we cannot view it as a work of art."[1] Yet how Euripides, by manipulating his audience, reverses the traditional tragic and mythic patterns remains a largely uncharted field.

Heracles

From the start, *Heracles* seems to follow the *Oresteia* in abounding with comments directing our attention to the possible outcome of the tragic conflict which arose after Heracles, now thought dead, went on a journey to Hades. The tyrant Lycus, usurper of Thebes, is threatening to kill Heracles' wife Megara and their children, who, along with Amphitryon, have sought refuge at an altar. "Is there any hope? What chance of rescue?" (79). Such questions naturally point to Zeus, who, as Heracles' father, should be concerned for his kindred (48, 170). If the god "intended justice here" (212), Lycus would suffer at Amphitryon's and Megara's hands rather than the reverse. When Lycus orders his henchmen to chop up oaken logs in order to have the suppliants burned alive, Amphitryon for a moment loses his faith in this justice of a god who, after all, made him a cuckold:

... I, mere man, am nobler than you, great god.
I did not betray the sons of Heracles.
You knew well enough to creep into my bed
and take what was not yours, what no man gave:
what do you know of saving those you love?
You are a callous god or were born unjust!   (342-7)

But the imminent threat of death restores enough of his confidence to make him implore Zeus for help (499ff). And the god seems to answer his supplications when Megara suddenly catches sight of Heracles approaching them from a distance: "He comes / to rescue us and Zeus comes with him" (521-2). Shortly afterwards, as the death screams of Lycus, killed by Heracles, ring out from within the house, the Chorus intones a hymn in praise of divine justice full of echoes from the *Oresteia*:

Justice flows back! O fate of the gods,
returning!
...
Die: you would have killed. Show your boldness now
as you repay to justice all you owe.

What lying mortal made that fable
that mindless tale
that slander on the blessed?
Who denied the gods are strong?
...
The gods of heaven do prevail:
they raise the good and scourge the bad.   (736-74)

The sudden disruption of these high-flown sentiments does not come as a total surprise. For expectation is built up in *Heracles* deliberately enough to border on parody. The choral propagators of divine justice who are about to be given a lesson in life's cruelty caricature themselves at every opportunity. Senile and decrepit, "mere words, ghosts that walk" (111), these old men of Thebes are a pitiful sight. Dancing, they assure each other of mutual support if any of them should collapse (122f). They are equally ludicrous in suggesting that the gods lack *their* wisdom because the gods have failed to distinguish good men from bad ones by a second youth (655ff). On the other hand, they can also play their traditional role in singing the praises of Heracles' labours (348ff) or, as in the lines quoted above (736ff), in eulogizing divine justice. Yet clearly comical again are the claims they derive from such activities:

I may not live without the Muses.
Let my head be always crowned!
May my old age always sing
of memory, the Muses' mother,
always shall I sing the crown
of Heracles the victor!

...

never shall I cease to sing,
   Muses who made me dance! (676–86)

The lines bristle with irony. This would-be poet is a caricature of the traditional tragedian as he was to appear in Aristophanes' comedies. But the humour has none of Aristophanes' benevolence. Instead, it is black and caustic. Soon after, the Chorus will totally reverse its plans.

What dirge, what song
shall I sing for the dead?
What dance shall I dance for death? (1025–7)

What has happened? In the middle of announcing how justice still finds favour among the blessed gods, the Chorus is suddenly sent into shrieking hysteria by a supernatural apparition: "*A crash of thunder. The figure of Madness, gorgon-faced and holding a goad, appears in a black chariot on the roof of the palace. On the other side of the roof Iris is seen*" (815). Hera has sent Madness to Heracles so that he will kill his wife and children. In the exchange that follows between Madness and Iris, Euripides seems to allude deliberately to *Prometheus Bound*, reinforcing a parallel hinted at earlier in the play. Heracles, in performing his various labours, is described as Prometheus's fellow champion of human progress. He promised "to civilize the world" (20), and his last and hardest task, after ridding the earth of its evil monsters, is the harrowing of hell, in progress during the play's first part. This mythical Hades and its unheroic counterpart – the potential hell that lives in all of us – form central thematic concerns of the play. In its first half, the hero is about to gain a victory similar to the one which the younger Olympian gods of reason, order, and light won over Earth and the Furies in *The Eumenides*. Heracles has not only conquered Hades, freed Theseus from infernal captivity, and brought back with him captive the triple-headed dog (611) but will also save his wife and children from their deathbound journey:

Rip from your heads those wreaths of Hades!
Lift your faces to the light; with seeing eyes,
take your sweet reprieve from death and darkness. (562–4)

"Mankind's benefactor, man's greatest friend" (1252) is close to celebrating his greatest triumph over the forces of death and darkness.

But the powers he thought to have conquered reappear to destroy the conqueror. The poisonous blood of the Hydra, into which, after killing the monster, Heracles dipped his arrows (1190), now kills his children. When he wakes from his fury and sees the corpses of his wife and children scattered all around him, hell seems to be there again:

> Have I come back to Hades? Have I run
> Eurystheus' race again?

But this is no hell of fabled distant realms. It is the real one, here and now, the hero's inner inferno:

> Hades? But how?
> No, for I see no rock of Sisyphus,
> no Pluto, no queen Demeter's sceptre.
> I am bewildered.   (1101–5)

This is not to say that Euripides has interiorized the mythological notion of Hades by turning it into a mere metaphor of insanity. True enough, his portrayal of Heracles' madness (867ff, 931ff), especially in the madman's own words as he wakes from his fit (1088ff), are worthy of a Shakespeare. But insanity as a mythic numen is just as real. And both are new in Greek drama.

Nowhere in either Aeschylus or Sophocles do we find madness depicted with this almost clinical accuracy. In Sophocles' *Ajax*, which otherwise bears resemblance to *Heracles*, the protagonist's mad fit is already over when we first encounter him. And nowhere even in Euripides' own plays do we find anything as theatrically effective as the staging of Madness. Her closest mythological kindred in Greek tragedy are Aeschylus's Furies. Like the gorgon-faced Madness, "child of blackest Night," "loathsome to the gods" (833, 845), the black-robed Erinyes are the daughters of Night, "loathed alike by men and the heavenly gods" (*Eumenides* 73, 321). They "come like gorgons" (*Libation Bearers* 1048) and strike their victim with madness. But the role of these pitiless barbaric vestiges of an obsolete cosmic order, who are taught better manners by the younger Olympians, is completely reversed in Euripides. Here the daughter of Night pleads mercy for the Promethean champion of mankind, whereas the Olympians, in the person of Zeus's wife Hera, are implacable in their revenge. This man, Madness tells Hera's messenger Iris,

> has won great fame on earth and with the gods.
> He reclaimed the pathless earth and raging sea,

and he alone held up the honors of the gods
when they wilted at the hands of evil men.
I advise you: renounce these wicked plans.
IRIS
Hera's scheme and mine need no advice from you.
MADNESS
I would place you on the better path: you choose the worse.
IRIS
Hera has not sent you down to show your sanity.
MADNESS
O Sun, be my witness: I act against my will. (8505–8)

In inverting the tragic patterns created by Aeschylus, Euripides thus again, in both a psychological and a mythical sense, seems to return to notions more archaic than those of the older tragedian. A daughter of Night and Uranos, Madness belongs to the earliest generation of the Hesiodic theogony, while the insanity she causes with such irresistible force corresponds to an understanding of man antedating that held by the older Sophists as well as by Socrates. Among these later philosophers, the Homeric notion of evil as due to possession by a demon was replaced by a growing belief in the moral perfectibility of man. The remnants of "barbarian silliness" in human society, they felt, could be extirpated by continuous reform of the social order. Virtue, according to Protagoras, could be taught. *Arete*, in Socrates' view, should be an object of scientific inquiry and knowledge.[2]

Apart from *Heracles*, there are several other of Euripides' plays which clarify the playwright's attitude towards this ethical optimism. Medea, for instance, has the barbaric traits which, the enlightened philosophers felt, could so easily be replaced by more civilized modes of behaviour. But this is by no means what the playwright seems to imply. About to murder her children, Medea implores her own heart not to "do these things" (1056), but in vain. Her alter ego, possessed by her *thumos* or passion, is, as she knows herself, stronger:

I know indeed what evil I intend to do,
But stronger than all my afterthoughts is my fury,
Fury that brings upon mortals the greatest evil.   (1078–80)

Video meliora proboque, deteriora sequor. Even more explicit is Phaedra's comment that people do evil while fully aware of the good. "There are many who know virtue," she argues. "We know the good, we apprehend it clearly. / But we can't bring it to achievement" (*Hippolytus* 378–80). Though put into Phaedra's mouth, the words are widely taken as Euripides' refutation of Socrates' optimism. The man whom Nietzsche misjudged as the "poet of esthetic Socratism"[3] is thus revealed as one of the staunchest opponents of the new rationalism.

E.R. Dodds argues that Euripides, while making Medea and Phaedra psychoanalyse their emotions, demythologizes their worlds.[4] This is partly true of *Medea* but not of *Hippolytus*, let alone *Heracles*, which Dodds fails to mention in this context. Even Medea's murderous passion, in a sense, is not without its mythological counterpart, for the heroine herself more and more assumes the supernatural dimensions otherwise missing in the play. A "bloody Fury raised by fiends of Hell" (1260), she even comes to resemble Madness in *Heracles*, especially when enthroned in her grandfather Helios's dragon-drawn chariot, the mangled bodies of her murdered children piled up beside her. Turning to Phaedra's madness in *Hippolytus*, we find that the mutual reinforcement of myth and psychology stands out even more clearly. The fact that her deadly passion was "sent from some god" (241) is well known to the heroine, and even more so to the audience. In the prologue the god, who is Aphrodite, has more or less told us in advance what will happen to her and her victim. Hippolytus, the son of Phaedra's husband Theseus, has blasphemed the goddess, who, in order to destroy the offender, has stricken his stepmother with a mad passion for him. Rejected and overwhelmed by guilt, Phaedra will commit suicide but also make sure to destroy Hippolytus by leaving behind a letter accusing him of having raped her. Phaedra is well aware that in doing so she, in fact, is assuming the role of the vengeful goddess herself. Authentic as her evil passion may be in a psychological sense, it is not less so in a mythological one. For ultimately, so Euripides seems to suggest, they are one and the same.

> I shall delight the Goddess who destroys me,
> the Goddess Cypris.
> Bitter will have been the love that conquers me,
> but in my death I shall at least bring sorrow,
> upon another, too.   (726-8)

Aphrodite, who uses the basically innocent Phaedra as a mere pawn, of course, differs radically from her Aeschylean namesake. In the fragment of the trilogy headed by *The Suppliant Maidens*, Aphrodite seems, like Apollo in *The Eumenides*, to argue for some just cause. By contrast, her Euripidean counterpart, as "Cypris of the Sea" (522), recalls the gruesome story of her birth in the *Theogony*. After Kronos, so Hesiod tells us, had castrated his father, Uranos's blood fell on to the earth, giving birth to the Furies and Giants, and from his genitals, thrown out into the sea, arose Aphrodite.[5] A power beyond good and evil, Euripides' Cypris is both the destroyer and creator from whom "everything, / that is, is born" (448-9). The Nurse in her confusion appropriately describes her true nature in a paradox. "Cypris, you are no God. / You are something stronger than God" (359-60). But for being amoral and non-anthropomorphic, she is all the more mythic if by that term we denote the numinous realm beyond the reach of strictly rationalist thought. She is the life-force deprived of the teleological superstructures of Aeschylean tragedy.

Euripides' *Heracles*, in which the protagonist's insanity finds its synonymous mythological counterpart in Madness, shows most clearly how the playwright's fatalistic vision thus tends to reveal itself in both its psychological and mythological dimensions simultaneously. Heracles, not unlike Phaedra, in a sense turns into the gorgon-faced monster who possesses him. The following scene, in which he kills one of his sons, finds a close analogue in *The Bacchae*, the poet's culminating achievement.

> "Dearest Father," he cried, "do not murder me.
> I am your own son, yours, not Eurystheus'!"
> But he stared from stony gorgon eyes,
> found his son too close to draw the bow,
> and brought his club down on that golden head,
> and smashed the skull, as though a blacksmith
> smiting steel.   (988–94)

But before he wrote *The Bacchae*, Euripides was to explore the absurdist and comical implications of his anti-tragic dramaturgy.

Heracles, for all the grimness of its vision, is not without its comedy-like elements. The Chorus largely acts in caricature of itself. The Messenger, when he first witnesses the eruption of Heracles' madness, does not know whether "to laugh or shudder" (950). The protagonist's pre-Socratic critique of traditional mythology, which has aroused unending critical debate, falls into the same category of black humour. Xenophanes, we remember, had reprimanded Homer and Hesiod for attributing to the gods "everything that is a shame and reproach among men, stealing and committing adultery and deceiving each other,"[6] while Anaxagoras found his true god in an abstract principle which he termed *nous*, "the finest of all things and the purest ... infinite and self-ruled."[7] Similar thoughts are voiced by Heracles when he rebuts Theseus's remarks about the gods' immoral nature. But we notice that they are ridiculed when we remember the injustices the hero has suffered through divine intervention:

> ... I do not believe the gods commit
> adultery, or bind each other in chains.
> I never did believe it; I never shall;
> nor that one god is tyrant of the rest.
> If god is truly god, he is perfect,
> lacking nothing. (1341–6)

It is a somewhat unsubtle joke to have the son of Zeus from an adulterous relationship with a mortal – the cause of all the suffering inflicted upon Heracles by the jealous Hera – protest that he cannot believe that the gods commit adultery. There are similar jokes in another of Euripides' anti-tragedies, jokes that may have been prompted by an actual comedy.

Orestes

Aristophanes' *The Poet and the Women* was staged in 411 BC. The "poet," of course, is Euripides. He is put on trial by an enraged mob of Athenian feminists for painting insulting portraits of their sex such as Phaedra and Medea. Euripides, in order to influence the assembly in his favour, sends his foul-mouthed friend Mnesilochus, who, somewhat clumsily dressed up as a woman, finds no trouble having himself arrested, put in the stocks, and guarded by a Scythian constable. But *deus ex machina* rescue seems at hand when Euripides, attired as Perseus, makes his swooping descent on to the stage. In the following parody of Euripides' *Andromeda*, which only survives in fragments, the uncomprehending Scythian with his pidgin Greek and common-sense disruptions provides most of the comic relief from the pseudo-tragic exchanges between Euripides (Perseus) and Mnesilochus (Andromeda):

EURIPIDES
Gods, to what barbarous country have I come
On my swift sandal, cleaving through the sky
My winged path? For Argos am I bound
And in my hand the Gorgon's head I bear.
SCYTHIAN
Gorgias da philosoph? You gotta his head? Hooray!
EURIPIDES
The Gorgon's head, I said.
SCYTHIAN
Da Gorgias' head, yeah, Hooray!
EURIPIDES
But soft, what rock is here? And what is this?
A beauteous virgin tied up like a ship?
MNESILOCHUS
Have pity, stranger, on my wretched fate,
And loose me from my bonds!
SCYTHIAN
You keep-a da mouth shut! You goin' to bloody die,
and you no keep-a da mouth shut?
EURIPIDES
Fair virgin, how my heart with pity fills
To see thee hanging there.

SCYTHIAN

No, no, he not any virgin, he just a dirty ol' man.

EURIPIDES

Oh, Scythian, thou art wrong:

This is Andromeda, the child of Cepheus.

SCYTHIAN

You no believe-a me? I show you. (*He lifts Mnesilochus'*
skirt.) Is big enough, yes?[8]

It is near unthinkable that Euripides would have missed a play whose
leading role was a caricature of himself. But instead of resenting *The Poet and the
Women*, he seems to have been sufficiently impressed by its parody of his
Andromeda to try to build something similar into one of his own plays. The
result is close enough to Aristophanes to suggest direct influence. Euripides, in
order to travesty his own tragedy, has a Phrygian slave play the role of
Aristophanes' Scythian constable and at one point seems to echo the earlier
play directly. Neither the Scythian nor the Phrygian can grasp the word
"Gorgon" when it is mentioned by Perseus (alias Euripides) and Orestes.
Aristophanes' constable asks, "Gorgias da philosoph?" Euripides' slave
retorts, "But this Gorgon thing / I do not know" (1521–2).

Compared with Aristophanes' buffoonish skit on *Andromeda*, Euripides'
self-parody in *Orestes* is a serious attack on the tragic mode. The Phrygian slave
may turn out to be the only character in the play to make us laugh, but at least
at first our reaction to him is one of great surprise. His appearance at the point
when we expect to see another *eccyclema* (like Agamemnon's corpse and those of
Clytaemnestra and Aegisthus being revealed in the *Oresteia*) is Euripides' most
stunning feat of anticlimactic audience manipulation next to the sudden
descent of Madness in *Heracles*. What has happened? Six days after Clytaemnestra's death, the starting-point of the play, Orestes and Electra are sentenced
to death by the Argive assembly. While ready to suffer death at first, they begin
to have second thoughts when Pylades and Electra propose a double plan of
revenge and possible salvation. As it happens, Menelaus, Helen, and their
daughter Hermione are in Argos on their return from Troy. Now Menelaus,
who has proved far more eager to gain the throne of Argos than to help
Agamemnon's children, becomes the indirect target of their revenge.

Pylades proposes that he and Orestes should murder Helen, while Electra
promises to make sure that her brother and his friend will be able to kidnap
Hermione. At first all seems to work to perfection. After Helen's "*Help me,
Menelaus! Help! I'm dying –*" (1301) has been heard from within the palace,
Hermione turns up just in time to walk into the trap set for her by Electra.
Even the Chorus helps to reinforce our expectations of the traditional *eccyclema*:

"Let me see," they exclaim, "dead Helen, lying in her blood" (1357–8). What we are made to see instead is without precedence in Greek tragedy: "*Breathless and incoherent with terror, a Phrygian slave bursts from the palace*" (1368). As Anne P. Burnett writes, "he is the only tragic messenger we know who has lost the power to speak in ordinary iambics. Indeed, his parody of the late Euripidean lyric monody is so exaggerated that his gestures, if they matched his music, must have been the most outrageous ever seen on the classic stage."[9]

After his opening dirge, the Phrygian, for all his confused jabber, makes clear to us that the revenge action, like everything else in the play, has ended in failure. About to cut Helen's throat, Orestes and Pylades were distracted by the arriving Hermione, and when they turned back to their victim, Helen, perhaps through magic or divine intervention, had disappeared. But for those sensitive to the nuances of Euripidean drama, Orestes' worst discomfiture is still to come. It takes the form of a lesson in anti-heroics which the cowardly but witty Phrygian slave delivers to the swashbucklingly obtuse protagonist. There is little in Brecht himself to illustrate more effectively the famous alienation effect of estranging the audience from certain established values (such as Orestes' anti-"barbarian" aristocratic valuations). At the same time this passage shows the degree to which Euripides infused Aristophanes' more strictly verbal and situational humour, which may have been his model, with his unmistakable complexity:

ORESTES (*lowering his sword still closer to the Phrygian's throat*)
Were all the Trojans as terrified by cold steel
as you?
PHRYGIAN
          Ooh, please, please, not so close!
All shiny bloody!
ORESTES
          What are you afraid of, fool?
Is it some Gorgon's head to turn you into stone?
PHRYGIAN
Not stone, corpse yes. But this Gorgon thing
I do not know.
ORESTES
          What? Nothing but a slave
and afraid to die? Death might end your suffering.
PHRYGIAN
Slave man, free man, everybody like to live.
ORESTES
Well spoken. Your wit saves you. Now get inside.

PHRYGIAN
You will not kill me?
ORESTES
    I spare you.
PHRYGIAN
        Oh, thank you, thank you.
ORESTES
Go, or I'll change my mind.
PHRYGIAN
      I no thank you for that. (*Exit Phrygian*) (1518–46)

In ways anticipating *Troilus and Cressida*, *Orestes* thus elicits multiple and contradictory responses in the audience. Before we are allowed to feel ambivalent about one issue, another and yet another claim our equally divided attention. To Shakespeare, the values he thus debunked (such as Ulysses' plea for a hierarchical order of society and Troilus's advocacy of chivalric honour and renown to be achieved in defence of Helen) were hold-overs from the late Middle Ages. Aeschylus's *Oresteia* provides the even more clearly identifiable background to the values and concepts called into question by Euripides' *Orestes*.

The plot of *Orestes*, we recall, is a non-stop sequence of traditional tragic actions ending in unexpected failure. Declared, like Electra, a matricide and outlaw by the people of Argos, Orestes approaches Menelaus as a suppliant. Grovelling on his knees, he implores Menelaus's help in the name of Agamemnon in his grave (675), but Menelaus is ready to promise no more than what can be achieved by "diplomacy and tact" (697). Orestes next decides to address the assembly, which is about to vote on his sentence, a self-help action which equally ends in failure. This is followed by Orestes', his sister's, and Pylades' botched attempt to take vengeance on Menelaus by killing Helen. Even their final trump card – threatening to kill Menelaus's kidnapped daughter unless they are let go – misfires. Menelaus seems quite prepared to sacrifice Hermione's life for the throne of Argos when he abruptly breaks off negotiations with the kidnappers by calling the knights of Argos to arms. It is only at this point that Apollo avoids further crime by his *deus ex machina* intervention.

What applies to the incidents is equally true of the arguments surrounding them. One by one, every single issue that is broached and solved in the *Oresteia* is left suspended, called into question, or reduced *ad absurdum*. Debating his crime with Menelaus and Clytaemnestra's father Tyndareus, Orestes runs the entire gamut of arguments that Aeschylus, via Apollo or the protagonist himself, had adduced in his defence: that killing a father was far worse than murdering a mother, since the man is the more crucial agent in procreation (546–64; compare *Eumenides* 625f, 660f); that, had he failed to murder Clytaemnestra according to Apollo's command, Agamemnon would have hounded him "with the Furies of a father's hatred" (582ff; compare *Libation Bearers* 269ff,

Eumenides 465ff); and that, in the final analysis, not he, Orestes, but Apollo, "the god.of Delphi, / navel and center of the world" (592–3), was to blame. But to his debating partners, the various components of the Aeschylean dialectic have turned into the interchangeable pseudo-arguments of a Sophistic antilogy. For a moment, Menelaus is ready to take the side of what Hegel was to call "the family as the natural ground of moral relations,"[10] arguing that it "is Greek custom ... to honour your kin." "But not to put yourself above the laws" (486–7), counters Tyndareus.

For in fact, or so at least we are made to believe, the new jurisdiction that is the culminating achievement of Aeschylus's dialectic is a *fait accompli* in the Argos of Euripides. The same arguments that in the *Oresteia* led to Orestes' acquittal therefore must bring about his condemnation here. Tyndareus argues this paradoxical but inescapable point with faultless logic. When will this endless chain of blood-lettings ever end, asked the Chorus towards the end of *The Libation Bearers*: "Where shall the fury of fate / be stilled to sleep, be done with?" (1075–6). We know how Aeschylus answered the question in *The Eumenides*. Where, asks Tyndareus,

> ... can this chain
> of murder end? Can it ever end, in fact,
> since the last to kill is doomed to stand
> under permanent sentence of death by revenge?   (510–13)

But to Clytaemnestra's father the answer was found long ago. His ancestors "stopped that endless vicious cycle / of murder and revenge" (517–18) through judicial reforms. By being killed, he admits, his daughter only got what she deserved, but Orestes was wrong to take the law into his own hands; he "should have haled his mother / into court" (499–500). For failing to do so he deserves death himself.

So far so good. But Tyndareus, supposedly representing the conciliatory spirit of *The Eumenides*, turns into a very Fury with vindictiveness when Orestes adduces the arguments which in the earlier play led to his acquittal. Invoking the "gods below" (620), he now wants to see executed not only Orestes but Electra as well:

> I will go to the Argives myself.
> They may resent it, but, by heaven, I'll hound them
> until they stone your sister and you to death!
> Yes, your sister too!
>   She deserves it,
> by god, even more than you! (611–16)

Any positive expectations the spectator may still entertain concerning the Argive assembly are equally disappointed. Instead of Aeschylus's divinely instituted Areopagus, we find a courtroom torn by rival factions, filled with corruption and bribery and ruled by whoever controls the mob. Nobody, including Prince Diomedes pleading for banishment instead of death or the honest farmer arguing for Orestes' acquittal, mentions the words justice or god. Purely pragmatic considerations, such as "Orestes' example was dangerous for parents" (893), are all that matter even to the protagonist in his self-defence. The rest, replacing Aeschylus's divine *Peitho* (Persusasion) in *The Eumenides* (971),[11] is demagoguery: a two-faced speech by Talthybises, another, glib and full of bluster, by a hired speaker arguing that Orestes and Electra be stoned to death – "while Tyndareus sat cheering him on" (915). Clytaemnestra's father has been true to his word. While acting the Fury, he knows how to fulfil this secularized mythic role to perfection. His hired orator, aided by his applause, carries the day.

But after all of the more metaphysical and civic values have been debunked, there remain friendship and love. No doubt Euripides wants us to take Electra's display of affection towards Orestes as seriously as the protagonist's madness, shame, and guilt. It is the same with Pylades' friendship. To hear Electra exclaim, "O gods, I cannot bear it! To see you now / for the last, last time ... No! No! No!" (1020–1) is as moving as the Messenger's description of Orestes and Pylades in the assembly,

> the one hunched down with sickness and despair,
> the other sharing his troubles like a brother
> and helping him along. (881–3)

Pylades may protest his friendship a little too often, but his commitment to it is strong enough to border on an obsession. Already he has been banished by his father for helping in Clytaemnestra's murder (765). Now he even wants to share Orestes' death:

> Wait!
> Stop, Orestes. I have one reproach to make.
> How could you think that I would want to live
> once you were dead? (1068–71)

As far as the author is concerned, this tone of shrill exaggeration is probably quite deliberate. We are in for another nasty surprise.

For all their love and friendship finally proves to amount to no more than what R.D. Laing describes as the ghetto morality of a group, living "in perpetual anxiety of what, to them, is an external persecuting world." "We" stand against "them," and any crime against "them" seems justified.[12] Sometimes the fears can be pure paranoia, but Orestes, Electra, and Pylades all have reason to feel threatened. Brother and sister have been sentenced to death and there is no hope of escape. Argos resembles a city under siege: "There are sentries posted everywhere" (761); "Armed men [are] patrolling the streets" (763). The plans for murdering Helen and kidnapping Hermione are made in this last-ditch situation, and the excitement surrounding it, Pylades praising the "beauty of [his] plan" (1132) and Orestes complimenting Electra on hers (1204f), has the all-too-natural ring of desperation. Of course, it never occurs to this young gangster trio, as it does to their critics, to think of the glaring inconsistency between their ill-concealed glee and their high moral sentiments about love and friendship.

Orestes' paranoid madness and the mafia ethos of his friends, then, have replaced Sophocles' pathos of the solitary hero nobly holding his own against a hostile world. Suffering has not made them wiser but simply more desperate both in their "love" towards the members of their clan and in their hatred against all others. Apollo's last-minute intervention provides this tale with its appropriate conclusion, suggesting that their virtues and their vices were simply what circumstances dictated to them. Orestes, who seconds earlier was holding a sword to Hermione's throat, is to marry his captive, and Menelaus, urged to do so by his worst enemy, Orestes, willingly gives him and his strangely assorted bride his blessing. Helen, whom Orestes thought to murder out of hatred for Menelaus, has joined the ranks of the immortals before his sword could reach her. So her cuckold husband had better marry again. Whatever mask Apollo may have worn in performance, a demonic grin at the vanity of man's emotions would suit this stage director of *la comédie humaine* to perfection.

There is something sordid about Apollo even in the way he arranges this "happy end." Orestes, while hailing the god for his prophetic oracles as the "True prophet, / not false!" expresses our own feelings in an afterthought:

> And yet, when I heard you speak,
> I thought I heard the whispers of some fiend
> speaking through your mouth.   (1666–70)

But to conclude that the play therefore marks yet another stage in Euripides' ongoing indictment of Apollo would be equal to claiming that *Waiting for Godot* is Beckett's arraignment of God the Father. On trial here is not a god but man with his wishful misconceptions and consequent denials of the divine. Orestes, while blaming Apollo for his crime (285), displays the behaviour of a man who has lost his faith. He fails to seek lustration, to take refuge at a local shrine, or to prostrate himself at his father's tomb.[13] His uncle, whatever else may divide him from the protagonist, completely shares this cynical attitude. When Orestes once again blames Apollo for Clytaemnestra's murder, Menelaus is all too glad to endorse the implied accusation:

MENELAUS

A callous, unjust, and immoral order.

ORESTES

We obey the gods – whoever the gods may be.

MENELAUS

Apollo, despite all this, refuses to help?

ORESTES

Oh, he will. In his own good time of course.   (417–21)

Theirs is a disillusioned and godless world, and nobody else in the play seems to offer an alternative. The divine, short of Apollo's appearance at the end, is simply absent. Even "those bitches with gorgon eyes, those goddesses / of hell" (261–2) haunting Orestes never appear visibly on stage as they do in the *Oresteia*. Electra, in fact, would like to deny their existence altogether. "These are only phantoms in your mind" (259) she shouts at her brother, trying to hold him down in his madness. And she is right, of course, especially when Orestes imagines that she is one of the Erinyes herself: "You're one of my Furies too? / You're holding me down to hurl me into hell!" (264–5). But interiorized as they have become, they are no less real than the remorse and bad conscience which Orestes talks about so feelingly (395, 398). If only, he tells Menelaus, "you knew the torture, knew how they hounded me!" (413). The gods, in sum, have turned into the inner demons of the godless. The once objective pantheon of divinities has shrunk to the size of an interior hell, and where the gods re-emerge from this psycho-dramatic inferno, their main appearance is sordid and destructive. All this is most powerfully dramatized in the play in which Euripides, while stepping beyond the boundaries of anti-tragedy, seems to exchange the tutelage of the Sophists for that of Heraclitus.

The Bacchae

"The lord whose oracle is in Delphi neither speaks out nor conceals, but gives a sign." Heraclitus's comment on Apollo is as cryptic as that on Dionysus. "For if it were not to Dionysus that they made the procession and sung the hymn to the shameful parts, the deed would be most shameless; but Hades and Dionysus, for whom they rave and celebrate Lenaean rites, are the same." The general meaning of both statements, however, becomes clear from other of the philosopher's remarks. Even before Aeschylus wrote his tragedies, Heraclitus had complained that the Greeks in their relation to the gods were driven by wishful thinking and anthropomorphic demands rather than genuine religiosity. They pray to the statues of the gods, he said, "as if one were to carry on a conversation with houses, not recognizing the true nature of gods or demi-gods."[14]

What then is the true nature of the gods? For one thing, Heraclitus seems to suggest, they are beyond good and evil. Men, he writes, "have supposed some things to be unjust, others just," whereas to the gods "all things are beautiful and good and just." Secondly, they have nothing to do with anthropomorphic notions such as teleology or dialectical progress. Heraclitus's emphasis on *panta rhei* or the eternal flux of things is well known. In fact, Aristotle's entelechies, ascribing purpose and direction to the whole of nature, a concept so crucial to his *Poetics*, stems indirectly from a refutation of the Heraclitean doctrine. Plato, so Aristotle reports, was under Heraclitus's influence before Socrates taught him how to define things. Hence he evolved his notion of changeless Ideas, from which Aristotle in turn derived his entelechies.[15]

Rather than a goal-oriented purposiveness, the gods, to Heraclitus, embody the ultimate paradoxes of life in its unending changes and transformations. God, Heraclitus writes, "is day night, winter summer, war peace, satiety hunger; he undergoes alteration in the way that fire, when it is mixed with spices, is named according to the scent of each of them."[16] Since the ascendance of Socratic rationalism there have been few philosophers who have seen much more than a cryptic superciliousness in such statements. Montaigne is one of the rare exceptions. Discussing the cyclical rebirth of life, a theme equally central to Shakespeare's last plays, he paraphrases Heraclitus in one of the final paragraphs of his "Apology for Raymond Sebond":

[We] foolishlie feare a kinde of death when as wee have already past, and dayly passe so many others. For, not only (as *Heraclitus* said) the death of fire is a generation of ayre; and the death of ayre, a generation of Water. But also we may most evidently see it in our selves. The flower of age dieth, fadeth and fleeteth, when age comes vppon vs, and youth endeth in the flower of a full-growne mans age: Childehood in youth, and the first age, dieth in infansie: and yesterday endeth in this day, and to day shall dy in to morrow. And *nothing remaineth or ever continueth in one state.*[17]

Euripides, like Shakespeare, may well have shared these beliefs. Heraclitus's sayings left no apparent traces in his plays, although an anecdote tells us that the poet once lent Socrates a text by Heraclitus, which Socrates found very difficult.[18] But even if he did not know them, Euripides no doubt would have appreciated Heraclitus's remarks on Apollo and Dionysus. For the philosopher's view that Apollo transcends our anthropomorphic interpretations, neither speaking out nor concealing but instead giving a sign, is what the playwright tried to demonstrate in plays like *Ion*, *Electra*, and *Orestes*. That Dionysus embodies the paradoxes of life, or creation and destruction, Dionysus and Hades in one, is something he more specifically dealt with in *The Bacchae*. A choral passage in *Hippolytus*, one of his earliest surviving plays, already hints at the same paradox in describing the god's mother Semele as "clasped in the arms of Death, / pregnant with Dionysus by the thunder king" (559–60).

Of course, Euripides had already – in, for example, *Orestes* – cast Apollo in a similarly dualistic role of creator and destroyer combined. But in Greek tradition Phoebus had come to embody civilization so thoroughly that any attempt to revise that tradition could hardly rise beyond a parodistic debunking of its values. In fact, such debunkings and denials by and large mark the limits of Euripides' transcendence of tragedy, especially when his works are compared with Shakespeare's romances and Goethe's *Faust*. Only *The Bacchae* comes close to being an exception to this rule. The play is no mere denial of the tragic vision of suffering: unlike Apollo, Dionysus gave Euripides a symbol to embody his new vision of life and suffering as neither meaningful nor absurd. But like the twentieth-century theatre of cruelty, on which it exerted considerable influence, *The Bacchae*, in its Dionysiac portrayal of the life-force beyond good and evil, puts most of the emphasis on destruction rather than creation.

Who then is Euripides' Dionysus?[19] *Prima facie* he simply acts the role of an offended divinity. Like Athena in *Ajax* or Aphrodite in *Hippolytus*, he takes revenge on the culprit. But there is a difference even on the level of pure story. The offence for which Pentheus is punished by death is not one of insult or negligence. He is punished for failing to acknowledge the godhead of Dionysus. Even Hippolytus, while calling Aphrodite the vilest of the gods (13), never denies her divine existence as such. But Agave declared Dionysus a "fraud" (30), and her more impulsive son calls him "one of those charlatan magicians, / with long yellow curls smelling of perfumes" (234–5). What Pentheus thus denies or, if you like, represses, is largely a figment of his imagination. Dionysus, who in Pentheus's view is given to "lechery and seducing women" (487), has no particular stake in promoting an unchained sexuality himself; it is the female Chorus of Asian proselytes, not he, that asks to be taken to Aphrodite's island, "homes of the loves that cast / their spells on the hearts of men!" (402–5). While admitting that Dionysus does not "*compel* a woman / to be chaste," Teiresias insists that "the chaste woman will not be corrupted" (314–18) by the god. Dionysus himself tells Pentheus that he will be surprised to see "how chaste the Bacchae are" (940). But in fact no such surprise is called for because Pentheus already has been told by an eyewitness that the Bacchae behave "all modestly and soberly" (689).

Yet Pentheus is so caught up in his fantasies that all such warnings fall on deaf ears. To him Dionysus's followers gather around "bowls brimming with wine," and then, one by one, "the women wander off / to hidden nooks where they serve the lusts of men" (221–3). Everything surrounding these "filthy mysteries" (260) is "rotten" (262), the god himself infecting the women of Thebes "with this strange disease and pollut[ing] our beds" (353–4). The whole "obscene disorder" (232) is deeply mortifying to Pentheus's easily shaken sense of order and propriety:

> Like a blazing fire
> this Bacchic violence spreads. It comes too close.
> We are disgraced, humiliated in the eyes
> of Hellas. (778–80)

What Pentheus rejects so violently, then, is largely a projection of his own fantasy. Yet he is quite prepared to translate impulse into fact. If Dionysus is a true god, he concludes sarcastically, then he should have a proper sacrifice. "His victims will be his women. / I shall make a great slaughter in the woods of Cithaeron" (797-8), and he calls on the entire Theban army, heavy-armoured infantry, cavalry, mobile squadrons, and archers (782-4), to perform this deadly mission in the name of purity, law, and order.

Pentheus invents and rejects his fantasies with equal compulsiveness. Upon first meeting Dionysus, he finds him surprisingly attractive, but he quickly corrects himself, adding, "at least to women" (453-4). The god, of course, is fully aware of how deeply Pentheus is attracted to the imagined sins and debaucheries for which he wants to punish him. "Would you like to *see* their revels on the mountains?" (812) he asks Pentheus, who is about to leave for the woods of Cithaeron. And within seconds the puritan turns voyeur, at first bashfully hypocritical about it but soon throbbing with unashamed anticipation of seeing the Bacchae "there among the bushes, / mating like birds, caught in the toils of love" (957-8).

As this interpretation begins to sound like a Freudian case history of repression, voyeurism, and self-destruction, a caveat may be called for at this point. For reasons too complex to be fully elaborated upon here, the notion of repression seems to me questionable when taken to be a universal law of what Freud called the psychic mechanism. Like other assumptions of psychoanalysis, it only applies to the human mind under specific cultural circumstances, such as, for instance, those of Greek, medieval, or seventeenth-century puritanical rationalism. What is more, Freud may partly owe his discovery of repression to the portrayals of its basic functioning process in such figures as Shakespeare's Angelo or Euripides' Pentheus. Just as the Freudian vocabulary, in other words, helps us to understand *The Bacchae*, so does the play itself offer an antecedent analysis of the cultural psycho-syndromes which prompted Freud's research and which alone make a concept like repression a widely useful one.

Be that as it may, Pentheus's prurient voyeurism is by no means the only indication that Euripides wants us to see the hero as a deeply neurotic. if not psychotic person. References to the fact that he is "excited and disturbed" (214), "mad, grievously mad," "drugged / with madness" (326-8), his mind "distracted" and in "sheer delirium" (332-3), that he suffers from the fantasies of a sick mind (312) and that he is obsessively prone to violence abound in the play. "With fury, with fury, he rages" (539), "this beast of blood / whose violence abuses man and god / outrageously" (555-7). As a raging beast – Agave will later identify her victim as a lion (1142, 1173) – Pentheus, of course, is not unlike the real Dionysus himself. The hero, dressed in women's clothes, a caricature of his former macho self and completely in the power of the god, suddenly catches a glimpse of Dionysus's true shape:

you are a bull
who walks before me there. Horns have sprouted
from your head. Have you always been a beast?   (920-2)

The answer is that Dionysus, unlike the Olympian gods but much in the way Heraclitus describes him, appears in multiple and particularly theriomorphic forms. A slightly effeminate man with long curly hair, he also assumes the shape of a bull-horned god (101) or wears a *chevelure* of living snakes (104). Equally diverse are his many functions and predilections. As the god of joy he "loves the goddess Peace" (412, 418). Usurping the functions of warlike Ares, he can strike panic into an entire army before battle (302-5). Calm, smiling (603), controlled (642), and full of Oriental wisdom, he bears a certain resemblance to the Buddha – and yet he "hunts the wild goat / and kills it. He delights in the raw flesh" (137-8). His Bacchic followers share their master's fiercely divided temperament: left to themselves, they live "modestly and soberly" (688-9), in peaceful harmony with poisonous snakes (697) and nature generally, but tracked down by voyeurs, they turn into ravaging monsters –

a single woman with bare hands
tear[ing] a fat calf, still bellowing with fright,
in two, while others clawed the heifers to pieces.   (737-40)

Dionysus, like nature herself, then, is the creator and destroyer in one. Particularly, he is "most terrible, and yet most gentle, to mankind" (861).

It is therefore wrong to view and judge Dionysus as if he were merely another character. The "god incognito, / disguised as man" (4-5; compare 55) whom we encounter on the stage is only the finite embodiment of a power much larger than himself. Dionysus himself repeatedly addresses and invokes that larger power in his own person, a force beyond good and evil immanent in all nature and all human beings. Euripides made especially clear that the violence which rages in and finally destroys Pentheus also is part of the force which Dionysus embodies in the most general, mythological sense. Pentheus, we remember, is described as a raging beast of blood who will be tracked down in the shape of a lion. Set in the context of an elaborate train of imagery in which the hunter becomes the hunted, Pentheus is finally made to act the role of the would-be hunter turned quarry.[20] Pentheus, in other words, destroys himself. "O Dionysus," demand the god's followers,

reveal yourself a bull! Be manifest,
a snake with darting heads, a lion breathing fire!
O Bacchus, come! Come with your smile!
Cast your noose about this man who hunts

your Bacchae! Bring him down, trampled
underfoot by the murderous herd of your Maenads!   (1016–21)

Since Aeschylus had also written plays on Dionysus, Euripides' portrait of
the god may well derive some of its traits from an inversion of their Aeschylean
counterparts. Yet inversion here probably meant the rehabilitation or neutral-
izing of a previously negative depiction of Dionysus. Of course, we don't know
what Aeschylus's two Dionysus tetralogies and kindred plays by other writers
may have been like.[21] But the Athenians had already purged the original Dionysiac rites of such uncivilized excesses as the dancing madness and the tearing
apart and eating raw of an animal body – hence, they took a distinctly hostile
stance when such primitivism was revived during the Peloponnesian
War. Sabazius, an Oriental counterpart of Dionysus, and certain other foreign
gods were put on trial and banished from Athens in a lost play by Aristophanes
entitled the *Horae*. Similar denunciations of the foreign gods and of female rites
under cover of darkness abound in other plays and writers both of the late fifth
and of the fourth century BC.

The Athenians, in short, probably tended to sympathize with Pentheus,[22]
perhaps to the point of seeing him as a Promethean rebel against the son of
Zeus. A caricature of this role survives in *The Bacchae*. Though condemning
him, the Chorus nevertheless seems to concede to Pentheus the stature of
somebody tracking "some boundless, superhuman dream" (398), "a giant in
wildness raging, / storming, defying the children of heaven" (543–4). And
lightning, as it strikes down Prometheus, is heaven's answer to Pentheus in
destroying his palace. But here the resemblances between *The Bacchae* and
Prometheus Bound come to an end. Pentheus, in the final analysis, is no Promethean promoter of civilization bringing benefits to mankind through his
suffering and self-sacrifice. Rather, his role is that of a psychotic anti-hero,
victim of civilization's discontents. When Pentheus is killed by his frenzied
mother Agave because both have blasphemed against Dionysus, their suffering is in no way made to appear meaningful or ennobling. And there is not the
slightest hint of any teleological progress. "Never shall my sufferings end"
(1360) exclaims Pentheus's grandfather Cadmus, while the Chorus of Asian
Bacchae, followers of Dionysus, concludes the play on a series of cryptic
aphorisms worthy of Heraclitus:

> The gods have many shapes.
> The gods bring many things
> to their accomplishment.
> And what was most expected
> has not been accomplished.
> But god has found his way

for what no man expected.
So ends the play.

It is tantalizing to speculate what kind of plays he might have composed had Euripides' career continued beyond *The Bacchae*. Would he have managed to shed the theatre-of-cruelty-like excesses of this work and evolved a more neutral, less brutal form of post-tragic drama? The works of Shakespeare, whose development followed similar lines, suggest such a possibility. But the parallels between Euripides and Shakespeare go beyond mere speculation.

The Greek playwright's anti-tragic techniques, we recall, dramatize a general questioning of values also found in fifth century BC Greek philosophy. For this reason they have to be seen as a distinct historical phenomenon in a specific cultural tradition so obviously absent, for instance, from Sanskrit or Nō drama. In turn, both tragedy and its transcendence as first observable in Euripides are again found in Western literature when circumstances come to resemble those surrounding the Greek playwright. Precisely this happened during the Renaissance, when once again established beliefs were questioned by men like Montaigne and Francis Bacon. Shakespeare's similar attitude towards orthodox assumptions can be derived from his plays. Thus the playwright, around the turn of the seventeenth century, developed new techniques of audience manipulation by presenting moral issues (such as the notion of justice in *Measure for Measure*) in ways "so that uncertain and divided responses to it in the minds of the audience are possible or even probable."[23] Such techniques seem to put into practice Montaigne's advice to his readers to suspend their judgment wherever possible. What they suggest and what the philosopher explains to us *expressis verbis* is that equally valid arguments can be found on both sides of a notion such as human justice.

Yet Shakespearian parallels with Euripides and the Sophists go even further. Shakespeare, in fact, could find in Montaigne most of the major critiques of traditional religion and philosophy which Euripides may have absorbed from contemporary philosophers. Xenophanes, we read in the "Apology for Raymond Sebond," "said pleasantly that if beasts frame any Gods vnto themselves, (as likely it is they doe) they surely frame them like vnto themselves, and glorifie themselves as we doe." Montaigne, in listing various conflicting accounts of the gods, also quotes the Sophist Protagoras's statement "that he had nothing to say, whether they were or were not, or what they are." Man being the measure of all things, as the same philosopher asserted, "there is nothing in Nature, but doubt." This general tendency to suspend judgment is particularly apparent with regard to a concept which Euripides, in his *Electra*, questioned in ways anticipating those of Shakespeare in *Measure for Measure*. Protagoras, writes Montaigne, "gave the justice of the lawes no other essence, but the authoritie and opinion of the Law-giver, and that excepted, both Good and Honest lost their qualities, and remained by vaine and idle names, of indifferent things."[24] In short, some of the Greek philosophers who helped Euripides evolve his anti-tragic denials may, via Montaigne, have had a similar impact on Shakespeare.

Shakespeare:
The Theoretical Background

OF THE THREE MAIN AUTHORS discussed in this volume, Shakespeare no doubt went furthest in transcending the traditional tragic mode. Because of the uniqueness of their vision, the romances, for lack of closer parallels in our own literature, have more than once been compared to the masterpiece of Hindu drama, Kālidāsa's *Sacontalá*.[1] Theodore Spencer even suggests that something analogous to the enlightenment of the Zen Buddhist, as described by D.T. Suzuki, must have happened to Shakespeare before he wrote the last plays:

Before a man studies Zen, to him mountains are mountains, and waters are waters; after he gets an insight into the truth of Zen through the instruction of a good master, mountains to him are not mountains and waters are not waters; but after this when he really attains to the abode of rest, mountains are once more mountains and waters are waters.[2]

However, such perspectives are more appropriately applied to Goethe, whose *Faust*, as we shall see, was directly influenced by *Sacontalá*. In the case of Shakespeare they are more likely to lead to distortions. After all, the playwright knew neither Zen Buddhism nor Sanskrit drama, nor is there a need to approach his romances from their vantage point. There is enough in Montaigne or Hermetic philosophy, with both of which Shakespeare was acquainted, to help us understand the general philosophy of the last plays. What is more, the genealogy of the romances can be traced to the playwright's gradual transcendence of tragedy, a development discussed in the following chapters.

For all that, we are confronted with a problem absent from the preceding analysis of comparable changes from a tragic towards a post-tragic vision of life in Greek drama. Aristotle, though writing long after the major tragedians, evolved a comprehensive theory of tragedy which helped us to ascertain the genre's transformations in Euripides. No comparable poetics is to be found in Shakespeare's England. Definitions of tragedy as setting forth "the dolefull falles of infortunate & afflicted Princes" are, of course, legion. Like our example from George Puttenham,[3] most of these fit the familiar *de casibus* pattern best known from Chaucer's "The Monk's Tale" and more recently studied by Willard Farnham.[4] But none of them accounts for the complexities of Shakespearian tragedy, let alone for the playwright's transcendence of the genre.

This is all the more surprising since Elizabethan critical writing to a large extent sprang up in reaction to the Puritan attack on play-acting and poetry in general.[5] But the apologists for literature proved for the most part to be as antagonistic to contemporary drama as the Puritan detractors. "I wish as zealously as the best that all abuse of playinge weare abolished," wrote Thomas Lodge in his *Defence of Poetry, Music, and Stage Plays*.[6] From Sir Thomas More to Joseph Hall,[7] critics inveighed against what Sidney called the typical "mungrell Tragy-comedie"[8] of the period, invoking ill-conceived Aristotelian unities of time and place[9] while ignoring Aristotle's complex assessment of the tragic with regard to plot structure, characterization, and catharsis. In evolving their terminology, the theoreticians of literature, by thus rejecting popular drama, excluded the realm in which the Elizabethan poetic genius was most innovative and powerful. Rather than follow the imaginative flights of a Shakespeare, the Puttenhams and Halls wrote with an eye to a Renaissance scholarly industry that had accrued around Aristotle's *Poetics* and other classical treatises. Hence little in their apologies and defences can help us to understand Shakespeare's intricate manoeuvres with the tragic, let alone his poetics in general.

The most striking discrepancy here stems from the critics' lack of a concept which Shakespeare, in Theseus's famous speech from *A Midsummer Night's Dream*, deals with in elaborate and colourful detail:

> The lunatic, the lover and the poet
> Are of imagination all compact.
> One sees more devils than vast hell can hold,
> That is the madman. The lover, all as frantic,
> Sees Helen's beauty in a brow of Egypt.
> The poet's eye, in a fine frenzy rolling,
> Doth glance from heaven to earth, from earth to heaven;
> And as imagination bodies forth
> The forms of things unknown, the poet's pen
> Turns them to shapes, and gives to airy nothing
> A local habitation and a name.
> Such tricks hath strong imagination,

That, if it would but apprehend some joy,
It comprehends some bringer of that joy;
Or in the night, imagining some fear,
How easy is a bush supposed a bear! (V.i)[10]

True enough, Elizabethan aestheticians were fond of invoking familiar
commonplaces such as the anonymous "Poeta nascitur, Orator fit" ("The
poet is born, the orator is made"), Plato's "celestial instinction," or Ovid's "Est
deus in nobis; agitante calescimus illo" ("God is in us; we warm by his
action").[11] Sidney, following Scaliger, went as far as to claim that the poet,
"lifted up with the vigor of his owne inuention, dooth growe in effect another
nature, in making things either better then Nature bringeth forth, or, quite a
newe, formes such as neuer were in Nature, as the *Heroes*, *Demigods*, *Cyclops*,
Chimeras, *Furies*, and such like."[12] But critics rarely explored the psychological
implications of such theorizing and, where they did, more often than not
ended up contradicting their high-flown premises.

Sir Philip Sidney's claim, in this sense, is even less than "marginal" (M.H.
Abrams)[13] to his poetics. The seeming apologist of an unbridled imagination
suddenly, when speaking in more specific terms, turns into a denunciator of
poetry tending towards the "*Phantastike*: which doth ... infect the fancie with
vnworthy obiects."[14] In the rare instances where critics discuss the imagination
directly, such suspicion tends to be the rule. God help us, exclaims Gabriel
Harvey, "when Ignorance and want of Experience, vsurping the chayre of
scrupulous and rigorous Iudgement, will in a fantasticall Imagination, or
percase in a melancholy moode, presume farther, by infinite degrees, then the
learnedest men in a ciuill Commonwealth."[15] As George Puttenham suggests,
the Platonic *furor poeticus*, or the notion that the poet-maker creates his poems
like God – "who without any trauell to his diuine imagination made all the
world of nought" – is only desirable to a certain degree. This is exceeded when
the imagination deviates from its role as "a representer of the best, most
comely and bewtifull images or apparances of thinges to the soule and
according to their very truth. If otherwise, then doth it breede *Chimeres* &
monsters in mans imaginations, & not onely in his imaginations, but also in all
his ordinarie actions and life which ensues."[16]

Equal misgivings were Ben Jonson's in assessing the "Phantsie" of a fellow
playwright. Shakespeare, he told William Drummond, "wanted Arte."[17]
Elsewhere he voiced his complaints about plays in which a baby turns
threescore within a few hours, "*Yorke* and *Lancasters* long iarres" are presented
with "three rustie swords," and a Chorus "wafts you ore the seas."[18] Ben
Jonson had often been told by "the Players" that Shakespeare "never blotted
out line" in "whatsoever he penn'd." To the actors such creative automatism
was something admirable, and when Ben Jonson remarked that Shakespeare
ought to have "blotted a thousand," they thought of it as "a malevolent

speech." What were they to make of a person who praised their "gentle" Shakespeare as an "open, and free nature," full of "excellent *Phantsie*; brave notions, and gentle expressions," but criticized him for flowing "with that facility, that sometime it was necessary he should be stop'd." "His wit was in his owne power," Ben Jonson concludes; "would the rule of it had beene so too."[19]

An Art That Nature Makes

Where, then, other than in the scattered and oblique comments the playwright made about his art,[20] will we find an account of his poetics? The answer is not an easy one. Shakespeare's sense of his craft and creativity, as seen in the context of Renaissance theories of literature, remains a largely uncharted field. Hence, whatever can be said about it prior to our discussion of his transcendence of tragedy remains by and large hypothetical. But let us begin with a concrete example. Perdita in *The Winter's Tale* is said to neglect certain flowers such as "carnations, and streaked gillyvors" because as products of a horticultural grafting process they are "Nature's bastards."[21] She has heard it said, she explains to Polixenes, that "There is an art, which in their piedness shares / With great creating Nature." The king feels called upon to refute this argument, however contradictory. All art, even in its most deliberate craftsmanship, he points out, is no more than a self-realization of nature:

> Say there be;
> Yet Nature is made better by no mean
> But Nature makes that mean; so over art,
> Which you say adds to Nature, is an art,
> That Nature makes. You see, sweet maid, we marry
> A gentler scion to the wildest stock,
> And make conceive a bark of baser kind
> By bud of nobler race. This is an art
> Which does mend Nature, change it rather; but
> The art itself is Nature.   (IV.iv)

It is distorting the facts to say that these words voice no more than an "orthodox" aesthetic position as found in some odd quotations from Plato's *Laws* – that the good legislator "ought to support the law and also art, and acknowledge that both alike exist by nature, and no less than nature" – and from Aristotle's *Physics* – "The best illustration is a doctor doctoring himself: nature is like that."[22] Nothing could be further removed from Plato's claim that art, in imitating mere phenomena, is twice removed from the truth of the Ideas.[23] Polixenes' words are equally at odds with Aristotle's claim that art imitates things not as they are but as they ought to be, finishing the job which nature left undone. More perceptive than many modern critics is Coleridge, to whom Polixenes' position amounts to a transcendence of the division between art and nature as initiated by Aristotle and Plato.[24]

There is a similar distortion in Northrop Frye's assertion that George Puttenham, in discussing the relationship between art and nature in his *Arte of English Poesie*, anticipated Polixenes' theory. "We feel that Puttenham, writing before Shakespeare," Frye argues, "had got properly started and two centuries earlier than Coleridge, has nonetheless well characterized the peculiar quality of Shakespeare's art."[25] In fact, Puttenham's analogy of the artist with the gardener, in which, like Perdita, he mentions the "gillifloure" and "carnation," points in the exactly opposite direction. Whereas art to Polixenes is no more than an extension of nature even where it "mends" or rather "changes" it, it works towards a definite improvement of nature in Puttenham's view:

In another respect arte is not only an aide and coadiutor to nature in all her actions but an alterer of them, and in some sort a surmounter of her skill, so as by meanes of it her owne effects shall appeare more beautifull or straunge and miraculous ... And the Gardiner by his arte will not onely make an herbe, or flowr, or fruite, come forth in his season without impediment, but also will embellish the same in vertue, shape, odour, and taste, that nature of her selfe woulde neuer have done, as to make single gillifloure, or marigold, or daisie, double ... any of which things nature could not doe without mans help and arte.[26]

In other words, Shakespeare, although he may well have drawn upon Puttenham's analogy, inverts his argument. The mental support for such inversion, if Shakespeare was ever in need of it, had to come from outside Elizabethan critical writing.

One source here may have been Montaigne, who states his preference for nature over art even more radically than Shakespeare himself. In the playwright's development from tragedy, which transforms reality teleologically, to romance, which simply "sisters" reality,[27] such a tendency is a fairly late one. With Montaigne it is a consistent position throughout. "I would naturalize arte, as much as they artize nature,"[28] he writes, arguing against Aristotle and others. This preference is made clearest in "Of the Caniballes," the essay from which Shakespeare is known to have borrowed for Gonzalo's speech about his Utopian commonwealth (*The Tempest* II.i).[29] Several parallels, such as the use of the words "wild" and "bastard," suggest similar borrowing from the same essay for Polixenes' speech. "Al our endevours or wit," Montaigne writes, "cannot so much as reach to represent the neast of the least birdlet, it's contexture, beavtie, profit and vse, no nor the webbe of a seelie spider." Or arguing in defence of primitive society, he claims that

we call those fruites wilde, which nature of hir selfe, and of hir ordinarie progresse hath produced: whereas indeede, they are those which our selves have altered by our artificiall devises, and diverted from their common order, we should rather terme savage. In those are the true and most profitable vertues, and naturall proprieties most livelie and vigorous, which in these we have bastardized, applying them to the pleasure of our corrupted taste. And if notwithstanding, in divers fruites of those countries that were never tilled, we shall finde, that in respect of ours they are most excellent, and as delicate vnto our taste; there is no reason, arte should gaine the point of honour of our great and puissant mother Nature.[30]

Shakespeare's Poetics, Montaigne, and Bacon

But there is more to the affinities between Shakespeare's and Montaigne's poetics than this instance involving possible influence. Shakespeare's spontaneous manner of composition, for instance, while eliciting Ben Jonson's criticism, no doubt would have found the essayist's full approval. To Montaigne, the poet "doth in a furie powre-out whatsoever commeth in his mouth, as the pipe or cocke of a fountaine, without considering or ruminating the same: and many things escape him, diverse in colour, contrary in substance, and broken in course." Though hardly a poet himself, Montaigne loved the "Poeticall kinde of march, by friskes, skips and jumps." Writing letters, he would "commonlie begin without project: the first word begets the second." Whenever he tried otherwise, by applying both labour and study, he found that the results were far inferior to his spontaneous effusions, written "in poste-haste, and so rashly-head long." He wrote in order to discover what he didn't know, just as poets "are often surprised and rapt with admiration at their owne labors, and forget the trace, by which they past so happie a carier."[31]

There is no need to impose form upon content. On the contrary, form, to use the terms of a more recent aesthetician, is "never more than an extension of content."[32] Or as Montaigne puts it, "the matter distinguisheth it selfe. It sufficiently declareth where it changeth, where it concludeth, where it beginneth and where it rejoyneth." As a result, Montaigne displays little interest in Aristotelian unity of plot or design. True poetry, "the good and loftie, the supreme & divine, is beyond rules, and aboue reason." The same applies to our response to it, especially regarding dramatic poetry:

It hath no communitie with our judgement; but ransacketh and ravisheth the same. The furie which prickes and moves him that can penetrate hir, doth also strike and wound a third man, if he heare it either handled or recited ... And it is more apparantly seene in theaters, that the sacred inspiration of the Muses, having first stirred vp the Poet with a kinde of agitation vnto choler, vnto griefe, vnto hatred, yea and beyond himselfe, whether and howsoever they please, doth also by the Poet strike and enter into the Actor, and consecutively by the Actor, a whole auditorie or multitude.[33]

In his general endeavour to "naturalize arte" as against those who "artize nature," the integration of the "*Chimeres* & monsters in mans imaginations," which caused such dismay to Puttenham and his fellow apologists for poetry, was one of Montaigne's primary concerns. Quoting Horace's disapproving remark about the kind of art that resembles a beautiful woman with the tail of a hideous fish (*Ars Poetica* 4), he concedes that his own writings are really no more than that – "monstrous bodies, patched and hudled-vp together of divers members, without any certaine or well ordered figure, having neither order, dependencie, or proportion." One of the reasons, in fact, why he began to write his essays, he says, was to study the "many extravagant *Chimeraes*, and fantasticall monsters" of his imagination by keeping a record of them.[34]

Although lacking Montaigne's radicalness of concrete detail, Francis Bacon shared some of the basic assumptions of this aesthetic. This may seem strange from the founding father of the Royal Society, which advocated a "naked natural way of speaking" purged of "the devices of Fancy, or the delightful deceit of Fables."[35] And Bacon's most general definition of poetry is rationalist enough. Poetry is a part of learning, he writes, "in measure of words for the most part restrained." But in all other points, he adds, it is "extremely licenced." The reason for this freedom is that it "doth truly refer to the imagination."[36] Bacon, of course, knew only too well that to Aristotle the imagination was to be subservient to reason.[37] But this is by no means what he believed himself. The imagination to him is "not tied to the laws of matter"; on the contrary, it "may at pleasure join that which nature hath severed, and sever that which nature hath joined, and so make unlawful matches and divorces of things."[38]

In formulating these phrases, Bacon, like Montaigne, alludes to Horace's line about the beautiful woman with the tail of a fish, implying that such imaginative feats of joining at pleasure that which nature has severed should be most welcome in poetry. More importantly, he refutes Aristotle's famous dictum that poetry is more philosophical and serious than historiography. He may pay lip service to the claim that poetry should imitate things not as they are but as they ought to be. But if poetry "feigneth acts and events greater and more heroical" than normal, it does so not because it affords us true philosophical insight but because it satisfies our wishful thinking. Bacon, in other words, severed the basic, traditional alliance between poetry and philosophy by attributing philosophy to reason, history to memory, and poetry to the imagination, a realm poetry shares with religion:

For we see that, in matters of Faith and Religion, we raise our Imagination above our Reason; which is the cause why Religion sought ever access to the mind by similitudes, types, parables, visions, dreams.[39]

Bacon and Montaigne, of course, were neither the first nor the only ones to replace the traditional concept of a rationalist imagination with its psychological counterpart. At about the time that Shakespeare began to write plays, Giordano Bruno defined the imagination as "the sole gate to all internal affections and the link of links."[40] Before him, Agrippa had claimed that man, thanks to his imaginative powers, "passes into the nature of a god as though he were himself a god; he has familiarity with the race of demons, knowing that he is issued from the same origin."[41] But such concepts derived from a heretical, underground body of thought compounded of neo-Platonism, Cabbala, and Hermeticism. By contrast, Bacon and Montaigne evolved their ideas by dismantling the mainstream tradition of essentialist thought in both philosophy and aesthetics.

Here poetry, operating in the service of speculative philosophy, had been supposed somehow to show things in their potential or actual perfection. Elizabethan critics, in invoking nature over art, may frequently strike a note which some scholars misinterpret as a pre-Romantic advocacy of the particular and concrete.[42] But as Rosemond Tuve has shown, the use of the concept simply takes its essentialist meaning for granted. "That which is most natural," to quote Quintilian, "is that which nature permits to be done to the greatest perfection."[43] Such perfection can appear in various philosophical trappings. To Spenser, "Rapt with the rage of [his] own ravisht thought, / Through contemplation of those goodly sights, / And glorious images in heaven wrought,"[44] these are Platonic. In Sidney they assume a more earthbound character. But even when he invokes "Nature's child," invention, or tells himself to look into his heart and write, Sidney was hardly in search of the stream-of-consciousness realism typical of some of Shakespeare's soliloquies.[45] While advocating a poetry written out of a certain "inward touch," he whole-heartedly subscribed to Aristotle's ruling "that Poetry is *Philosophoteron* and *Spoudaioteron*, that is to say more Philosophicall and more studiously serious then history." The difference between a first- and a second-rate poet is like that between "the meaner sort of Painters (who counterfet onely such faces as are sette before them) and the more excellent, who, hauing no law but wit, bestow that in cullours vpon you which is fittest for the eye to see."[46]

It was Montaigne's and Bacon's achievement to discharge poetry from this traditional role as a mouthpiece of philosophical insight and to evolve the concept of an autonomous poetic imagination freed from its traditional subservience to reason. All this was the outcome of a general critique of essentialist philosophy in which Montaigne and Bacon, despite their obvious differences, again share basic premises. Montaigne, for instance, denounces the human mind as "a vagabond, dangerous, and fond-hardy implement,"[47] while Bacon calls it "an enchanted glass, full of superstition and imposture, if it be not delivered and reduced."[48] To the British philosopher, this distorting mirror was compounded of four major fallacies, which in fact had all been previously discussed by Montaigne. In doubting "whether man be provided of all naturall senses,"[49] for instance, the essayist gives an example of what Bacon meant by the *Idola tribus*, or "false appearances ... imposed upon us by the general nature of the mind"[50]:

> I see divers creatures, that live an entire and perfect life, some without sight, and some without hearing; who knoweth whether wee also want either one, two, three, or many senses more? For, if we want any one, our discourse cannot discover the want or defect thereof. It is the senses priviledge, to be the extreame boundes of our perceiving.[51]

In calling reason "that apparance or shew of discourses, which every man deviseth or forgeth in himselfe,"[52] he with equal aptness characterizes the *Idola specus*, or "false appearances imposed upon us by every man's own individual nature and custom."[53]

To be sure, Montaigne, as most of these examples can show, is usually both more radical and original than Bacon. "Wee easily pronounce puissance, truth and justice; they be words importing some great matter, but ... wee cannot possibly see, nor conceive or apprehend the same,"[54] Montaigne writes, as if to illustrate the *Idola fori*, or "false appearances ... imposed upon us by words."[55] Or he gives the example of a language game which points beyond Francis Bacon to the philosophy of Wittgenstein:

> I demaund what Nature, voluptuousnesse, circle and substitution is? The question is of wordes, and with wordes it is answered. A stone is a bodie: but he that should insist and vrge; And what is a body? A substance: And what a substance? And so goe-on: Should at last bring the respondent to his Calepine or wittes end.[56]

The last of the four idols, *Idola theatri*, reflecting the world in the distorting mirror of our traditional metaphysical systems, more than all others shows how Bacon's reductionist epistemology freed the poetic imagination from its subservience to metaphysics. Here again, Montaigne's contention that philosophy "is nothing else but a sophisticated poesie" and Plato "but a loose Poet"[57] would probably have struck Bacon as slightly extreme. But his own denunciation of traditional metaphysics as "the conceit of antiquity" says little else. For "the Forms of Substances," in Bacon's view, "are not to be enquired," and Plato, who in trying to do so displayed a "wit of elevation situate as upon a cliff," confused proper metaphysics with theology, "wherewith all his natural philosophy is infected."[58]

Basically, Bacon is in agreement with Montaigne that there "can be no principles in men, except divinitie hath revealed them vnto them." And both philosophers would have been ready to add that such revelation, while closed to the speculative philosopher, could choose as its medium the religious prophet as well as the vatic poet. In Montaigne's view poetry "is the originall language of the Gods"[59] and in Bacon's "was ever thought to have some participation of divineness." While its "Kalendars of doubts" register deficiencies in every imaginable realm of mental activity, *The Advancement of Learning* "can report no deficience" in "poesy." Partly this is due to an organic understanding of poetry which is as prematurely Romantic as Bacon's concept of the imagination.

For being as a plant that cometh of the lust of the earth, without a formal seed, it hath sprung up and spread abroad more than any other kind. But to ascribe unto it that which is due, for the expressing of affections, passions, corruptions, and customs, we are beholding to poets more than to the philosophers' works.[60]

Suspending One's Judgment

Shakespeare's spiritual kinship with Montaigne perhaps is strongest in plays which, like *Measure for Measure*, present moral problems in "such a manner that we are unsure of our moral bearings, so that uncertain and divided responses... in the minds of the audience are possible or even probable."[61] *Measure for Measure* deals with moral issues in ways reminiscent of Euripides' *Electra*. Isabella faces the sacrifice of a family member with self-righteousness equal to that of Euripides' heroine. Her brother Claudio has been sentenced to death for incontinence, but his life could be saved if Isabella were prepared to yield her virginity to Claudio's corrupt judge Angelo. Merciful thoughts such as these, however, can hardly tempt Isabella's icy saintliness: "Then, Isabel, live chaste, and brother, die: / 'More than our brother is our chastity'" (II.iv) she decides categorically. Right to the very end, when Claudio is thought to have been executed, she maintains that her brother "had but justice" (V.i), a claim that almost everything and everyone in the play (except for the legalistic Angelo) seems to contradict.

It would be superfluous to show in detail how Shakespeare thus makes the "enskied and sainted" (I.iv) Isabel the mouthpiece of an overly legalistic concept of divine justice with the result of casting doubt on that very notion. The task has been painstakingly performed by Ernest Schanzer, who demonstrates in particular how Shakespeare transformed his major source, Whetstone's *Promos and Cassandra*, so as to make his audience respond to Isabella in an uncertain, divided, and varied manner. Shakespeare's and Whetstone's presentations of their heroine's choice are found to be in complete antithesis: "Whereas Weststone keeps his heroine divided and wavering but his audience single-minded and free from doubts, Shakespeare keeps his heroine single-minded and free from doubts but his audience divided and wavering."[62]

Such strategies might best be viewed as Montaigne's "Suspend your judg-ment" cast into the dramatic mode. Problems handled as in *Measure for Measure* and similar plays "desire to be contradicted," as the philosopher puts it, "thereby to engender doubt, and suspense of judgement, which is their end and drift." By way of illustrating this "pure, entire and absolute surceasing and suspence of judgement," Montaigne gives an example suggesting the central theme of *Measure for Measure*:

That humane justice is framed according to the modell of physike, according to which, whatsoever is profitable is also just and honest: And of that the Stoickes hold, that Na-ture her selfe in most of her workes, proceedeth against justice: And of that which the Cyrenaiques hold, that there is nothing just of it selfe: That customes and lawes frame justice.[63]

Such relativism was enhanced by a new global perspective from which Montaigne scrutinized the heretofore undisputed assumptions of Western culture as if he were looking at some exotic tribe with the eyes of a visiting anthropologist. Regarding the relativity of justice, for instance, he referred to the superior jurisdiction of China, "the policie, arts and governement of which kingdome, having neither knowledge or commerce with ours, exceede our examples in divers partes of excellencie; and whose Histories teach me, how much more ample and diverse the World is, than either we or our forefathers, could ever enter into." Elsewhere he discusses the mores of cannibals to the detriment of inquisitorial torture; or, comparing "our maners vnto a Turke, or a Pagan," he finds that "we must needes yeeld vnto them."[64]

Such examples were gathered from multicultural lore as it invaded Renais-sance Europe from all corners of the newly explored globe. What is more, this influx of esoteric data was compounded by the recently unearthed treasures of ancient manuscripts and the emerging natural sciences. So great was this information explosion that most scholars were unable to cope with it other than by filtering it through the specious order of their commonplace-books, in which quaintly obsolete chapter headings are thrown into confusion by the sheer abundance of the examples. Amplification, for good reason, was one of the most prevalent stylistic and argumentative devices of the time.

Montaigne, then, was only one of many who, like Robert Burton in *The Anatomy of Melancholy*, were content with listing the several theories concerning a specific issue rather than arguing their way towards a new one. The French philosopher may pursue this suspension of judgment as a deliberate method; for most others it was the only way of keeping their heads above a welter of conflicting opinions that otherwise threatened to engulf them. But the results were similar, in a sense. For who, after discussing the opinions of some three dozen philosophers concerning God, as does Montaigne, or an equal number of theories concerning the divine, as does Burton, could in good faith conclude such a catalogue by offering the reader his own opinion on the subject? A more honest reaction was Burton's: he, after his survey, felt "almost giddy with roving about" while admitting that he "could have ranged farther yet, but I am an infant, and not able to dive into these profundities or sound these depths, and not able to understand, much less to discuss."[65]

A similar multicultural relativism inspired the diverse geographical and cosmological settings of Shakespeare's plays, from pre-Christian England to Cleopatra's Egypt of Isis-worship or Caliban's island of airy spirits. It also caused him to probe into the perverse vindictiveness of a Hamlet, a syndrome which Montaigne diagnosed as our unsurpassable Christian "hostilitie."[66] Also reminiscent of Montaigne is how Shakespeare in *Lear* dramatizes contradictory concepts of God while mainly working through non-Christian mythology. The play only mentions the Christian God once (as against nineteen such references in *Hamlet*, for instance) – and that at the point when the protagonist, in a gesture of final self-delusion, looks forward to the blissful life he hopes to share with Cordelia. Instead of a traditional Christian order, *King Lear*, as Geoffrey Bullough points out,[67] contains four levels of religious reference: Graeco-Roman gods, the goddess of nature, the idea of a moral divinity, and more specific Judaeo-Christian notions.

To make matters worse, Shakespeare juxtaposes in *King Lear* conflicting accounts of the gods in unresolved contrast. At one point he tells us that

> As flies to wanton boys, are we to th' gods;
> They kill us for their sport   (IV.i)

and the next moment that "The gods are just" (V.iii). Similarly, he sets the possibility of a Christian theodicy against the gloomy background of a fatalistic Manichean cosmology. In this, Shakespeare's deliberately excessive invocations of the gods and heavens part company with both Burton's whimsical oddity and Montaigne's cheerful scepticism. In *Lear* and other plays, they form part of the playwright's anticlimactic audience manipulation, as when the assurances of a divine justice are violated by the actual events or when our worst fears, as articulated in the following words by Albany, come true with crushing brutality:

> If that the heavens do not their visible spirits
> Send quickly down to tame these vile offenses,
> It will come,
> Humanity must perforce prey on itself,
> Like monsters of the deep.   (IV.ii)[68]

Explorations of the Self

This general scepticism goes hand in hand with a questioning of the self from which a later philosopher, René Descartes, made his way back into rationalist thought via his "Cogito, ergo sum." By contrast, neither Shakespeare, Montaigne, nor Burton resorted to the traditional belief in the substantiality of the ego. Instead they delved into realms of the psyche whose scientific investigation had to await the rise of clinical psychology in our own time. Montaigne's one central activity for years had been to "study nothing but [his] selfe" by way of delving into "the thicke-covered depths of these internall winding cranks":

To the end I may in some order and project marshall my fantasie, even to dote, and keepe it from loosing, and straggling in the aire, there is nothing so good, as to give a body, and register so many idle imaginations as present themselves vnto it. I listen to my humors, and harken to my conceites, because I must enroule them.[69]

As a result, Montaigne had a hard time believing in the permanency of the human soul. "Of a thousand there is not one perfectly ... setled but one instant of her life, and question might be made, whether according to her naturall condition she might at any time be so." A person's ego has not only to reify itself anew at any given moment; it will assume different personae as the introspective gaze changes its point of view. "Sometimes I give my soule one visage, and sometimes another, according vnto the posture or side I lay hir in." In the effort to record this stream of consciousness, inconsistencies are inevitable. For Montaigne's aim was not to describe "the essence, but the passage," and the result was an account "of diuers and variable accidents, and irresolute imaginations, and sometimes contrarie: whether it be that my selfe am other, or that I apprehend subiects, by other circumstances and considerations." Nor does it make sense to Montaigne to try to fix a person in terms of a moral character:

Shamefast, bashfull, insolent, chaste, luxurious, peevish, pratling, silent, fond, doting, labourious, nice, delicate, ingenious, slowe, dull, froward, humorous, debonaire, wise, ignorant, false in wordes, true-speaking, both liberall, covetous, and prodigall. All these I perceive in some measure or other to bee in me, according as I stirre or turne my selfe; And whosoever shall heedefully survay and consider himselfe, shall finde this volubilitie and discordance to be in himselfe, yea and in his very judgement.[70]

Such self-analyses form an important precedent to the soliloquies of a Troilus or Hamlet, which themselves mark a definite stage of divided self-consciousness in Shakespeare's work. They may also coincide with what Robert Ellrodt diagnosed as the rise in European literature of a "simultaneous awareness of experience and the experiencing self."[71] In turn, there is little doubt that Shakespeare and Montaigne explored most of the introspective vicissitudes usually thought to have been discovered in our own century. Like Montaigne, Hamlet, for instance, likes to imagine the innumerable roles that he *might* play:

I could accuse me of such things that it were better my mother had not borne me: I am very proud, revengeful, ambitious, with more offenses at my beck than I have thoughts to put them in, imagination to give them shape, or time to act them in.   (III.i)

Clearly aware of his own reveries, he catches himself unpacking his heart "like a whore" (II.ii) or recognizes his schizoid disposition in attributing his violence towards Laertes to "when he's not himself" (I.ii). This divided self, which reveals itself to the character in the very process of talking, is most fully and graphically worked out in Troilus's monologue after he witnesses Cressida's unfaithfulness:

> This is not she. O madness of discourse,
> That cause sets up with and against itself:
> Bifold authority where reason can revolt
> Without perdition, and loss assume all reason
> Without revolt. This is, and is not, Cressid
> Within my soul there doth conduce a fight
> Of this strange nature that a thing inseparate
> Divides more wider than the sky and earth. (V.ii)[72]

All this, of course, has often been analysed.[73] What is usually ignored, however, is the extent to which Shakespeare's self-dramatization in the sonnets anticipates or at least parallels his most self-analytically divided characters. Typical here is Ellrodt, who, in an otherwise penetrating essay on "Self-consciousness in Montaigne and Shakespeare," claims that the sonnets "seldom show him self-absorbed in a brooding self-examination."[74] It may be true that the simultaneity of self-revelation and dramatic utterance observable in the plays tends to be statically formalized in the sonnets. But a divided self, fatefully in love against all better reason, is the troubled focus of many sonnets, particularly those about the dark lady. In fact, Ellrodt's argument that Montaigne laicized Christian self-examination by stripping it of its allegorical trappings – the forces of good and evil fighting their *psychomachia* for the conquest of the human soul – is strikingly illustrated in Sonnet 144. The traditional good and bad angels have become rivals in a sexual triangle, leaving the speaker in a quandary about his own precarious role in this sexomachia:

Two loves I have, of comfort and despair,
Which like two spirits do suggest me still;
The better angel is a man right fair,
The worser spirit a woman colored ill.
To win me soon to hell, my female evil
Tempteth my better angel from my side,
And would corrupt my saint to be a devil,
Wooing his purity with her foul pride.
And whether that my angel be turned fiend
Suspect I may, yet not directly tell;
But being both from me, both to each friend,
I guess one angel in another's hell.
　　Yet this shall I ne'er know, but live in doubt,
　　Till my bad angel fire my good one out.

The sonnet is one out of two published in *The Passionate Pilgrim* of 1599[75] – that is, well before *Troilus and Cressida*, *Hamlet*, and *Measure for Measure* as well as Thorpe's edition of the complete sonnets of 1609. The other, Sonnet 138, reveals the poet's divided self and wilful self-betrayal in a psychogram which is as complex as any in either Thorpe's volume or the plays:

When my love swears that she is made of truth,
I do believe her though I know she lies,
That she might think me some untutored youth,
Unlearnèd in the world's false subtleties.
Thus vainly thinking that she thinks me young,
Although she knows my days are past the best,
Simply I credit her false-speaking tongue;
On both sides thus is simple truth suppressed.
But wherefore says she not she is unjust?
But wherefore say not I that I am old?
O, love's best habit is in seeming trust,
And age in love loves not to have years told.
　　Therefore I lie with her, and she with me,
　　And in our faults by lies we flattered be.

The "truth" which the speaker understands so clearly is completely uprooted by the force of what he experiences. Emotionally it turns out to be an untruth, and that on two levels. Despite his better knowledge, the speaker not only believes that his mistress is faithful but "vainly" thinks that she thinks him young. In R.D. Laing's terms,[76] there is a double mystification of experience which proves stronger than all the speaker's analytical insight into his self-deceptive strategies. It forces him into the pseudo-logic of the final quartet, in which an obvious untruth is affirmed as what is true in his particular situation. A twofold play on the words "truth" (alias "faithfulness") and "lie" (alias "sleep with") is the appropriate verbal correlative for this deadly serious game.

The tone, as when the speaker analyses various other syndromes of self-division (for example, "But my five wits nor my five senses can / Dissuade one foolish heart from serving thee" Sonnet 141; "Canst thou, O cruel, say I love thee not, / When I against myself with thee partake" 149) and deliberate self-delusion (for example, 140, 151), remains witty and satirical. But anguish and self-disgust are never far beneath the surface, and in a sonnet such as the one about "lust in action" (129) they prove strong enough to sweep aside all self-conscious witticism and to break forth with the breathless vehemence of a person who loathes himself for what he cannot stop himself from doing. Here, at least, one would agree with W.H. Auden that most of Shakespeare's sonnets give the impression "of naked autobiographical confession."[77]

Shakespeare's self-division and disgust rarely assume the distinctly Christian dimensions we find in, say, John Donne's "Oh, to vex me, contraries meet in one." But what Robert Burton's *Anatomy of Melancholy* somewhat later was to diagnose as the "Horror of Conscience" becomes all the more terrifying for that very lack of a religious framework. A Christian like Donne can refer his anguish to the threat of eternal damnation. To Shakespeare it seems to open up into the bottomless pit of a more nameless horror. Had Burton been familiar with his works, he might have found reason to discuss Shakespeare along with those who feel "the pains of hell in [their] soul ... They think evil against their wills, that which they abhor themselves, they must needs think, do, and speak."[78] Sonnet 129 fits Burton's analysis to perfection. Like Sonnet 144 and several others it evokes the secularized *psychomachia* of someone to whom hell and damnation have become the parameters of his actual existence here and now. And again, the speaker's ability to analyse this dilemma only makes it worse. Few other sonnets begin with a definition:

> Th'expense of spirit in a waste of shame
> Is lust in action.

But his continued effort to define what plagues him only leads to the recognition of his "madness":

> and, till action, lust
> Is perjured, murd'rous, bloody, full of blame,
> Savage, extreme, rude, cruel, not to trust;
> Enjoyed no sooner but despisèd straight;
> Past reason hunted, and no sooner had,
> Past reason hated as a swallowed bait
> On purpose laid to make the taker mad;

Mad in pursuit, and in possession so;
Had, having, and in quest to have, extreme;
A bliss in proof, and proved, a very woe,
Before, a joy proposed; behind, a dream.

The final couplet sums up the nightmare of a Christianity bereft of everything but its horror of conscience. "Never was any living creature," writes Burton, "in such torment before, in such a miserable estate, in such distress of mind, no hope, no faith, past cure." The speaker of Shakespeare's sonnet is trapped in a similar conviction that his madness is "past cure":

All this the world well knows, yet none knows well
To shun the heaven that leads men to this hell.

From Tragic to
Anti-tragic Closure

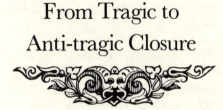

THE EVIDENCE OF THE LAST PLAYS seems to suggest that Shakespeare, if ever he inhabited these depths himself, found his way out of them by radically changing his spiritual context. The most obvious sign for this is an almost total absence of explicit Christian references in the plays after *Antony and Cleopatra*.[1] Antony, Pericles, Posthumus, Leontes, and Prospero, too, go through a spiritual hell. But their inferno is transitional, as we shall see, towards some form of rebirth. Gone is Othello's fear of eternal damnation when looking at the strangled Desdemona:

> When we shall meet at compt,
> This look of thine will hurl my soul from heaven,
> And fiends will snatch at it.   (V.ii)

Where Othello sees himself separated from his beloved by the abyss dividing hell from heaven, Antony and Cleopatra will share a future life in the lovers' paradise of the Elysian fields:

> Where souls do couch on flowers, we'll hand in hand,
> And with our sprightly port make the ghosts gaze:
> Dido and her Aeneas shall want troops,
> And all the haunt be ours.   (IV.xiv)

But the path towards this new vision[2] was a long and arduous one, involving a transcendence of tragedy in both the Christian and the classical senses.

Nearly all of Shakespeare's tragedies end on a note of reconciliation.[3] After the deed of horror is done, order is restored and there is the prospect of a better future, sometimes attained through the very suffering we have witnessed. In this the playwright followed a pattern he first evolved in *Richard III*. Richmond, the future king, announces the end of the Wars of the Roses, voices his hopes for future peace and prosperity, and looks back on the tragic past now set aright by "God's fair ordinance":

> England hath long been mad, and scarred herself;
> The brother blindly shed the brother's blood,
> The father rashly slaughter'd his own son,
> The son, compell'd, been butcher to the sire.

From *Romeo and Juliet* to *Macbeth*, tragedy after tragedy ends on a similar note. In *Romeo and Juliet* itself, there is the friar's circumstantial report of how the star-crossed lovers met their final end. Mark Antony, standing over Brutus's dead body, points out how this "noblest Roman of them all" was the only conspirator against Caesar who acted not out of envy but "in a general honest thought / And common good to all." Hamlet's main concern before his death is to have himself and his cause reported "aright / To the unsatisfied," and Horatio, obedient to his friend's wish, promises to explain "to th' yet unknowing world / How these things came about":

> So shall you hear
> Of carnal, bloody, and unnatural acts,
> Of accidental judgments, casual slaughters,
> Of deaths put on by cunning and forced cause,
> And, in this upshot, purposes mistook
> Fall'n on th' inventors' heads. All this can I
> Truly deliver.

Othello asks to have his own destiny reported with neither malice nor extenuation, and both Cassio and Lodovico seem eager to comply, the one by praising the dead hero as one "great of heart," the other promising to relate his "heavy act" to the Venetian senate with a "heavy heart." *Macbeth*, more closely than any of the tragedies preceding it, returns to the original pattern of *Richard III*. Briefly recalling the deaths of the protagonist and his wife, the future king offers rewards to his friends, vows to arrest the surviving allies of Macbeth, and promises to restore order "by the grace of Grace."

King Lear, of all of Shakespeare's works (including *Antony and Cleopatra*, a play directly leading to the romances), deviates most drastically from this pattern. Recent critics who speak of the play as a comedy of the grotesque or absurd[4] were not the first to notice this singularity. Dr Johnson was so shocked by its final scenes that he could not bear to reread them till he "undertook to revise them as an editor." In most tragedies, A.W. Schlegel wrote, "the sudden blows of fate still seem to honour the head which they strike," whereas Lear is "given up a prey to naked helplessness." In other words, the tragic in this play, as Coleridge put it, "has been urged beyond the outermost mark and *ne plus ultra* of the dramatic." To Lamb it simply seemed "painful and disgusting."[5] Hegel is probably the first who therefore associated the play with what seemed to him a deplorably modernist trend in the arts – "the humour of the abominable thing, a kind of burlesque simulation of irony."[6]

The phrase aptly describes the moment in *King Lear* when Albany is about to deliver the kind of speech typical of the conclusions in Shakespeare's other tragedies:

> What comfort to this great decay may come
> Shall be applied. For us, we will resign,
> During the life of this old majesty,
> To him our absolute power: [*To Edgar and Kent*] you, to your rights;
> With boot, and such addition as your honors
> Have more than merited. All friends shall taste
> The wages of their virtue, and all foes
> The cup of their deservings.   (V.iii)

But circumstances force this well-rounded rhetoric into a sudden dissonance by disrupting the final couplet towards which Albany seems to be heading.[7] "O, see, see!" he exclaims, and everybody's eyes are riveted on Lear, who, bent over the strangled Cordelia, dies in the delusion that his daughter may still be alive.[8] Death to Lear brings no more comfort than to a man tortured on the rack. It relieves him of his agony while silencing all further oratory about the woes that are past, the order that will be restored, and the brighter future that lies ahead. Albany, who still had such hopes only a moment ago, can now think of nothing but general woe. Although the obvious successor to Lear, he entrusts Kent and Edgar with his task to sustain the "gored state." In his turn, Kent declines the request, wishing no more than to follow his master into death, while Edgar, in a brief speech which concludes the entire drama, explicitly denies himself Albany's reassuring rhetoric, which Lear's death disrupted so brutally:

> The weight of this sad time we must obey,
> Speak what we feel, not what we ought to say.

Instead of being ennobled or improved by human suffering, a once-heroic world has shrunk to the size of mere existence:

> The oldest hath borne most: we that are young
> Shall never see so much, nor live so long.

Although many critics have remarked on the singularity of this ending, few attempts have been made to determine its place in Shakespeare's development as a tragic poet. Of course, there are good reasons for this omission, and any attempt to amend it will have to begin by setting out its own caveats. Thus, development here is not to be misunderstood as an irreversible trend in which new modes evolve and decline, never to reappear again. *King Lear*, for instance, probably finds its clearest antecedent in *Titus Andronicus*, written even before *Romeo and Juliet*. Similarly, *The Comedy of Errors*, which of all of Shakespeare's plays before 1608 most clearly prefigures the last plays, may well have been the poet's first. Yet despite such erratic leaps, of which several more could be listed, a rough outline of Shakespeare's development emerges from the mere sequence of his work as well as from specific data such as his reading of Florio's Montaigne or his possible involvement in the Hermetic movement as more recently documented by Frances A. Yates.[9] It is generally recognized that comedies and history plays dominate Shakespeare's beginnings, tragedies and the newly evolved problem plays the middle period, and romances the final one. Whatever more specific developments we might discern within the tragic mode will have to be seen against this wider background.

In *Titus Andronicus*, chronologically speaking the first of the "tragedies" printed in the 1623 Folio, Shakespeare as yet showed little concern for the redemptive closure patterns he had already evolved in *Richard III*. Lucius, the new emperor, orders that the defiantly evil Aaron be starved to death and his dead paramour thrown to the beasts:

> As for the ravenous tiger, Tamora,
> No funeral rite, nor man in mourning weed,
> No mournful bell shall ring her burial;
> But throw her forth to beasts and birds to prey.
> Her life was beastly and devoid of pity,
> And being dead, let birds on her take pity.

These words, worthy of the contemporary theatre of cruelty rather than of classical tragedy, conclude the First Quarto of *The Most Lamentable Romaine Tragedie of Titus Andronicus* (1594). But only six years later the typical last scene of Shakespearian tragedy already seems to have been firmly enough established in people's minds to make the printer or editor of the Second Quarto change this unconventional ending by adding four more lines:

> See justice done on Aaron, that damned Moor,
> By whom our heavy haps had their beginning;
> Then afterwards to order well the state,
> That like events may ne'er it ruinate.[10]

Romeo and Juliet

The perfect model for what has already turned cliché here is found in *Romeo and Juliet*. *Titus Andronicus* is Shakespeare's Senecan revenge drama *par excellence*. Had the playwright been more than just remotely familiar with Aeschylus, Sophocles, and Euripides, one would be tempted to assume that *Romeo and Juliet* was modelled directly on Greek tragedy. Being well versed in its myths, a Greek audience, for instance, would in most cases recognize the story of a play from its mere title. In a similar way, Shakespeare reveals the main content and the outcome of his plot before the beginning of the actual play. Brooke's *Tragicall Historye of Romeus and Juliet*, Shakespeare's "main and perhaps sole source,"[11] may have been an influence here. But whereas Brooke's "Argument" merely sums up the story, Shakespeare's "chorus" focuses on certain themes which the play shares with Greek tragedy:

> Two households, both alike in dignity,
> In fair Verona, where we lay our scene,
> From ancient grudge break to new mutiny,
> Where civil blood makes civil hands unclean.
> From forth the fatal loins of these two foes
> A pair of star-crossed lovers take their life;
> Whose misadventured piteous overthrows
> Doth with their death bury their parents' strife.

Here, as in, for instance, Aeschylus's *Oresteia*, the emphasis is on the power of fate and even more importantly on how a seemingly unending "chain of blood-lettings" (*Libation Bearers* 433) is finally brought to an end through the suffering of the tragic protagonists.

None of this is found in Brooke's "Argument" or preface "To the Reader," which purports to treat of some "tragicall matter" within a simplistic framework of divine retributive justice. In "hastyng to most unhappye deathe," the lovers, instead of incurring a destiny "hanging in the stars," pay the price for "thralling themselves to unhonest desire" and "abusyng the honorable name of lawefull mariage." Without doubt the poem itself is more complex than that. But despite the occasional mention of the "fatall sisters three," "fatall desteny," or even the "starres above," Brooke's main scapegoat for the lovers' tragic deaths is Fortune, with her "hasty ronning wheele," who is frequently invoked several times on the same page. In this he followed the *de casibus* tradition, which, by way of exculpating God, attributes the mischances of man to the goddess who casts down mighty kings as well as poor lovers – "frayle unconstant Fortune, that delyteth still in chaunge, / Who, in a moment, heaves her frendes up to the height / Of her swift turning slippery wheele, then fleetes her frendship straight."[12]

Shakespeare changed this cosmological framework considerably.[13] Romeo may call himself "fortune's fool" (III.i), or Juliet, on taking leave of her husband, exclaim, "O Fortune, Fortune! All men call thee fickle" (III.v). But far less casual and also more frequent are references to the stars, the heavens, and "black fate" (III.i). Never throughout the entire play are we allowed to forget that the lovers are "star-crossed." Romeo defies the stars in returning from banishment (V.i), tries to shake off their yoke by committing suicide (V.iii), and, even before he meets Juliet, has forebodings of

> Some consequence yet hanging in the stars
> Shall bitterly begin his fearful date
> With this night's revels and expire the term
> Of a despisèd life, closed in my breast,
> By some vile forfeit of untimely death.   (I.iv)

This shift from fortune to fate in the play's imagery only reinforces what we witness in the plot. Shakespeare, by adding to and altering the events found in Brooke's *Tragicall Historye*, gave them an aspect of inescapable doom. Although desperately trying to escape the tragic fate which he foresees so clearly, Romeo is forced to kill Tybalt after Tybalt has treacherously murdered his friend Mercutio. Lacking in the source, as is Mercutio's murder, is the death of Paris, whom Romeo, again forced by circumstance, kills against his will. With such additions Brooke's narrative canter turns into a breath-taking race against time in which every happy scene is overshadowed by the evil forebodings of a preceding one. Even before Romeo exchanges first words with Juliet, Tybalt has vowed vengeance for the protagonist's unwelcome visit at his uncle's feast – a brief scene that Shakespeare again added to his source. The lovers' union in *The Tragicall Historye* "doth last a month or twayne"[14] before it is ended by Romeo's murder of Tybalt and his banishment; by contrast, Shakespeare allows them but one Monday night, and already Tybalt has been slain, Romeo banished, and, what is more, Juliet's marriage with Paris scheduled for the following Thursday (III.iv).

All this adds to the coincidences of miscarried letters, erroneous messages, and fateful precipitations which critics have found both excessive and unconvincing. Yet none of it would have offended Aristotle, who points out that a "convincing impossibility" is preferable to "an unconvincing possibility."[15] Certainly, *Romeo and Juliet* in no way puts greater strains upon our willing suspension of disbelief than Aristotle's model tragedy, *Oedipus Rex*. To disapprove of the play by implying that its tragic conclusion should have been made to arise from the characters, as in *Macbeth* or *Othello*, is to judge it by standards alien to those Shakespeare seems to have set himself.[16]

Whether or not the playwright knew Aristotle's *Poetics*, *Romeo and Juliet* meets the Aristotelian criterion that characters be secondary to the coherent concatenation of the incidents. By deliberately transforming Brooke's story, Shakespeare makes fate the overruling determinant not only in the outward events but also in the characters' innermost thoughts. Romeo's forebodings of "Some consequence yet hanging in the stars" probably stem from a dream which he is never allowed to tell because, instead, the loquacious Mercutio has to convince everybody that dreams are "nothing but vain fantasy" (I.iv). Ironically, it is Mercutio himself who first falls victim to the evil foreseen by Romeo. Like the oracles in Greek tragedy, such dream prophecies often speak in riddles, as when Romeo

> ... dreamt my lady came and found me dead
> (Strange dream that gives a dead man leave to think!)
> And breathed such life with kisses in my lips
> That I revived and was an emperor.   (V.i)

The lines are typical of an almost heavy-handed use of dramatic irony for which *Oedipus Rex* again provides striking parallels. Just as Oedipus draws calamities upon his head in cursing the murderer of King Laius, so the lovers unwittingly invoke their tragic destiny, Romeo by protesting that his life were better ended by the families' hate than by losing his love (II.ii), Juliet by imploring her mother to make her bridal bed in "that dim monument where Tybalt lies" (III.v), by fearing that her "grave is like to be [her] wedding bed" (I.v), or by suddenly visualizing her departing lover down in the orchard "As one dead in the bottom of a tomb" (III.v). The only time Fortune is actually invoked in the play, the goddess herself turns out to be an instrument of such dramatic irony: Juliet again is hardly aware of what she calls upon herself in imploring Fortune to be as fickle as men call her and send her lover back from banishment quickly (III.v).

Thus the incidents of the play converge in raising one central question about a possible rationale behind the ingeniously fated deaths of the lovers. Shakespeare again misses no opportunity to articulate this crucial concern in the characters' own words. "Is there no pity sitting in the clouds / That sees into the bottom of my grief?" (III.v) exclaims Juliet. But the heavens, of course, answer her question with silence, so that her attitude, like Romeo's, towards their undeserved fate remains one of uncomprehending bewilderment, right up to their deaths:

> Alack, alack, that heaven should practise stratagems
> Upon so soft a subject as myself!   (III.v)

Both the friar and Prince Escalus come up with their own answers but fail to rise above a simplistic explanation of "this work of heaven" (V.iii) in terms of divine retribution. "The heavens do low'r upon you for some ill; / Move them no more by crossing their high will" (IV.v), Friar Lawrence warns the Capulets. "See what a scourge is laid upon your hate, / That heaven finds means to kill your joys with love" (V.iii), concludes the prince after all the evil is done. Neither they nor anyone else goes deep enough to explain to us what the Chief Watchman calls "the true ground of all these piteous woes" (V.iii). But the audience, of course, has been told already. So all along, as the protagonists wonder about their undeserved fate, we know that the heavens intend more than a mere punishment. By killing Romeo and Juliet they will "bury their parents' strife" (prologue viii).

Although the general questioning of fate was one of Shakespeare's major additions to his source, Brooke's *Tragicall Historye* probably gave him a hint concerning the answer. Throughout Brooke's poem, the hope that the lovers' marriage will finally bring their families "such a peace as ever shall endure"[17] is voiced by Romeo and Juliet as well as by the friar. In Shakespeare's play, its sole spokesman is Friar Lawrence, who thereby justifies his otherwise questionable strategems. In promising Romeo that he will marry him to Juliet, he speculates that "this alliance may so happy prove / To turn your households' rancor to pure love" (II.iii). Even after his initial plans have misfired, he sends Juliet into her deathlike trance in the name of the same hoped-for reconciliation – "To blaze your marriage, reconcile your friends, / Beg pardon of the Prince" (III.iii).

Little does he know that his goal is to be reached through the very suffering of the lovers that he most tries to avoid. The secret dialectics of destiny are as baffling to the Christian friar as to the lovers themselves. "A greater power than we can contradict / Hath thwarted our intents" (V.iii), he finally concludes. Yet he never realizes the clearly defined though ironic role he has been made to play in a teleologically unfolding order of destiny so clearly of Greek rather than Christian descent. Hegel believed that the dialectical unfoldings of Eternal Justice are realized in the very injustices suffered by tragic heroes, and few scenes illustrate that claim more clearly than the finale of *Romeo and Juliet*, which Shakespeare again added to his source. As the tragedy draws to a close, a pageant-like glorification of its protagonists takes over. Old Montague and old Capulet, while shaking hands, vie with each other in promising to have the victims of their family feud cast into statues of golden splendour:

> CAPULET O brother Montague, give me thy hand.
> This is my daughter's jointure, for no more
> Can I demand.
> MONTAGUE But I can give thee more;
> For I will raise her statue in pure gold
> That whiles Verona by that name is known,

> There shall no figure at such rate be set
> As that of true and faithful Juliet.
> CAPULET As rich shall Romeo's by his lady's lie –
> Poor sacrifices of our enmity!

Troilus and Cressida

As Shakespeare wrote several years later, "The end crowns all, / And that old common arbitrator, Time, / Will one day end it." The words are Hector's in *Troilus and Cressida* (IV.v), a play which by its very title invites comparison with *Romeo and Juliet*. But Shakespeare, though others were busy providing his untragic *Titus Andronicus* with a proper Shakespearian ending, proved an unlikely person to imitate his own model tragedy. Nothing, at least in the Shakespearian canon, could be more untragic than the ending of *The Tragedie of Troylus and Cressida*. A pimp, groaning with venereal disease which he plans to bequeath to the audience, orates not *de casibus virorum illustrium*, or of the fall of famous men, but of his own "fall":

> Good traders in the flesh, set this in your painted cloths:
> "As many as be here of Pandar's hall,
> Your eyes, half out, weep out at Pandar's fall;
> ...
> Some two months hence my will shall here be made.
> It should be now, but that my fear is this,
> Some gallèd goose of Winchester would hiss.
> Till then I'll sweat and seek about for eases,
> And at that time bequeath you my diseases."

While perhaps its most daredevil feat, this anticlimactic ending is only part of a penchant for a general questioning of accepted values, beliefs, and artistic modes which characterizes Shakespeare's work around the turn of the century. The general manifestations of this new mentality are as obvious as they are difficult to account for. In *Julius Caesar*, for instance, Shakespeare, according to Ernest Schanzer, first evolved the problem play. Here a moral problem is "presented in such a manner that we are unsure of our moral bearing"[18]:

> O hateful Error, Melancholy's child,
> Why dost thou show to the apt thoughts of men
> The things that are not?   (V.iii)

asks one of the characters in the play. Shakespeare's answer seems to proclaim error universal, so that the audience, in witnessing Brutus's murder of Julius

Caesar as such, still is given sufficient reason to question its own verdict. In the same spirit Shakespeare began to experiment in dislogistic rhetoric, having his characters argue two diametrically opposed points of view concerning the same issue with equally convincing effect.[19] The practice ultimately derives from the Greek Sophists, whose *dissoi logoi*, as we have seen, influenced the dramatic techniques of Euripides. Shakespeare, if he was ignorant of both, could have learned about an even more radical relativism from Montaigne, whose *Essays* in the translation of John Florio he probably started to read while working on *Hamlet*. Instead of *dissoi logoi*, Montaigne evokes the "rejoynders, double, treble, qvadruple, with this infinit contexture of debates"[20] that can surround an argument.

Of all of Shakespeare's plays, it is probably *Troilus and Cressida* which comes closest to the relativist spirit of the French philosopher. Twentieth-century critics were not the first to be confused by the drama. In the Folio of 1623, the printer had just begun to set it following Shakespeare's model tragedy *Romeo and Juliet* when it was withdrawn, then finally squeezed in at the last minute between the histories and the tragedies under the title *The Tragedie of Troylus and Cressida*. Earlier, it had appeared as *The Historie of Troylus and Cresseida* in the quarto (first state) of 1609. To make matters worse, the quarto (second state) of the same year adds an epistle in which the play is described as being "passing full of the palme comicall." In believing that "there is none more witty than this,"[21] the anonymous writer seems to anticipate Ionesco's conviction that "Nothing is comic. Everything is tragic. Nothing is tragic, everything is comic."[22]

Troilus and Cressida poses problems – such as the traditional belief in cosmic order – the way a Renaissance magus like Giovanni Battista della Porta, author of *Magiae Naturalis Libri* (Neapoli 1589), would place, say, his own face in a circular hall of mirrors, with the result that "ex multis reflexionibus infinitae propemodum facies numerabuntur" ("an almost infinite number of faces can be counted from the many reflections"). One of Shakespeare's scenes seems to transform the stage into such a "speculum theatralis."[23] Cressida's flirting with Diomed in front of Calchas's tent is presented to us from four different angles. The lovers' mutual cat-and-mouse play would be enough in itself to make us see their behaviour as role-playing. But hiding, perhaps behind some bush, so that the "torch may not discover" them, are Troilus, Cressida's former lover, who spying becomes the agonizing witness of his betrayal, and Ulysses, knowing, realistic, and cynical, who tries to control Troilus's passionate outbursts. And standing apart from either group but close enough to Ulysses that he can parrot his words is Thersites, who chorus-like declares all to be no more than "wars and lechery; nothing else holds fashion" (V.ii).

From the start, there is hardly an assertion made in the play, be it about the heroics of war, courtly love, or the hierarchical order of the universe, which the ensuing action does not undercut or violate. Critics like Theodore Spencer[24] and R.A. Foakes[25] have shown in detail how again and again specific audience expectations are thus aroused and cut short. And Hector's "The end crowns all" are not the only words in the play to encourage the audience to expect a tragic ending. Even after it has become obvious that Cressida is not to die like a second Juliet, Troilus retains some of the characteristics of a tragic hero. Furthermore, there is Hector, whom Shakespeare endows with even greater tragic potential, including an Aristotelian flaw of character, his "vice of mercy" (V.iii). But here again Shakespeare uses a deliberate technique of anticlimactic audience manipulation. At one point the sons of Priamus debate whether they should accept Nestor's proposal of ending the war by returning Helena. Hector, after first pleading that she should be let go, finally yields to Troilus's passionate rhetoric about "valiant and magnanimous deeds," announcing that he has sent "a roisting challenge" among the Greeks (II.ii). Although largely unread in Homer's *Iliad*, Shakespeare's audience was familiar enough with the matters of Troy to associate such a challenge with Hector's heroic death at the hands of Achilles.

In order to frustrate these expectations, Shakespeare had to alter his sources drastically. None of them anticipates the cowardly brutality of the scene in which Hector falls victim not to a superior warrior, as in Homer, but to a perfidious braggart. Achilles, too feeble to dare do so himself, has his Myrmidons kill the unarmed Hector, who, minutes before, after defeating Achilles, had deigned to pursue what he thought to be a dishonourable advantage. What follows is quite in tune with this untragic death of a potentially tragic hero.

Troilus, the only character to make a speech comparable with the concluding words of a Richmond, Mark Antony, or Horatio, has no thoughts concerning a restoration of order or a brighter future, let alone the benefits others might reap by the suffering of the dead hero. There is textual evidence that Shakespeare may have thought of giving the play a conclusion other than the one we know.[26] Such an ending is reached when Troilus suddenly rounds off his speech with a couplet that in fact anticipates Edgar's "The weight of this sad time we must obey, / Speak what we feel, not what we ought to say" in the concluding speech of *King Lear*.

> Let him that will a screech owl aye be called
> Go in to Troy, and say there Hector's dead.
> There is a word will Priam turn to stone,
> Make wells and Niobes of the maids and wives,
> Cold statues of the youth, and in a word
> Scare Troy out of itself. But march away.
> Hector is dead; there is no more to say.[27]

What follows this is little better than the four wretched lines about a restoration of order added to the Second Quarto of *The Tragedy of Titus*

Andronicus (1594). The hero suddenly changes his mind, telling the soldiers whom he has just asked to "march away" to "Stay yet." He then bursts forth into a vapid tirade about the "vile abominable tents" of the Greeks and about haunting the "great-sized coward" Achilles, who, as we know from Homer, will kill him. With such empty promises he again dismisses the soldiers:

> Strike a free march to Troy. With comfort go;
> Hope of revenge shall hide our inward woe.

If Shakespeare's intention here was a double parody of the closure patterns of his tragedies, he was probably the first to notice that such irony was too subtle for most of his audience. Hence the play concludes with Pandarus's speech, whose heavy-handed sarcasm would not be lost even on the most "dull and heauy-witted worldlings."[28] For that, the playwright had only to bring Pandarus back on the stage and send Troilus away, which Shakespeare managed by letting the disabused lover curse his former go-between:

> PANDARUS But hear you, hear you!
> TROILUS Hence, broker, lackey! Ignominy and shame
> Pursue thy life, and live aye with thy name.
> *Exeunt all but Pandarus.*

What follows – Pandarus proclaiming his fall and bequeathing his diseases to the audience – is shocking but in an almost haphazard way. In fact, the scene was put together by borrowing the quick exchange between Pandarus and Troilus from an earlier scene (V.iii.112ff), where it can still be found in the 1623 Folio.

In Theodore Spencer's view *Troilus and Cressida* was "the kind of experiment ... necessary before *King Lear* could be written."[29] This is true in ways even more specific than the critic realized. In *Lear*, the arousal and subsequent violation of certain expectations – a technique brought to the utmost of cynical sophistication in the earlier play – has the effect of a hammer blow which gathers its force from the movement of the entire play. Like *Troilus and Cressida*, *King Lear* questions, negates, and inverts the tragic patterns to which it alludes, but it does so more subtly, less parodically, and altogether more powerfully.

King Lear

A look at the sources shows how radically Shakespeare both preserved and altered a near-parable of parental unkindness and filial ingratitude in order to achieve the play's anti-tragic effects. Put in the simplest terms, he kept the beginning while inverting the conclusion. A happy ending, in which the good are rewarded and the evil punished, is turned into one in which calamity seems to strike down good and bad alike. Shakespeare's principal source, *The True*

Chronicle Historie of King Leir, more or less dramatizes an ending already found in Holinshed, where Gonorilla and Regan reap the just reward for their "unkindnesse" and "unnaturalnesse":

Aganippus [Cordeilla's husband] caused a mightie armie to be put in a readinesse, and likewise a great navie of ships to be rigged, to passe over into Britaine with Leir his father in law, to see him againe restored to his kingdome ... Hereupon, when this armie and navie of ships were readie, Leir and his daughter Cordeilla with hir husband tooke the sea, and arriving in Britaine, fought with their enimies, and discomfited them in battell, in the which Maglanus and Henninus were slaine: and then was Leir restored to his kingdome, which he ruled after this by the space of two yeeres, and then died, fortie yeeres after he first began to reigne.[30]

This conclusion, plus the opening in which Leir, grown "unweldie through age ... thought to understand the affections of his daughters towards him" by asking them how well they loved him, takes up more than half of Holinshed's narrative, a proportion not too different from that found in *The True Chronicle Historie*. It is the proper framework for a tale which in the play's words purports to "warne all ages that insueth, / How they trust flattery, and reject the trueth":

> O just *Jehova*, whose almighty power
> Doth governe all things in this spacious world,
> How canst thou suffer such outragious acts
> To be committed without just revenge?

asks Leir's faithful follower when the king is threatened with murder. But never once are we made to doubt that, to quote another of the play's characters, "The heavens are just, and hate impiety, / And will (no doubt) reveale such haynous crimes."[31] Shakespeare has his dramatis personae ask similar questions and give comparable assurances. But all of them are either answered by silence, proven wrong, or simply ignored. This is most apparent regarding the character who is to utter the play's anticlimactic last words. The *Lear* world, as John Reibetanz shows in detail, "ironically crushes every one of his hopes as soon as he voices them ... Edgar is being schooled in the *Lear* world. His hopes are crushed as ours will be in the last scene, during *our* education."[32]

To put it somewhat differently, our education towards the play's final disillusionment in the last scene begins with the very first one. It has confused more than one critic that Shakespeare, while changing almost everything else, should have followed his sources in their most unrealistic details at the beginning of the story. By eliminating some of the motivation for Lear's intemperate behaviour (Leir's wife has died recently, while Gonorilla and Regan use his love-test to lay a plot for Cordeilla), he even increased its parable and fairy-tale character. Thus, condemnations of the play's opening are as widespread and time-honoured as those of its ending. "Let the first scene of *Lear* have been lost," suggested Coleridge, "and let it be only understood that a fond father had been duped by hypocritical professions of love and duty on the part of two daughters to disinherit a third, previously, and deservedly, more dear to him, and all the rest of the tragedy would retain its interest undiminished."[33] Just as Coleridge was perturbed by an ending which urged the tragic beyond the "*ne plus ultra* of the dramatic*," he failed to appreciate that the opening of *King Lear* was deliberately designed to prepare him for such anti-tragic shock therapy.

In the actual play, other factors help to reinforce and frustrate expectations derived from its opening. *King Lear*, for instance, repeatedly recalls the Book of Job, to the point of echoing some of its notions and phrases.[34] "I will be the pattern of all patience" (III.ii), exclaims the protagonist. And even if his behaviour for the most part belies these words, there is nobody who resembles him more in this than self-righteous Job, who expostulates with heaven pleading his innocence and undeserved suffering. So Lear in the tempest strives "to outscorn / The to-and-fro-conflicting wind and rain"[35] and bids the "all-shaking thunder" to "Strike flat the thick rotundity o' th' world" (III.i.2). But Job's claims are heard and vindicated, while Lear's are answered by silence. What is more, Lear, clamouring for justice in the storm, is a man gone mad; he has become a parody of his Biblical prototype.

Titus Andronicus shows that Shakespeare was trying out similar effects long before *King Lear*. Like Lear, its protagonist throws away an empire and goes mad over the ingratitude of man. In his insanity he sends messengers to the underworld to summon up Justice. He receives the answer that he can have revenge but no justice because Justice is busy with Jupiter in heaven. Titus Andronicus therefore shoots petitions into heaven with his bow and arrows, pleading with Jupiter and the other gods "To send down Justice for to wreak our wrongs" (IV.iii). A little later a Clown arrives whom Titus mistakes for a heavenly messenger carrying a divine message. "What says Jupiter?" Titus asks him, and the Clown answers with a pun which is one of the most profound and sinister in all of Shakespeare. "Ho, the gibbet maker! He says that he hath taken them down again, for the man must not be hanged till the next week." A few minutes later this unwitting herald of a gallows justice in heaven is taken to be hanged himself (IV.iv).

Even Lear's growth in wisdom, from one who "hath ever but slenderly known himself" (I.i) into a person who knows that he is but "A poor, infirm, weak, and despised old man" (III.ii), is anticlimactic or at least highly ambivalent. Thus, some of Lear's statements which appear wise to us must have impressed some of Shakespeare's spectators as rather blasphemous and heretical. His "Thou art the thing itself; unaccommodated man is no more but such a poor, bare, forked animal as thou art" (III.iv), for instance, may be said to be in the best spirit of Montaigne, who concluded that man is little more and often less than an animal.[36]

But agreement with Montaigne was hardly a guarantee for common approval. According to Thomas Aquinas, anyone "ignoring...the order of his place in the universe" by thinking himself "beneath certain creatures above whom he is placed"[37] by God himself was a fit candidate for the stake. The Church of early seventeenth-century England might have considered such punishment overly severe but would still have concurred with the Catholic theologian in condemning such non-anthropocentric thought as heretical. While his namesake in the anonymous *True Chronicle Historie* becomes the true model of contrition, enlightenment, and God-fearing right-mindedness, Lear, despite moments of deep human insight, never completely regains sanity and right to the end retains some of his irascible blindness. One of the last lines he utters is a curse on all those who are only there to help him: "A plague upon you, murderers, traitors all!" (V.iii)

This final relapse into blindness is set against the story of a man who, while actually blinded, acquires truly tragic enlightenment in his suffering. Shakespeare borrowed the Gloucester plot that he superimposed on the main story from Sidney's "Tragedie"-like tale of paternal "wickedness," of a bastard son's "poysonous hypocrisie" in supplanting his half-brother and blinding his father, and of the true son's "fillial piety" in saving his father from suicide.[38] "He childed as I fathered" (III.vi), exclaims Edgar, who, contemplating Edmund's treachery and Lear's insanity, "is almost mad" (III.iv) himself. The parallels reach an emblematic climax when the mad Lear finally meets his blind alter ego and protests that even without his eyes Gloucester can "see how this world goes":

> GLOUCESTER I see it feelingly.
> LEAR What, art mad? A man may see how this
> world goes with no eyes. (IV.vi)

The Gloucester story, while paralleling and contrasting with the protagonist's, also protracts our sense of Lear's suffering. Gloucester's "As flies to wanton boys, are we to th'gods, / They kill us for their sport" (IV.i) in that sense applies to Lear rather than to the man who utters it. Had Shakespeare ended the play towards the middle of act IV, King Lear, who has fallen from the heights of fortune but also become a wiser man in the process, could easily have been made to undergo a tragic end. Instead, the playwright renews the king's suffering. From there till the play's end Lear is seen as a man tortured upon the "rack of this tough world" (V.iii). The tragedian-playwright has turned into a puppeteer-manipulator of slowly drawn-out suffering.

The final turn of the screw comes with the last scene. In contrast to the sources, the French king's army has been defeated, Lear and Cordelia thrown into prison, and a captain dispatched by Edmund with a commission to murder them both. What follows has the suspense of a thriller. There is still

hope that Lear and Cordelia might be saved while we seem to hear the
captain's footsteps strutting towards the prison from backstage. But a series of
events, which paradoxically conform to either the heroic, the *de casibus*, or the
tragic mode, precludes this rescue. The noble Edgar defeats his evil half-
brother Edmund in single combat. Goneril and Regan meet their deserved
deaths, which Albany, not inappropriately in this narrower context, interprets
as a "judgment of the heavens" (V.iii).

But more than by anything else, the audience is made to bristle with
impatience by Edgar's long-winded accounts of his father's death and his
encounter with Kent. Particularly in the first monologue, Edgar does the very
opposite of what he advises in the play's final words: instead of speaking just
what he feels, he utters what he ought to say. His "brief tale" of Gloucester's
end is an example *par excellence* of Shakespearian tragic closure, both in its
circumstantial account of the woes past and in the almost epigrammatic
description of a truly tragic death fusing passion, joy, and grief:

> List a brief tale;
> And when 'tis told, O, that my heart would burst!
> The bloody proclamation to escape
> That followed me so near – O, our lives' sweetness,
> That we the pain of death would hourly die
> Rather than die at once! – taught me to shift
> Into a madman's rags, t'assume a semblance
> That very dogs disdained: and in this habit
> Met I my father with his bleeding rings,
> Their precious stones new lost; became his guide,
> Led him, begged for him, saved him from despair;
> Never – O fault! – revealed myself unto him,
> Until some half-hour past, when I was armed,
> Not sure, though hoping, of this good success,
> I asked his blessing, and from first to last
> Told him our pilgrimage. But his flawed heart –
> Alack, too weak the conflict to support –
> 'Twixt two extremes of passion, joy and grief,
> Burst smilingly.   (V.iii)

Ironically, this highly pathetic account almost leads to the rescue of Lear
and Cordelia, which, however, is prevented by Edgar's eagerness to tell his
second tale:

> EDMUND This speech of yours has moved me,
> And shall prechance do good: but speak you on;
> You look as you had something more to say.   (V.iii)

Edgar indeed has more to say, and by the time he finishes talking about Kent, who in turn has told him "the most piteous tale of Lear," the thought of the actual Lear has been blotted out in the minds of his listeners. It needs Kent's sudden arrival, coming "To bid [his] king and master aye good night," to remind Albany of that "Great thing of us forgot." But by the time the now-repentant Edmund sends his own sword to stop the captain from murdering Lear and his daughter, Cordelia has already been killed. "Is this the promised end?" asks Kent when Lear walks on to the stage, his strangled daughter cradled in his arms. This certainly is not the conclusion which the play's beginning promised us, nor does it reveal Lear's death to have meaning, purpose, or nobility. The king's "If it be so, / It is a chance which does redeem all sorrows," when in his self-delusion he sees a feather stir in front of Cordelia's mouth, suggests the very opposite. For Cordelia's fate is beyond repair, and all else, as Kent observes, is "cheerless, dark and deadly." The remainder of the scene has already been discussed. It more than frustrates our expectations. Albany's tragic rhetoric is stifled by the sudden spectacle of Lear's death. In a final twist of audience manipulation, Edgar's tale of his father's genuinely tragic death becomes a means towards that anti-tragic end. But the well-meaning and loquacious Edgar has learned his lesson. His and the play's final words express a new, less hopeful, but also more realistic sense of life beyond the tragic:

> The weight of this sad time we must obey,
> Speak what we feel, not what we ought to say.
> The oldest hath borne most: we that are young
> Shall never see so much, nor live so long.

In sum, *King Lear*, like *Troilus and Cressida*, inverts the mainly classical paradigms of tragedy more directly embodied in *Romeo and Juliet*. The suffering which in *Romeo and Juliet* leads to the reconciliation of two families is shown in *Lear* to be neither purposeful nor ennobling. Although the king temporarily achieves *pathei mathos*, or learning through suffering, he dies in sheer misery and madness, mouthing curses against his best friends. Nor are we purged of fear and pity in watching his slowly drawn-out agonies, any more than we are in witnessing Hector's cowardly murder. Although the expectation of such tragic effects has been aroused in us, we find ourselves experiencing their opposites.

Once-climactic peripeteia has been replaced by a series of nasty surprises. Where we expect the traditionally promised end in which something decisive is accomplished through suffering, all concludes in final arbitrary disaster. Tragedy, in retrospect, reveals what at first surprised us by its randomness to be a consistent chain of causes and effects. In *Lear* and *Troilus* we are simply made to see how blind fate rules men's lives. The two plays seem to make such randomness their very subject matter. What they present, in short, is how things are, not how they ought to be.

But Shakespeare's anti-tragic impulse by no means exhausted itself in thus negating the tragic vision of classical derivation. *Hamlet*, in this respect, differs notably from both *Lear* and *Troilus*. Unlike these, with their pagan or multi-religious background, it has a distinctly Christian ambience. Furthermore, it lacks the kind of audience manipulation which is the primary means of anti-tragic inversion in *Troilus* and *Lear*. What then, if anything, allows us to discuss *Hamlet* in the same context? Would it not be more appropriate to treat it simply as a tragedy, even though one of Christian derivation? As such, Hamlet's suffering and death could be seen, for instance, as helping to unfold the dark plans of divine providence.

This, indeed, is the way in which *Hamlet* is understood by some critics. "At the end of the play," writes one of them, "Hamlet learns to accept the order of the universe and to become a passive instrument in the hands of a purposive and benevolent God."[39] But such a view only raises further questions. Are we really meant to see Hamlet as fulfilling his self-appointed role of "scourge and minister" (III.iv) of mankind? Does he really act in the name of providence and set the world aright through his suffering and self-sacrifice? To say so, I think, amounts to identifying Shakespeare's own attitude with that of Hamlet, a character whom S.L. Bethell rightly calls the "spoilt favourite among Shakes-pearean characters."[40] As I shall try to show, *Hamlet* as a whole by no means warrants such identification; instead, it seems to offer a subtle but incisive critique of the Christian notions embraced by the protagonist. At the same time, it questions and throws doubt on the tragic paradigms associated with Hamlet: the play's implied critique of Christianity generally, and particularly of the corrupt Christianity practised by Hamlet, turns tragedy into anti-tragedy.

Hamlet, or the Slave-Moralist
Turned Ascetic Priest

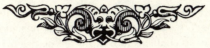

THE VERY OPENING SCENE of *Hamlet* sets the play's dominant mood. Fears of damnation seem to hang like a looming shadow over every person and action. An infernal harbinger of destruction appears to a country already "sick almost to doomsday" (I.i) with evil forebodings. It tells Hamlet not only about the murder but also about hell's nameless horrors amid "sulf'rous and tormenting flames"[1]:

> But that I am forbid
> To tell the secrets of my prison house,
> I could a tale unfold whose lightest word
> Would harrow up thy soul, freeze thy young blood,
> Make thy two eyes like stars start from their spheres,
> Thy knotted and combinèd locks to part,
> And each particular hair to stand on end,
> Like quills upon the fretful porpentine.   (I.v)

Everywhere in the play, "Heaven's face ... With heated visage, as against the doom" (III.iv)[2] seems to glower over men's destinies; and the fear of eternal damnation either determines or inhibits their actions. Hamlet is afraid that the Ghost may be a devil in disguise out to damn him (III.ii) and proceeds to test it. He wants to send his uncle to hell, not simply to kill him, and finding Claudius at prayer desists for fear that he might send the murderer to heaven instead (III.iii). Laertes, eager to revenge himself on Hamlet, risks and defies damnation (IV.v), tells the priest who wants to bury Ophelia in unsanctified ground that she will be a ministering angel when the priest lies howling (V.i), and finally asks Hamlet's forgiveness, assuring him of his own, so that their mutual crimes may not damn them (V.ii).

Hamlet's Suicidal Nature, Freud, and Eliot

If the ubiquitous menace of hell provides the play's metaphysical circumference, its psychological core seems to be Hamlet's suicidal will to nothingness. Suicide is on the protagonist's mind throughout the play, and suicide, rather than revenge, marks his end. His conviction that God has set "His canon 'gainst self-slaughter" (I.ii) prevents him from killing himself, but biblical scripture paradoxically confirms him in his self-destructive resolution in the end. Paraphrasing Matt 10:28–31, Hamlet defies the evil forebodings of his heart, which tells him not to fight, and walks into death:

... we defy augury. There is a special providence in the fall of a sparrow. If it be now, 'tis not to come; if it be not to come, it will be now; if it be not now, yet it will come. The readiness is all.   (V.ii)

. In posing suicide as a moral and psychological problem, *Hamlet* differs markedly from Shakespeare's other plays. None of the dozen or so suicides in the Shakespearian *oeuvre* seems to share Hamlet's scruples or arouse the moral indignation of the survivors.[3] The other exception is Ophelia, whose doubtful death provokes the priest who presides over her burial to restate Hamlet's earlier concern that suicide to a Christian is a mortal sin.

Suicidal impulses also seem to inhere in Hamlet's mysterious delays in avenging his father. Even before the Ghost tells him about the murder, Hamlet proves unable to do what he most wants to do, which is to kill himself. But the reasons here are anything but mysterious: just as in his most famous soliloquy, Hamlet himself tells us why. It is not that he is afraid to take his life in true Roman fashion. What stops him are the nameless horrors of damnation which his father, a direct messenger from hell, has evoked so vividly (I.v). As Hamlet concludes,

> Thus conscience does make cowards of us all,
> And thus the native hue of resolution
> Is sicklied o'er with the pale cast of thought,
> And enterprises of great pitch and moment,
> With this regard their currents turn awry,
> And lose the name of action.   (III.i)

Syntactically, the lines refer back to Hamlet's discussion of suicide, not to his delay in avenging his father. But in his unconscious mind the two acts have fused, or so at least Shakespeare seems to suggest in making Hamlet use an expression, "enterprises of great pitch and moment," which befits a heroic deed such as avenging a royal father rather than the act of killing oneself.

In other words, Hamlet's suicidal tendencies and fears of damnation may provide the answer to a problem which has continued to puzzle critics to date. Why does Hamlet delay in avenging his father while showing both determination and resolution in most other activities, including murder? Of course, there is Freud's answer. Yet even if judged in its own terms, the Oedipal explanation of Hamlet's procrastinations is not without loopholes. Like any male child, Hamlet, argues Freud, loved his mother and wanted to murder his father. Now he is asked to kill the man who has done both – in other words, to punish his own mirror image. As a result, Hamlet delays.[4] With equal justification one might argue that given this situation, Hamlet has all the more reason to kill his uncle because he would "thereby punish that aspect of himself which he repudiates, thus sparing himself much guilt."[5]

But this or similar disagreements with the Oedipal *Hamlet* interpretation apart,[6] there is a more crucial objection. As Freud seems to admit himself, his reading of the play relies almost exclusively on proof *ex negativo*. It imposes an explanation from outside for lack of a better one which could be deduced from the play itself. People, Freud writes, "have remained completely in the dark as to the hero's character. The play is built up on Hamlet's hesitations over fulfilling the task of revenge that is assigned to him; but its text offers no reasons or motives for these hesitations." In other words, Shakespeare himself must have been in the dark about it and only wrote the play because, at the time, he suffered from the Oedipus complex himself. Freud, who discovered the complex within months of his own father's death, found the relevant clues to this effect in a book by Georg Brandes:

Hamlet was written immediately after the death of Shakespeare's father (in 1601), that is, under the immediate impact of his bereavement and, as we may well assume, while his childhood feelings about his father had been freshly revived.[7]

Curiously enough, this interpretation comes close to that of Eliot, who otherwise shared few ideas with Freud. Where Freud's Hamlet suffers from an Oedipal father-fixation, Eliot's is paralysed by an inexplicable excess of disgust for his mother, a feeling, so Eliot seems to suggest, shared by Shakespeare:

Hamlet is up against the difficulty that his disgust is occasioned by his mother, but that his mother is not an adequate equivalent for it; his disgust envelops and exceeds her. It is thus a feeling which he cannot understand; he cannot objectify it, and it therefore remains to poison life and obstruct action.

Shakespeare, in other words, "tackled a problem which proved too much for him." As he failed to provide us with more obvious clues for seeing Hamlet as a potential Oedipus, he found no objective correlative to account for the protagonist's disgust, which thus appears to be "in excess of the facts as they appear." In sum, the play to Eliot is an "artistic failure."[8]

However, there is little reason to agree with this verdict. Far from failing to find an objective correlative for an emotion he only half understood himself, Shakespeare, in *Hamlet*, develops a critique of Christian morality that would encompass Eliot's own stance as a distinctly puritanical Anglo-Catholic. In several cases Hamlet's Christianity, as Roy Battenhouse has shown,[9] is corrupt even if judged by orthodox theological standards. In others, it simply partakes of a corruption which, at least in post-Nietzschean terms, is typical of traditional Christianity itself.

No doubt, the villain in *Hamlet* is Claudius. His murder of the protagonist's father was deliberate and motivated by greed. Hamlet's murders, by comparison, are either accidental, as in the case of Polonius, or perpetrated in the name of some justification, as in the case of Rosencrantz and Guildenstern. Since they all result from Hamlet's delays, one might also see them as psychologically motivated. But whatever they are, the prince, in causing these deaths, can hardly be called "evil" in the traditional sense we attach to Claudius, who in this becomes a foil to Hamlet.

The protagonist, in fact, is clearly blameless of any real crime before he kills Polonius. Nevertheless, he is convinced of his utter depravity. Hoping that Ophelia may remember all his sins in her prayers, he accuses himself "of such things that it were better [his] mother had not borne [him]" (III.i). Yet there is little motivation for such self-incrimination in the incidents of the play itself. The death of his father and hasty remarriage of his mother may have unleashed his general disgust with life. But his first soliloquy reveals in its very opening line that the deeper roots lie elsewhere: "O that this too too sullied flesh would melt" (I.ii).[10] Why should a thirty-year-old son feel suicidal because of his widowed mother's hasty remarriage to a despised uncle? Indignation and anger would be a more natural response. It seems more likely that these events made him conscious of a general feeling of sinfulness of which the former courtier, soldier, and scholar was only half-aware.

Even before the Ghost tells him about the murder, Hamlet's self-disgust has spilled over to make him see the entire world as an "unweeded garden that grows to seed" (I.ii). As Eliot was right to point out, this disgust envelops and exceeds his mother and everybody else – Ophelia, Polonius, Claudius, Rosencrantz and Guildenstern. All of these he despises, reprimands, and castigates for their real or imagined depravity. It "therefore remains to poison life and obstruct action." But Eliot fails to see (or perhaps to acknowledge) that behind Hamlet's disgust are the sense of his sinfulness and the fear of damnation. Even before he is asked to avenge his father, Hamlet reveals the cause of his self-avowed weakness and melancholy; his subsequent self-incrimination for delaying his revenge therefore can hardly surprise us. The fact that Hamlet, according to actual events, has no reason to call himself a rogue, peasant slave,

John-a-dreams, or coward (II.ii) serves to emphasize that his delays have little to do with the specific task. Instead, they reflect the behaviour pattern of a man caught in a vicious circle in which his basic will to nothingness is turned upon itself by fears of eternal damnation.

Hamlet's second monologue on suicide (III.i), uttered in the very next scene, reinforces these links. Hamlet calls himself a coward for failing both to kill himself and to avenge his father. In both cases his self-incrimination reflects a Christianity corrupted by despair. A true Christian would ultimately welcome what detains him from suicide or revenge as the voice of his good conscience. Not so Hamlet, who equates man's "godlike reason" (IV.iv) with his lust for revenge, the "native hue of resolution" (III.i) with his will to nothingness, or a phrase like "enterprises of great pitch and moment" (III.i) with both. At the same time, Christianity, or the debased form of it practised by Hamlet, has corrupted his will to the point where his behaviour, as his mother recognizes so clearly, swings between deadly lethargy and impulsive rashness:

> And thus a while the fit will work on him.
> Anon, as patient as the female dove
> When that her golden couplets are disclosed,
> His silence will sit drooping.   (V.i)

This switching back and forth between "a jealousy of doubt" and an extreme "vehemancy of ... affections once raised" was well known to Elizabethan psychologists like Timothy Bright, who discussed it in *A Treatise of Melancholie* (London 1586).[11] No wonder that Hamlet, former student and scholar, to a large extent acts as his own analyst. When he first decides to play the madman, his reasons for doing so seem to be largely unconscious. But Hamlet gradually comes to understand his new role as it turns into a more and more fitting mould for his split temper. In recent psychological jargon, Hamlet is stuck in a double-bind impasse.[12] The same Christian phobias that have filled him with guilt, self-disgust, and a will to nothingness transform his suicidal impulse into a long, drawn-out agony of mental self-destruction. The resultant schizophrenic disposition is aptly described in Hamlet's own account of how he forgot (V.ii) or, rather, lost himself in his double when fighting with Laertes:

> Was't Hamlet wronged Laertes? Never Hamlet.
> If Hamlet from himself be ta'en away,
> And when he's not himself does wrong Laertes,
> Then Hamlet does it not, Hamlet denies it.
> Who does it then? His madness. If't be so,
> Hamlet is of the faction that is wronged;
> His madness is poor Hamlet's enemy.   (V.ii)

As Shakespeare's more erudite spectators would realize, Hamlet's corrupt Christianity is an example only of a general trend within much of Christian theology. "Fecemi la divina potestate, / La somma sapienza e'l primo amore" ("The divine power made me, / The supreme wisdom, and the primal love"), we read above the gate of hell in Dante's *Inferno* (III.5–6).[13] "What my laughter, my joy and exultation," exclaims Tertullian, when at the last judgment he will see some "groaning in the depths of darkness," others liquefying in flames.[14] Similarly, Hamlet's only moment of genuine enthusiasm, which even makes him burst forth in song, follows his catching the conscience of the king with "The Mousetrap." Revenge has turned into vindictiveness, and although Hamlet may curse himself for the consequent delays, he takes thorough delight in his actions. The same subliminal relish inspiring his plans to strike the king to the soul with his play (II.ii) makes him anticipate how by delaying his revenge he will be able to send Claudius straight to hell (III.iii).[15]

The Scourge and Minister of Mankind

Furthermore, Hamlet turns vindictiveness into a self-righteous concern with a supposedly divine order of the universe. Before he learns about his father's murder, the world's corruption, which more than anything else reflects his self-disgust, suggests to him this new role. Horatio's account of the Ghost makes him augur foul deeds that will rise, "Though all the earth o'erwhelm them, to men's eyes" (I.ii); and as the Ghost beckons him to follow, a growing sense of his fated destiny turns his customary indecisiveness into a new strength of will "As hardy as the Nemean lion's nerve" (I.iv). His dead father's request for revenge completes this transformation. Reluctantly, yet with utter conviction, Hamlet assumes his mission:

> The time is out of joint. O cursèd spite,
> That ever I was born to set it right!   (I.v)

Unlike Laertes, who knows that he will risk damnation in avenging his father (IV.v), Hamlet in his missionary zeal may have doubts about the Ghost but never questions the ethics of his revenge. Nor, as he procrastinates or refines his actual task, does the growing number of his more or less innocent victims in any way deter him from believing that he was sent out to set the world aright. On the contrary, when the first of them dies on his sword, he refers his deed directly to the working of divine justice:

> ... heaven hath pleased it so,
> To punish me with this, and this with me,
> That I must be their scourge and minister.   (III.iv)

Yet while he repents of inadvertently slaying Polonius, his wilful murder of Rosencrantz and Guildenstern does not at all come near his conscience. Having made "love to this employment" (V.ii) but probably unaware of their deadly mission, the former friends may have deserved castigation, but hardly death. None the less, Hamlet again tries to make sure of sending his victims straight to hell. He orders their instant execution upon arrival in England, "Not shriving time allowed." Telling Horatio how he engineered this infernal justice, he again invokes divine providence for his deeds:

> There's a divinity that shapes our ends,
> Rough-hew them how we will   (V.ii).[16]

Nor does it ever occur to Hamlet to think of the sinister role he has played in the life of Ophelia, other than by protesting that he loved her more than forty thousand brothers (V.i). Here, and in his behaviour towards his mother, his self-elected role of minister and scourge of mankind assumes its most sinister dimension. For by presuming to save them from their corruption, he seems to infect them with his own disease. At the same time, the imagery of sickness and corruption which is the play's most dominant leitmotiv gains in intensity.[17] Ophelia is driven mad where Hamlet feigns madness; she kills herself where he is unable to commit suicide. And if we ask for the causes, the answers can again be found with the protagonist. In a studied piece of horror drama, probably contrived to test his "antic disposition" on the most impressionable victim, Hamlet first visits Ophelia in the shape of another ghost "loosèd out of hell" (II.i) and sends her into a tail-spin of fear. Her subsequent description reveals as much of her empathetic and compassionate nature towards Hamlet as of what Dr Johnson called Hamlet's "useless and wanton cruelty"[18] towards her. While taken in and confused by his vaudeville display of madness, Ophelia senses his obsession with hell and suicide:

> He raised a sigh so piteous and profound
> As it did seem to shatter all his bulk
> And end his being.   (II.i)

Hamlet intimidates and manipulates Ophelia by various means. His central strategy, to which sexual provocation and spookish horror tricks lend the necessary reinforcement, is to convince his victim of her utter depravity.[19] Thus, in the nunnery scene, he first questions her honesty, then breaks forth into a sermon-like tirade against the general corruption of mankind and of woman in particular, and concludes with further personal insults. Although Ophelia is convinced of Hamlet's madness and, as a practising Christian, would be familiar with some of his rhetoric, its impact, coming from the mouth of the man she loves, is devastating:

And I, of ladies most deject and wretched,
That sucked the honey of his musicked vows
...
T'have seen what I have seen, see what I see!   (III.i)

Ophelia goes insane when her lover, who has already poisoned her soul,
kills her father. As a result her mad fantasies revolve around the dead Polonius,
sexual guilt, and salvation. Again and again she invokes the beyond, hoping
that "'a made a good end," wishing that "God 'a' mercy on his soul" and on
"all Christian souls." Or, expressing her own fears, she calls upon the Lord,
saying, "we know what we are, but we know not what we may be." Her own
weirdly insightful interpretation of the statement "when they ask you what it
means, say you this" tells the story of a lover who, somewhat like Hamlet, has
aroused her sexuality, only to blame and reject her on account of it:

Young men will do't if they come to't,
   By Cock, they are to blame.

Quoth she, "Before you tumbled me,
   You promised me to wed."

He answers:
"So would I'a'done, by yonder sun,
   An thou hadst not come to my bed."   (IV.v)

In his role of scourge and minister of mankind, Hamlet not only "Make[s]
mad the guilty" (II.ii), as in Claudius's case, but actually maddens the innocent, as in Ophelia's. Gertrude stands half-way between the two, but as with
Polonius and Rosencrantz and Guildenstern, Hamlet's missionary fervour by
far exceeds its provocation. While ignorant of her previous husband's murder
at the hands of the present one, she is aware of her "o'erhasty marriage" (II.ii).
But she fails to see why marrying her dead husband's brother should be
considered a crime; thus, she responds to Hamlet's oblique or direct accusations with incomprehension and bewilderment. Especially when Hamlet in
the closet scene purports to "wring her heart" with the catalogue of her crimes,
she at first reacts with understandable defiance:

What have I done that thou dar'st wag thy tongue
In noise so rude against me?   (III.iv)

The logical answer would be that she is married to a murderer and living in
incest. But neither argument really establishes Gertrude's guilt, and, as if
half-aware of this fact, Hamlet instead bursts forth into another sermon-like
harangue. So Gertrude remonstrates again: "Ay me, what act, / That roars so

loud and thunders in the index?'' Hamlet's answer once more fails to establish Gertrude's crimes. But his name-calling diatribe against Claudius and her lust that would "batten on this moor" at an age when the "heyday in the blood" should be tame completely overwhelms her.

Hamlet's aim to "speak daggers" is a total success. Meanwhile, his rhetorical fantasies about "making love / Over the nasty sty" in the "rank sweat of an enseamèd bed" or his detailed evocation of sexual intimacies between Claudius and Gertrude more than anything else reveal his own overheated imagination:

> Not this, by no means, that I bid you do:
> Let the bloat King tempt you again to bed,
> Pinch wanton on your cheek, call you his mouse,
> And let him, for a pair of reechy kisses,
> Or paddling in your neck with his damned fingers,
> Make you to ravel all this matter out.   (III.iv)

Yet his words act as a powerful contagion through which Gertrude catches her son's disease. Convinced of her basic innocence until now, she breaks down in utter contrition and guilt, her heart "cleft ... in twain," her eyes, like Hamlet's, turned into her soul to stare at "black and grainèd spots / As will not leave their tinct."

The World Turned Prison-house

Thanks to Hamlet and his infernal prompter, almost everybody in the play is finally stricken with guilt, maddened, or sent to eternal damnation. The "prison-house" of hell (I.v) so vividly evoked by the Ghost has found its replica in a world to which Kafka's *The Trial* and Orwell's *Nineteen Eighty-four* provide the twentieth-century analogues. Spying, dissimulation, and subterfuge, secret plots, hidden traps, and back-door stratagems – all conducted under the eyes of a hellish ghost – predominate in *Hamlet* as in no other play by Shakespeare. Almost every other scene involves multiple espionage and counter-espionage.[20] To at least two characters spying has become second nature even before there is any immediate motivation for it. Polonius sends out Reynaldo to spy on his son in Paris, suggesting methods at which even his servant demurs. Before he uses Ophelia for spying on Hamlet, he kept the lovers' encounters under close surveillance (I.iii). Polonius's only equal in gratuitous intriguing, and, at the same time, his master, is Hamlet himself. Dressed in an "inky cloak," his "veilèd lids" avoiding the eyes of others, Hamlet appropriately introduces himself in a furtively spoken aside (I.ii). He feigns madness in order to spy on enemies and friends and openly admits to his delight in anticipating the lethal stratagems he will employ against Rosencrantz and Guildenstern:

> For 'tis the sport to have the engineer
> Hoist with his own petard, and't shall go hard
> But I will delve one yard below their mines
> And blow them at the moon. O, 'tis most sweet
> When in one line two crafts directly meet.   (III.iv)

In sum, the world of *Hamlet* is a prison with "many confines, wards, and dungeons, Denmark being one o' the' worst" (II.ii). And there is no escape from it in either this life or the next. Its central symbol is "The Mousetrap," the play within the play with which Hamlet, trying to catch Claudius's conscience, lays a trap for himself in which he in turn entraps his pursuers. His exclamation – "O, villainy! Ho! Let the door be locked" (V.ii) – before he kills the king, witnesses the death of Laertes, and dies himself suggests the appropriate scenario for the play's murderous finale. And as death engulfs him, Hamlet's will to nothingness celebrates its ultimate triumph: without incurring the risk of damnation, he finds the death he wished for,[21] while also fulfilling his mission as the scourge of mankind. Horatio is to tell his cause to the unsatisfied and perhaps continue on his dead friend's devious paths.

Shakespeare, of course, gives us a further perspective on Hamlet's world. The protagonist never questions his mission as mankind's scourge and minister, but he does have an inkling of the disease which made him escape into this missionary role. Thus, other alternatives, more reminiscent of his previous life as courtier, soldier, and scholar, offer avenues of escape, be they the heroic rodomontades of the actors or the actual, though questionable, heroism of Fortinbras. The latter, in particular, prompts Hamlet's most consistent and incisive self-criticism. In the process, Fortinbras emerges as a counter-image to the protagonist,

> ... a delicate and tender prince,
> Whose spirit, with divine ambition puffed,
> Makes mouths at the invisible event,
> Exposing what is mortal and unsure
> To all that fortune, death, and danger dare,
> Even for an eggshell.   (IV.iv)

Hamlet's attempt and failure to model himself on his peer underscore the contrast. In emulating another person, he acts even here from an ulterior motive. For Fortinbras, unlike Hamlet, seems to act entirely for the sake of action. His attempt to wage war against Denmark with an army of "lawless resolutes" (I.i) is foiled by Claudius's instant countermanoeuvres. So he decides to attack Poland instead (II.ii), requesting permission to cross with his army through Denmark. Yet the quicksilvery hotspur we expect to meet completely surprises us with his commanding yet diplomatic presence when he appears on the stage (IV.iv).

The contrast becomes complete when Fortinbras, after his victorious campaign against Poland, returns in the nick of time to claim the Danish throne. To the new king, the sight of the slain suggests no images of doomsday or damnation. What he is made to think of instead seems to be the old Scandinavian belief, reported by Saxo Grammaticus and others,[22] of the eternal battle of life, in which the warriors who fall each day are resurrected in time for the feasting in Odin's Valhalla in the evening:

> This quarry cries on havoc. O proud Death,
> What feast is toward in thine eternal cell
> That thou so many princes at a shot
> So bloodily hast struck?   (V.ii)

A Nietzschean Reading of *Hamlet*

Montaigne is the only one among Shakespeare's contemporaries who readily comes to mind when we look for analogues to what the playwright attempted in *Hamlet*.[23] "There is no hostilitie so excellent," we read in Florio's translation, "as that which is absolutely Christian. Our zeale worketh wonders, when ever it secondeth our inclination toward hatred, crueltie, ambition, avarice, detraction, or rebellion." Also applicable to *Hamlet* is Montaigne's observation that "Sadnesse or Sorrowe," far from reflecting "uertue, and conscience," deserve to go by the name of "malignitie; for, it is a quality ever hurtfull, ever sottish; and as ever base and coward."[24]

But such randomly thrown-out remarks fail to amount to the complex psychological critique found in *Hamlet* of Christian morality in both its corrupt and orthodox manifestations. In fact, not before Nietzsche's *Genealogy of Morals* do we find insights equal to Shakespeare's. Like the playwright, Nietzsche probes into the life-debilitating impact of a religion which makes eternal damnation the measure of man's potential sinfulness, or in which the saved are thought to enjoy watching the tortures of the damned. Had Nietzsche used *Hamlet* to illustrate his critique of Christianity,[25] his interpretation might well have gained the importance of Freud's, not least of all by putting the Oedipal approach into its proper perspective. For despite his attempts to prove religion an illusion, Freud remained deeply indebted to the Judaeo-Christian tradition; at least, it seems difficult to imagine how else he could have posited the Oedipus complex as both "the nucleus of all neuroses" and "the beginnings of religion, morals, society and art."[26] For crucial to our tradition, which in this differs from many others, is God the Father as righteous judge and punisher.

Nietzsche's analysis of this figure serves to underscore Freud's mistake of translating into a universally human complex what is more likely to be a specifically Judaeo-Christian obsession.

According to the *Genealogy of Morals*, God the Father did not emerge till after the "slave revolt in morals." In Nietzsche's primordial society there were only masters and slaves, and the slaves had quietly to suffer the punishments inflicted upon them for whatever debts they could not defray. Gradually their instincts turned inwards, took arms against themselves, developed into a sense of guilt and, at a later stage, into a feeling of resentment against the masters. This "rancor of beings who, deprived of the direct outlet of action, compensate by an imaginary vengeance" gave birth to the pseudo-values of slave morality. On its momentum the slaves eventually managed to overthrow the masters. But this change left a frightening vacuum in the slaves' guilt-ridden minds, and groping for a substitute they found a new instrument of self-torture: instead of being in the master's debt, they now thought themselves to be indebted to God:

[They] projected all [their] denials of self, nature, naturalness out of [themselves] ... as God (the divine Judge and Executioner) ... as endless torture, as hell, as the infinitude of guilt and punishment.[27]

In Nietzsche's view, then, God the Father is not the mythic equivalent of a universally human complex but the projection of a mind burdened by a specific cultural heritage. It is a god turned demon. Similarly, in *Hamlet*, the father who exhorts and upbraids his son can, in one sense, be seen as a figment of a diseased mind. In another he is an envoy from hell who, in Eleanor Prosser's words, does everything "to taint Hamlet's mind with lacerating grief, sexual nausea, hatred, and fury."[28]

Within this general symbolic framework, Hamlet seems to perform the role of Nietzsche's rancorous man, who, as minister of mankind, ends up infecting others with his disease. In *The Genealogy of Morals* Nietzsche, in fact, derides Dante's description of hell as a creation of eternal love. He also quotes the lines in which Tertullian expresses his anticipated delight in watching the agonies of the damned in hell. This is a pleasure, as we have seen, shared by Hamlet. To Nietzsche, such priestly vindictiveness is only the last refinement of the slave's perversion of the will, his

will to poison the very foundation of things with the problem of guilt and punishment ... his will to erect an ideal (God's holiness) in order to assure himself of his own absolute unworthiness.[29]

The "native hue of resolution" has been "sicklied o'er" by the fear of hell and damnation; the original "beast of action,"[30] who seems to survive in Fortinbras, has been transformed into a mad, sick animal; the world has turned into what Hamlet, half-aware of his dilemma, sees as the "distracted globe" (I.v). The thought of eternal punishment inhibits every thought and action; a terrible heaviness weighs on man and makes him, like Hamlet, "swing between brooding and emotional explosions," between "drugged tranquillity" and uncontrollable outbursts of "bottled-up aggressions." The will to life has become a "will to nothingness, a revulsion from life, a rebellion against the principle conditions of living."[31]

There is no escape from this labyrinth of obsessions. As God's canon is set against self-slaughter, the only outlet for this suicidal impulse is revenge. But not the revenge of the strong, who react and forget: "When a noble man feels resentment, it is absorbed in his instantaneous reaction and therefore does not poison him."[32] The rancorous man, by contrast, turns vengeance into poisonous resentment: "he condemns, disparages, curses 'the world' – himself not excluded."[33] And resentment vents itself in vindictiveness, taking revenge in the name of divine justice or "love." Everything around him, as around Hamlet, turns into a labyrinth of traps and subterfuges, spying and intrigues. "His soul squints; his mind loves hide-outs, secret paths, and back doors."[34] "I must be cruel only to be kind," says Hamlet (III.iv) as he invokes divine justice for sending his enemies to hell. "Me, too, eternal love created" are the words which Dante put over the gate of hell with similarly disconcerting naïveté.[35] Here as elsewhere, of course, Nietzsche lashes out in vehement anti-Christian invective, whereas Shakespeare, in *Hamlet*, is content with presenting his critique of Christian morality by mere innuendo. The result is a characteristically Shakespearian paradox. Though in content the playwright's critique resembles Nietzsche's, in tone it is more like Montaigne's – and Montaigne, we know, remained a practising Christian throughout his life.

The general urge "to discharge an inner tension in hostile actions and ideas" finds its most forceful embodiment in the ascetic priest. Like Hamlet driven by his own sickness, he turns himself into a scourge of mankind. To this "poison-spider of life," the notions of sinfulness, last judgment and eternal damnation become "instruments of torture" and "forms of systematic cruelty ... capable of exciting disgust at the sight of mankind."[36] Like Hamlet with Gertrude and Ophelia, he saves his victims from the sickness he spreads himself: "in order to cure he must first create patients. And even as he alleviates the pain of his patients he pours poison into their wounds."[37] Curiously enough, Hamlet, as a former student at Wittenberg, seems to be linked with Luther, in Nietzsche's view one of the most prominent representatives of the Christian ascetic priest besides St Paul, Tertullian, and St Thomas. Luther, driven by "an insatiable thirst for revenge as a moral-religious duty,"[38] managed to submerge a sudden resurgence of the pagan spirit within the bosom of the Catholic church in the "plebeian rancor of the German and English Reformation."[39] What have he and other "spiritual men" of Christianity done for Europe so far? Nietzsche's answer uses a well-known expression from *Hamlet* as a key phrase:

Stand all valuations *on their head* ... And break the strong, sickly o'er great hopes, cast suspicion on the joy in beauty, bend everything haughty, manly, conquering, domineering, all the instincts characteristic of the highest and best-turned-out type of "man," into unsureness, agony of conscience, self-destruction – indeed, invest all love of the earthly and of dominion over the earth into hatred of the earth and the earthly.[40]

For all that, Nietzsche apparently failed to reread *Hamlet* while writing his later works,[41] or he might well have noticed how strikingly Shakespeare's play bears out his critique of Judaeo-Christian morality. Instead, he found similar corroboration in Dostoyevsky's *Notes from Underground*, whose anti-hero turned saviour, like Shakespeare's pigeon-livered John-a-dreams turned heaven's scourge and minister to mankind, can also be shown to resemble Nietzsche's rancorous man become ascetic priest.[42] Nietzsche himself ranked this find, made at age forty-three, with his previous discoveries of Schopenhauer at twenty-one and of Stendhal at thirty-five.[43] Dostoyevsky, Nietzsche later wrote in *Twilight of the Idols*, was "the only psychologist ... from whom I had anything to learn."[44]

One thing Nietzsche may have learned from *Notes from Underground* relates to the psychology of acting and role-playing, which also covers a major trait in Hamlet's enigmatic character. Nietzsche, of course, was aware of how the Christian *psychomachia* turns every man into the self-conscious protagonist of his private *teatrum mundi*. To the philosopher, man's "interpretation of his own petty destiny as if everything were contrived and sent with a view to the salvation of his soul," making God "the director" of his play, simply bespeaks infantile presumptuousness. Yet Nietzsche little more than comments upon the psychological consequences whereby every act becomes a self-conscious performance in either one's own or somebody else's game. Priests, he jotted down in a posthumously published note, "are the actors of something superhuman ... the shrewdness of their actor's art must above all aim at giving them a good conscience."[45] Both *Hamlet* and *Notes from Underground* are explorations of this phenomenon in all its psychological complexity. But here again, of course, Shakespeare merely implies what Dostoyevsky, like Nietzsche, spells out in analytic detail.

Right from the start, Hamlet plays mocking games with the king and preaches a little sermon against the "actions that a man might play," all the while protesting his own innocence: "But I have that within which passes show" (I.ii). As he turns protagonist in the Ghost's revenge drama, Hamlet in turn assumes his antic disposition, making others participants in his own play. Embedded in all this, "The Mousetrap" becomes a play within the play of a play. Yet while Hamlet delights in his games with Claudius and others, his response to the actors reflects his psychological confusion. Watching how these performers "drown the stage with tears / And cleave the general ear with horrid speech, / Make mad the guilty" (II.ii), he accuses himself of cowardice for being unable to act like them. It never occurs to him that they *act* only in a theatrical sense, a talent he already masters to perfection. So instead of taking action, Hamlet indeed play-acts to the very end and, in his self-elected role as minister and scourge of mankind, captures the conscience of the king, maddens Ophelia, and cleaves his mother's heart.

By comparison with Hamlet, who remains for the most part unaware of his dilemma, Dostoyevsky's anti-hero in *Notes from Underground* comes close to being his own Nietzschean analyst. In a way his problems have become worse, for where Hamlet's neuroses are contained within a religious framework, the anti-hero's seem to run amok in a chaos of social phobias or idealistic obsessions. Already in childhood, his sense of guilt was so strong that, like Hamlet, he would admit to crimes he had not even committed. Yet all this self-knowledge does not save the anti-hero from the dilemma he shares with Hamlet. His attempt to escape from it makes him slip into the same role of the Nietzschean ascetic priest who infects others with his own sickness. The anti-hero, too, is deeply disgusted with his own person, calling himself a "highly conscious mouse," a "nasty obscene fly," and other dirty names. Like Hamlet, he has "never been able to look anybody straight in the face."[46]

Permanently brooding over "poisonous accumulation of unsatisfied wishes," his imagination likes to dwell on death, cemeteries, and decay, with such emotional involvement that he suddenly feels a lump rising in his throat.[47] This again recalls Hamlet, who, looking at Yorick's skull in the cemetery, exclaims: "how abhorred in my imagination it is! My gorge rises at it." Just as Liza checks the anti-hero's flights of morbid fantasizing when he describes the burial of another prostitute, Horatio feels that " 'Twere to consider too curiously to consider so" when Hamlet asks: "Why may not imagination trace the noble dust of Alexander till 'a find it stopping a bungh-hole?" (V.i) When not absorbed by their morbid imaginings, both protagonists either burst into feverishly ill-directed activity or sink "voluptuously into inertia, silently and impotently gnashing [their] teeth." For this they partly blame a conscience that makes cowards of us all or "is man's supreme misfortune"[48]; at the same time, they take a distinct delight in what Nietzsche called the "conscience-vivisection and self-crucifixion"[49] which has plagued us for over two millennia. More so even than Hamlet, the anti-hero "would gnaw and nibble and probe and suck away at [himself] until the bitter taste turned at last into a kind of shameful, devilish sweetness."[50]

As in the case of Hamlet, we can observe how the anti-hero's bottled-up aggressions turn into resentment until resentment, as in Nietzsche's *Genealogy of Morals*, turns creative, "giving birth to values."[51] Hamlet, from early on, has a sense of his mission and, despite his doubts, grows stronger and stronger in his conviction. By contrast, Dostoyevsky's anti-hero, like a *fin de siècle* ascetic priest, plays the saviour mainly for "the fascination of the game" and can be totally cynical about his mission. As he explains to his victim Liza, "I had been humiliated, so I wanted to humiliate somebody else; I had been treated like dirt, so I wanted to show my power ... That's what happened, and you thought I'd come on purpose to rescue you, didn't you? ... It was power, power ... I wanted to get your tears, your humiliation, your hysterics."[52] Nevertheless, his impact on Liza resembles Hamlet's on Gertrude or Ophelia. According to Nietzsche, the ascetic priest "must be deeply akin to all the shipwrecked and diseased" but at the same time strong and "master over himself ... with a will to power that is intact."[53] The anti-hero suddenly grows into that role upon realizing that there is a kinship between him and the prostitute Liza:

"Damn it, how very interesting that we should be *akin*!" I thought, almost rubbing my hands ... "Why did you come here?" I began again, now somewhat masterfully.[54]

From then on, though mockingly aware of voicing his "cherished *little ideas*" in orating about domestic bliss versus the prostitute's dissolute life, he talks himself into the fervour of a Savonarola. And, as in the case of Ophelia and Gertrude, the impact of this penitential oratory is devastating. The cynicism with which the anti-hero enjoys his new role, however, is quite unlike Hamlet's misplaced though more questioning sense of his mission. For all his self-awareness, the anti-hero enjoys his new role. "I sat down beside her and took her hands; ... there was a smile on her lips ... with a glance that seemed to be pleading for forgiveness for something." All of a sudden she acts towards him "as if [he were] some higher kind of creature who knew everything without being told." Even after Liza has left him, he keeps dreaming about how she will come back, throw herself at his feet, and declare that he is "her saviour."[55]

Like *Hamlet*, *Notes from Underground* is about the protagonist's failure to take revenge. The anti-hero's complaint that he is incapable of taking his "revenge on anybody for anything"[56] seems to echo Hamlet's self-incriminations after speaking to Fortinbras's captain:

> Now, whether it be
> Bestial oblivion, or some craven scruple
> Of thinking too precisely on th'event –
> A thought which, quartered, hath but one part wisdom
> And ever three parts coward – I do not know
> Why yet I live to say, "This thing's to do,"
> Sith I have cause, and will, and strength, and means
> To do't.   (IV.iv)

But Hamlet is unaware of why he delays. By contrast, the anti-hero not only understands but explains to us the dilemma he shares with Shakespeare's protagonist:

I couldn't even take my revenge on anybody for anything, because I should probably find it impossible to make up my mind to take any steps, even if I could. Why not? I should like to say a word or two about that in particular.[57]

Like Nietzsche comparing the slave with the master, Dostoyevsky's anti-hero distinguishes between himself, the "man of heightened awareness," and "l'homme de la nature et de la vérité." This man of action, who recalls Fortinbras, "considers his revenge to be no more than justice," goes straight to his goal, and, when faced with an insuperable obstacle, simply steps aside. He acts and forgets.[58] By contrast, the man of heightened awareness delays and remembers. In literally writing down the Ghost's last words, "Adieu, adieu, adieu. Remember me," so that nothing but its commandment will live "Within the book and volume of [his] brain" (I.v), Hamlet performs a gesture which is as incongruous under the circumstances as it is characteristic of his temperament. What governs Hamlet from the start is not the will to act but what Nietzsche calls "a veritable 'memory of the will'; so that, between the original determination and the actual performance of the thing willed, a whole world of new things, conditions, even volitional acts, can be interposed."[59]

This "active not wishing to be done with it, [this] continuing to will what has once been willed"[60] is equally typical of Dostoyevsky's anti-hero, who, like Hamlet, broods over an ever-growing accumulation of shameful memories without ever being able to shake them off. Hamlet curses his own self-deprecations, calling himself a whore who unpacks her heart with words and falls "a-cursing like a very drab" (II.ii). The anti-hero is simply "ashamed of [his] fantasies, but all the same ... will always be remembering them and turning them over in [his] mind, inventing things that never happened because they might have done so, and forgiving nothing." Both of them, in protracting their revenge and brooding over the delays, accumulate "so many other unresolved problems in addition to the original problem" that they involuntarily collect around themselves "a fatal morass" of "doubts and agitation." When they finally rouse themselves to action, they take their revenge "somehow in little bits, in snatches, furtively, anonymously." Here as elsewhere, the anti-hero analyses his own dilemma with a Nietzschean perspicacity that Hamlet seems to lack. He knows that his haranguing of Liza is a sadistic game of vicarious revenge, that love with him always begins with hatred and ends with moral subjugation, and that, generally speaking, "if civilization has not made man more bloodthirsty, it has certainly made him viler in his thirst for blood."[61]

Yet for all that, there seems to be little reason for calling Shakespeare's play an "artistic failure."[62] True enough, the protagonist does not fully understand his dilemma. There is also, perhaps, no concrete set of objects, no situation or chain of events that could provide the formula to account for the suicidal self-disgust that poisons Hamlet's life and obstructs his actions. But the play's implied critique of Christianity seems to account sufficiently for the protagonist's state of mind – except to those, perhaps, who, like Eliot, insist upon safeguarding orthodox Christianity and Aristotelian standards of the rational in literature. To be sure, Shakespeare wrote a play and not a *Genealogy of Morals*, and for better, rather than worse, this dramatic presentation of this nexus lacks the analytic precision of its nineteenth-century analogue. So Nietzsche, as well as Dostoyevsky, can serve tentatively to elucidate what Shakespeare's intuitive genius remained content to imply. But neither *Notes from Underground* nor *The Genealogy of Morals* is indispensable to our understanding of *Hamlet*. The play's internal evidence, as has been shown, is sufficient to solve the riddle of Hamlet and his problems.

Such a solution, of course, is only apparent if *Hamlet*, like *King Lear*, is read, as it were, on a double level. Superficially speaking, both plays seem to follow the tragic pattern. But at a deeper stratum these patterns – "Through suffering, learning" in *King Lear*, suffering in the service of divine providence in *Hamlet* – are reversed into their opposites. In *King Lear* this is achieved through elaborate techniques of audience manipulation; in *Hamlet* it results from the play's critique of Christianity. Not unlike Richmond in *Richard III*, which set the model for Shakespearian tragic closure, Hamlet repeatedly sees himself as pursuing his revenge by providential ordination. But the play as a whole leaves no doubt that Hamlet's god is an infernal demon, or that, translated into psychological terms, his mysterious oscillations between suicidal lethargy and uncontrollable vindictiveness are prompted by his obsessive concern with hell and damnation. His self-destructive tendencies are the direct result of these fears, which at the same time forbid him to perpetrate what they inspire. Hamlet is caught in a double-bind situation which Nietzsche was to describe as the hallmark of Christian civilization in general.

Shakespeare's perhaps greatest achievement was to transcend this antitragic vision, evident in *Lear*, *Hamlet*, and *Troilus*. For it is one thing to question and invert a specific genre, but it is quite another to evolve a new one which will be meaningful and captivating without relying on a tradition which it negates. Shakespeare's last plays draw on sources going back to the late Greek romances. As philosophical and theatrical artefacts they may, however, have more in common with, say, Sanskrit drama than with any of the major plays of the West.[63] Even compared to works by contemporaries like Beaumont and Fletcher, Shakespeare's romances stand out as unique creations. Rather than adventure stories in quaintly idealized no-man's lands ruled by love and honour, they are carefully designed post-tragic alternatives to the way in which his tragedies and anti-tragedies had answered the questions raised by human suffering.[64]

The Post-tragic Vision
of Romance

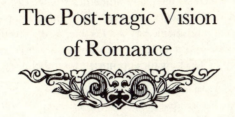

JUST AS BRUTUS or Othello in Shakespeare's tragedies, Pericles, Posthumus, Leontes, and Ferdinand in his romances go through a temporary season in hell. But this journey, instead of ending in a death that is either meaningful or meaningless, culminates in a spiritual rebirth. After undergoing a "melancholy state" which takes him to the brink of insanity, Pericles is given "another life" when he is reunited with his daughter (V.i). Jupiter assures Posthumus's dead relatives now inhabiting Elysium's "never-withering banks of flow'rs" that the hero will be "happier much by his affliction made" (*Cymbeline* V.iv). Leontes is cured of his despair when the victim of his unjustified jealousy is resurrected from the dead. Ferdinand, after successfully undergoing the tests imposed upon him by the godlike Prospero, feels that he is receiving "a second life" (V.i) through his marriage to Prospero's daughter Miranda.

Death and Rebirth in Shakespeare and Montaigne

These shamanistic destinies are set against an overwhelmingly pagan mythological background of mostly Hellenic divinities. Many of them, like Lucina in *Pericles*, Jupiter in *Cymbeline*, Proserpina in *The Winter's Tale*, Ceres in *The Tempest*, and Venus in *The Two Noble Kinsmen*, are connected with birth, fertility, death, and procreation. All seem to be centred around "great creating Nature" (*Winter's Tale* IV.iv) and her negative counterpart Time, who, as "the king of men," is "both their parent and ... their grave" (*Pericles* II.iii). But these human and supernatural embodiments of rebirth provide no more than the larger figurative patterns in a series of tapestries containing numerous smaller but, at the same time, more colourful configurations to the same effect.

A few instances at this point must suffice to show the density of these symbolist weavings. Almost everywhere we find the imagery of seasonal change, flowers and tombs, "things dying" and "things new born" (*Winter's*

Tale III.iii) intertwined with equally numerous shipwrecks, seeming deaths, and resurrection ceremonies, along with their attendant paraphernalia of tombstones, corpses, and magic.[1] When Perdita, at the sheep-shearing feast, wishes to strew Florizel "o'er and o'er" with flowers, her lover half-jokingly asks "What, like a corpse?" eliciting the appropriately symbolist reply from Perdita:

> No, like a bank for Love to lie and play on;
> Not like a corpse; or if, not to be buried,
> But quick and in mine arms. (*Winter's Tale* IV.iv)

What is an organic part of the dramatic context here becomes a somewhat laboured set piece in the inscription on the tombstone of Marina, whom her father Pericles falsely believes to be dead:

> "The fairest, sweetest, and best lies here,
> Who withered in her spring of year.
> ...
> On whom foul death hath made this slaughter.
> Marina was she called; and at her birth
> Thetis, being proud, swallowed some part o'th'earth.
> Therefore the earth, fearing to be o'erflowed,
> Hath Thetis' birth-child on the heavens bestowed. (IV.iv)

The brevity of Gower's inscription –

> O ye that this beholde,
> Lo here lieth she, she whiche was holde
> The fairest, and the floure of all,
> Whose name Thaisis men call –

shows even more clearly how Shakespeare exploits the symbolic implications of the dramatic situation beyond the limits of its theatrical potential.[2] Many other passages could exemplify this rebirth imagery of the romances. Except for minor details, such images in the last plays are almost interchangeable:

> Oxlips, in their cradles growing,
> Marigolds, on death-beds blowing ... (*Two Noble Kinsmen* I.i)

> With fairest flowers,
> Whilst summer lasts and I live here, Fidele,
> I'll sweeten thy sad grave ...
> ...
> Yea, and furred moss besides, when flow'rs are none,
> To winter-ground thy corse ... (*Cymbeline* IV.ii)

It's a near-formulaic language in which the playwright bodied forth his final beliefs.

For some of these Montaigne again provides a noteworthy precedent to Shakespeare. "Great Nature" (*Cymbeline* V.iv), whom the romances again and again invoke as the good and wise goddess, is Montaigne's "mother Nature," whom human rationalist endeavour has managed to transform into a "most injust and partiall stepdame." "Wee have forsaken nature, and yet wee will teach her her lesson: Shee, that lead vs so happily, and directed vs so safely." What Shakespeare suggests to us in the last plays is also the aging Montaigne's repeated advice to his readers:

Rowze vp your selfe, and you shall finde forcible arguments against death to be in your selfe; most true and very proper to serve and steade you in time of necessitie ... *We cannot erre in following Nature* ... the soveraigne document is, for a man to conforme himselfe to hir.[3]

However, neither Shakespeare nor Montaigne romanticizes nature. "*Those which we call monsters are not so with God*," writes the philosopher. "We call that against nature, which commeth against custome. There is nothing, whatsoever it be, that is not according to hir."[4] Nature is Janus-faced: her alter ego Time destroys what she creates.[5] In *The Two Noble Kinsmen*, Mars, that "great corrector of enormous times," is said to heal "with blood / The earth when it is sick" and cure the world "O'th'plurisy of people" (V.i). Montaigne quotes Lucretius's *De Rerum Natura* by way of affirming a similarly Heraclitean understanding of time:

> Of th'vniversall world, age doth the nature change,
> And all things from one state must to another range,
> No one thing like it selfe remaines, all things doe passe,
> Nature doth change, and drive to change, each thing that was.

The inescapable fact that "*The birth, encrease, and augumentation of every thing, is the alteration and corruption of another*," as Montaigne puts it,[6] is what Nietzsche and Artaud were to describe as the "cruelty" ("Grausamkeit," "cruauté") of life.[7] But Montaigne and Shakespeare, at least towards the ends of their lives, for the most part focused on the more positive aspects of this phenomenon. Their main concern was not destruction but how the "decay of one life, is the passage to a thousand other lives."[8]

The anguished expectation of a death in the company "Of those that lawless and incertain thought / Imagine howling" (*Measure for Measure* III.i) has been replaced by a trust in great creating nature and her endless cycles of death and rebirth. As the concluding lines to *The Two Noble Kinsmen* suggest, Shakespeare shared Montaigne's opinion that, considering the "thousand ridiculous associations" man has fabricated between himself and God, "*The wisest judging of heaven, is not to iudge of it at all*"[9]:

> Let us be thankful
> For that which is, and with you leave dispute
> That are above our question. Let's go off,
> And bear us like the time.

Metaphysically speaking, we know little more about the absolute than what is obvious from birth and death, spring, summer, autumn and winter. At best we can tell a winter's tale about the coming of spring. Neither Montaigne nor Shakespeare, however, seems to have extended this trust in the renewal of life into a belief in metempsychosis. At least to Montaigne, that creed was as unconvincing as Plato's "that it shall be the spirituall parte of man that shal enjoy the recompences of the other life." All the keener therefore is his interest in the cycles of death and rebirth we can observe in life itself. Montaigne may not share Shakespeare's emphasis on the possibility of spiritual rebirth. But his insistence on individual death and rebirth as they interconnect with the life-rhythms of the entire universe is as strong as the playwright's. Just as "the death of fire is a generation of ayre; and the death of ayre, a generation of Water," he writes,[10] quoting Heraclitus, so do we constantly die and revive in our lives.

To this infinite flux of life corresponds an eternity of the here and now. Our traditional understanding of eternity is temporal: to Thomas Aquinas, for instance, the only way to arrive at a proper understanding of God's eternity is through linear time.[11] Not so to Montaigne, to whom God in eternity is "*not according to any measure of time, but according to an immoovable and vnmooving eternitie, not measured by time.*" By "*one only* Now *or* Present," God "*filleth the* Ever."[12] Montaigne here employs the international language of mystics, who have described the ineffable in the same paradoxical terms throughout the ages. Similar terms are used by Shakespeare where Florizel describes Perdita as the very symbol of this eternity found in the here and now of life:

> When you do dance, I wish you
> A wave o'th'sea, that you might ever do
> Nothing but that – move still, still so,
> And own no other function. Each your doing,
> So singular in each particular,
> Crowns what you are doing in the present deeds,
> That all your acts are queens.   (*Winter's Tale* IV.iv)

The first of Shakespeare's romances shows with what force this new vision of life must have invaded Shakespeare's consciousness.

Pericles

Pericles displays all the crudeness of an experiment, and in none of his other romances did the playwright remain so close to his sources.[13] In terms of

Shakespeare's development, then, the importance of the old tale of Apollonius of Tyre can hardly be overestimated; there was enough in the story itself to hold the interest of a poet about to evolve a whole new dramatic symbolism of death and rebirth. The protagonist barely escapes death after divining the incest between the woman he wooed and her father. During his flight, he saves a city from starvation and wins himself a royal bride but loses her again in a tempest shortly after she has borne him a daughter. After also losing this child, he falls into a deep melancholy. But rescue is at hand from those whom the protagonist thought dead. His wife has been brought back to life through the craft of a certain "medicus nomine Cerimon."[14] Before Diana, in a vision, directs the protagonist to her temple in Ephesus, where his wife has become a priestess, he is reunited with his daughter, who cures him of his depression.

Shakespeare follows the general outline of this story, found in Gower's *Confessio Amantis* and Laurence Twine's *The Patterne of Painefull Adventures*, in often minute detail. However, he deviates from his source in two respects: one is due to the elimination of Christian references, the other to the substitution for them of a new network of symbolist imagery centred around the notions of life, death, and rebirth. Both Gower and Twine refer to pagan divinities such as Diana and Neptune, but, like the repeated mention of Fortune in Gower, these are part of the story's exotic mythological décor rather than of its religious essence. In Gower this is located in "goddes purveance, / Whiche doth mercy forth with justice," in Twine in the "providence of almightie God," his "just judgement," "goodness" and "grace."[15]

Both authors make their characters pray to their "mercifull God, which beholde[th] heaven, earth and hell, and discovere[th] all the secretes therein." Shakespeare omits these prayers, except in one case where his changes are more revealing than what he retained. Marina's counterpart in Gower's *Confessio Amantis* implores the man about to murder her to permit, "for the love of god allmight,"

> for a litell stounde,
> She mighte knele upon the grounde
> Towarde the heven for to crave
> Her wofull soule that she maie save.

In Twine's version her request is granted, and "the providence of God" sees to it that certain pirates come to the maiden's rescue while she is "devoutly making her praiers."[16] In *Pericles* the situation is reversed. Here it is the murderer who exhorts his victim to fall to her prayer, an opportunity Marina simply ignores. Instead she protests her innocence and, in a skilful manoeuvre of flattery, praises her murderer's goodness of heart. In all this, Shakespeare never once invokes Gower's and Twine's Christian God but, as elsewhere in the play, has his character address an unspecified number of divinities:

LEONINE If you require a little space for prayer,
I grant it. Pray; but be not tedious, for
The gods are quick of ear. (IV.i)

In Gower the vision takes the form of a mere command sent to the protagonist by the "hie god"; in Twine "there appeared an Angell in his sleepe."[17]

Instead of this Christian pantheon, then, Shakespeare makes the gods of pagan antiquity preside over a world which he fills with the symbols, emblems, and shorthand parables of a specific philosophy of life. The opening scenario shows the king's palace at Antioch "with heads displayed upon its walls," a detail already mentioned by Twine and Gower.[18] New, however, is the description of Antioch's daughter, who, "appareled like the spring," enters to the sound of music. As her father points out, Lucina, the goddess of childbirth, reigned at her conception; nature gave her beauty as a dowry, and

> The senate house of planets all did sit,
> To knit in her their best perfections.

Also, there is abundant talk about life and death, though in a moralizing tone of Christian persuasion that stands in striking contrast to later comments of a similar type. Death remembered, Pericles himself points out, "should be like a mirror, / Who tells us life's but breath, to trust it error" (I.i).

Similar symbolist embroideries are added to subsequent events. After giving back "life" to the citizens of Tharsus, "whom hunger starved half dead" (I.iv), Pericles undergoes one of several shipwrecks, is saved from the "wat'ry grave" (II.i) of the Mediterranean, immediately involves his rescuers in a debate about life and death, retrieves a rusty suit of armour which his father, upon his deathbed, had given him, saying, "Keep it, my Pericles; it hath been a shield / Twixt me and death" (II.i), and duly proceeds in it to a tournament held in celebration of Simonides' daughter's birthday, his shield displaying a device appropriate for this knight errant on his repeated journeys through death and rebirth:

> A withered branch, that's only green at top;
> The motto, *In hac spe vivo.* (II.ii)

Simonides reminds Pericles of his dead father, which makes the protagonist conclude that "Time's the king of men; / He's both their parent and he is their grave" (II.iii). Simonides' daughter, sitting "like Beauty's child, whom Nature gat / For men to see and seeing wonder at" (II.ii), recalls Antioch's daughter, but with the difference that Thaïsa embodies what her fake double presents in mere appearance. This contrast is reinforced by Antioch's and his daughter's subsequent "fall" when, "Even in the height and pride of all his glory," they incur the vengeance of the "most high gods" and, struck by lightning, reap the just reward for their sin (II.iv). Such a *de casibus* destiny has little in common with Pericles' basically unmerited ordeals. But we are again invited to compare and contrast the two when the protagonist, upon Marina's birth during a tempest, invokes the help of the goddess who, according to Antioch, presided over the conception of his daughter:

> Lucina, O
> Divinest patroness and midwife gentle
> To those that cry by night, convey thy deity
> Aboard our dancing boat; make swift the pangs
> Of my queen's travails!   (III.i)

A subsequent scene shows Shakespeare's pursuit of a specific symbolism going so far as to interfere with a consistent unfolding of his plot. In Twine, Marina's counterpart Tharsia has a nurse who, before passing "into the state of life everlasting," reveals the heroine's true parenthood.[19] This is the reason why Tharsia frequently visits the nurse's sepulchre, where she eventually encounters the man sent to kill her. In *Pericles* this piece of information is thrown in, so to speak, as an afterthought when Marina is already face to face with the murderer (IV.i.). Yet what is awkwardly contrived in the story creates crucial links in the play's symbolic network. Marina happens to be picking flowers for Lychorida's grave *"near the seashore,"* where she is in easy reach of the pirates who are about to rescue her:

> No, I will rob Tellus of her weed
> To strew thy green with flowers; the yellows, blues,
> The purple violets, and marigolds,
> Shall as a carpet hang upon thy grave,
> While summer days doth last. Ay me, poor maid,
> Born in a tempest, when my mother died,
> This world to me is as a lasting storm.   (IV.i)

To tell the rest of the story in this way would be tantamount to multiplying examples of a similar kind. Shakespeare's often awkward closeness to his sources seems to be in direct proportion to his lack of interest in the story as such. What made this "mouldy tale" attractive to him was its situational symbolism, and he missed no opportunity to exploit its potential to the utmost. Our sense of saturation in reading the play derives from the many further instances of this kind, such as, for instance, the inscription on Marina's tombstone (IV.iv) or Pericles' words when, upon retrieving sanity, his new lease on life is almost cut short by the joy of being reunited with his daughter:

> Give me a gash, put me to present pain;
> Lest this great sea of joys rushing upon me
> O'erbear the shores of my mortality,
> And drown me with their sweetness. O, come hither,
> Thou that beget'st him that did thee beget;
> Thou that wast born at sea, buried at Tharsus,
> And found at sea again!   (V.i)

This occurs shortly before the protagonist's reunion with his wife, who in turn swoons from joy ("PERICLES What means the nun? She dies!"), only to recover in order to talk about "birth and death" and to be "buried / A second time" in Pericles' arms (V.iii). In no other play before or after *Pericles* did Shakespeare pursue a specific symbolism with greater insistence. In this, much as in the way in which he associates rebirth with art and magic, Shakespeare is seen experimenting with ideas which found their perfect dramatic expression not in this first of his romances but in *The Winter's Tale*.

Marina is Perdita's predecessor, sharing the fate of a daughter lost and retrieved by her father, to whom, before the final recognition, she appears like the double of his wife, equally thought dead. Like Perdita, she, too, turns into the human embodiment of nature, the divinity central to the play's cosmological framework. As such she also comes to stand for an art that is a mere extension of nature. In Aristotle's view, we remember, art finishes the job which nature has left undone. By contrast, the later Shakespeare is content with trying to "sister" the perfection of nature. Marina, as he makes Gower tell us,

> ... sings like one immortal, and she dances
> As goddesslike to her admired lays;
> Deep clerks she dumbs, and with her neele composes
> Nature's own shape of bud, bird, branch, or berry,
> That even her art sisters the natural roses.   (V.i)

Such talents help her to give spiritual rebirth to her father, who, "*unkempt and clad in sackcloth*," has for a period of three months "not spoken / To anyone, nor taken sustenance / But to prorogue his grief" (V.i) over the supposed death of his daughter. Also, there are the visitors of the brothel who, like Lysimachus, her future husband, are morally reformed by her fair words, so that the Bawd, when he hears Marina invoke the gods, has reason to suspect that she conjures (IV.vi). But the person through whose art and magic the gods most clearly show their power is Cerimon. A mere "medicus" and "physition" in Gower and Twine,[20] he has in Shakespeare been aggrandized to a semi-divine Renaissance Hermetic magus. Reverend sir, Pericles addresses him in the last scene, "The gods can have no mortal officer / More like a god than you" (V.iii).

In rewriting the role of Gower's and Twine's learned doctor, who resurrects the protagonist's wife from her deathlike state, Shakespeare may well have drawn on certain Hermetic texts which, like the *Asclepius* from the *Corpus Hermeticum*, proclaim "a holy and most solemn restoration of nature."[21] Cerimon, if we can trust some of the play's editors, is a student of such literature. I have read, he says,

> Of some Egyptians, who after four hours' death
> Have raised impoverished bodies, like to this,
> Unto their former health.   (III.ii)[22]

Other of Cerimon's studious endeavours are no less Hermetic than his reading. In their pursuit he has come to share Bruno's presumption that a man may turn himself into a god by his "Virtue and cunning," which are "endowments greater / Than nobleness and riches":

> 'Tis known, I ever
> Have studied physic, through which secret art,
> By turning o'er authorities, I have,
> Together with my practise, made familiar
> To me and to my aid the blest infusions
> That dwells in vegetives, in metals, stones;
> And I can speak of the disturbances
> That nature works, and of her cures.   (III.ii)

What follows is a resurrection ritual, complete with music, incantation, magical instruments, and the magician's accompanying description. But as Shakespeare makes sure to remind us, this resurrection, instead of pointing towards an eternal life, is a rebirth simply towards another death:

> THAISA O dear Diana,
> Where am I? Where's my lord? What world is this?
> SECOND GENTLEMAN Is not this strange?
> FIRST GENTLEMAN Most rare!
> CERIMON Hush, my gentle neighbors!
> Lend me your hands; to the next chamber bear her.
> Get linen. Now this matter must be looked to,
> For her relapse is mortal.   (III.ii)

Cymbeline

Pericles with its rebirth symbolism was not the only experiment needed before Shakespeare was ready to transform tragedy into post-tragedy in *The Winter's Tale*. The other was *Cymbeline*, which, from the moral innocence of *Pericles* and its protagonist, takes us back to the ill-starred errors and passions of an Othello. Just as Iachimo has his most notable predecessor in Iago, so Posthumus, while foreshadowing the jealous rages of Leontes, speaks in the near-demented accents of the Moor or, even more notably, of the poet's own voice in the dark sonnets:

> O, all the devils!
> This yellow Iachimo in an hour, was't not?
> Or less? At first? Perchance he spoke not, but,
> Like a full-acorned boar, a German one,
> Cried "O!" and mounted; found no opposition
> But what he looked for should oppose and she
> Should from encounter guard. Could I find out
> The woman's part in me! For there's no motion
> That tends to vice in man but I affirm
> It is the woman's part. Be it lying, note it,
> The woman's; flattering, hers; deceiving, hers;
> Lust and rank thoughts, hers, hers; revenges, hers;
> Ambitions, covetings, change of prides, disdain,
> Nice longing, slanders, mutability,
> All faults that have a name, nay, that hell knows,
> Why, hers, in part of all, but rather all.   (II.v)[23]

Although Posthumus is about to re-enact Othello's murder of his beloved, this tragic ending turns into its opposite when Imogen, whom he believes dead, is reborn to him in the final scene. Here as elsewhere in the play, Shakespeare deploys some of the rebirth symbolism first developed in *Pericles*. In a rather gratuitous scene Cymbeline's kidnapped sons plan to bury Fidele, alias Imogen. Resolved that her head, contrary to Christian fashion, should lie "to th'east" (IV.ii), they articulate the usual imagery of seasonal changes, flowers sprouting from graves, and "furred moss besides, when flow'rs are none, / To winter-ground thy corse" (IV.ii).

This distinctly pagan atmosphere is reinforced when the dramatis personae worship either "divine Nature" (IV.ii), the "holy sun" (IV.iv; compare III.iii), Jupiter, or simply the gods, letting their "crooked smokes climb to their nostrils / From our blest altars" (V.v). Just as Diana appears to Pericles, Jupiter makes himself known to Posthumus, assuring the protagonist that his prolonged trials are a sign of the god's special concern. He also leaves him with an oracle which, in its central prediction ("when from a stately cedar shall be lopped branches which, being dead many years, shall after revive, be jointed to the old stock, and freshly grow; then shall Posthumus end his miseries" V.iv), makes Jupiter the guarantor of the multiple rebirths we witness in the final scene. Here the Soothsayer expounding the prophecy is not the only one to ensure that we appreciate the events on their symbolic and oracular level. "O, what am I?" exclaims Cymbeline when he finds that his two sons as well as Belarius, a faithful old retainer whom he banished unjustly, are still alive:

> A mother to the birth of three? Ne'er mother
> Rejoiced deliverance more.

At the same time, we are given to understand that all these rebirths are not to be confused with a resurrection into eternity. Cymbeline fears that the gods mean to strike him "To death with mortal joy," while Posthumus, when embraced by Imogen, tells his beloved: "Hang there like fruit, my soul, / Till the tree die!"

Although more examples to similar effect could be adduced, the rebirth symbolism in *Cymbeline* is far less pervasive or deep-rooted than in *Pericles*. In fact, there is something perfunctory about it, as if the poet, while pointing to it as his main concern, was absorbed in related but as-yet unexplored matters. One of these is the question of moral responsibility left untouched by the innocent protagonist of *Pericles*; the other is the attempt, only partially realized in the earlier romance, to give the rebirth theme a structural correlative in the cyclical patterns of the dramatic narrative.

Just as Posthumus, contrary to Pericles, causes his own and others' misfortunes by his quarrelsome temper, so he, unlike his predecessor, is given a chance to repent. After concluding act II with his curse on women, he remains absent from acts III and IV only to reappear at the beginning of act V, an "ugly monster" (V.iii) cursing himself for having murdered his wife and eagerly seeking death, first in battle, then by pretending to be a Roman soldier. "I am merrier to die than thou art to live," he tells the jailer who is about to haul him off to execution.

> JAILER Come, sir, are you ready for death?
> POSTHUMUS Over-roasted rather; ready long ago. (V.iv)

No doubt the protagonist has learned his lesson, and his repentance (like Leontes' in *The Winter's Tale*) has struck to the very roots of his life. But Posthumus's enlightened remorse is final neither in a tragic nor in a moral sense. Life goes on, and the cyclical patterns Shakespeare evolves in order to portray it counteract such closure.

Cymbeline, of all of Shakespeare's plays, is, as B. Evans has shown, the greatest achievement in "exploitation of discrepant awareness." Even more than *Pericles*, it is a deliberate experiment "with the dramatic effects of uncertainty."[24] The final scene, a *tour de force* in happy-ending revelations, only deepens this uncertainty. For as the dramatis personae's ignorance persists to the very last, the playwright assumes the role of a puppeteer who, on a mere whim, decides to resolve his puppets' all-too intricate problems in an all-too implausible conclusion. We know that without this *deus ex machina* intervention a disastrous ending would be almost certain – what happens, in other words, happens by mere chance. Fortune, as Pisanio predicted, "brings in some boats that are not steered" (IV.iii).

To make matters worse, the characters are shown to be the playthings not only of fate but also of their psychological conditioning: while ignorant of the outer circumstances of their situation, they blindly repeat the mistakes that led them there. Just before Cymbeline has reason to call himself "mother to the birth" of Belarius, Arviragus, and Guiderius, he is about to make himself their executioner, passing judgment with the same intemperance with which, deceived by two villains, he banished Belarius twenty years earlier. When confronted with Pisanio, Imogen repeats her previous error of cursing the man who saved her: "Thou gavest me poison. Dangerous fellow, hence; / Breathe not where princes are" (V.v). Ironically, these are her first words after recovering from a blow by Posthumus which sent her reeling to the ground. For even Posthumus, despite his genuine repentance, is not immune to acting out of his inveterately evil temper when Fidele, moved by his grief over her alter ego Imogen, tries to reveal herself to him. To call such irony diabolical is hardly to overstate the case:

> POSTHUMUS ... O Imogen!
> My queen, my life, my wife! O Imogen,
> Imogen, Imogen!
> IMOGEN Peace, my lord. Hear, hear –
> POSTHUMUS Shall's have a play of this? Thou scornful page,
> There lie thy part. [*Striking her; she falls.*] (V.v)

The incident is pregnant with a rebirth symbolism *à rebours*, and Shakespeare makes sure to articulate this underside of his major theme as clearly as possible. Pisanio's comment that Posthumus "ne'er killed Imogen till now" is true in a deeper than the literal sense, while Cymbeline's "Does the world go round?" hints at more than the apparent confusion which makes him ask the question. Even before the play is finished, its symbolical wheel has come full circle, and we know that it will keep on revolving in a similar manner beyond the somewhat artificially tagged-on happy ending. Amid all this blind bewilderment, even the prophecies of the gods are called into question. The Soothsayer expounding the rebirth symbolism of Jupiter's oracle was wrong in predicting "Success to th'Roman host" (IV.ii) before the battle, and his *post factum* rectification of this error strikes one as mere casuistry (V.v). "Here's a maze trod indeed / Through forthrights and meanders," as Gonzalo in *The Tempest* puts it (III.iii).[25] But before Shakespeare created the Borgesian labyrinth of the later romance, he wrote the play that would give perfect expression to the themes and issues initiated in *Pericles*.

From *King Lear* to
The Two Noble Kinsmen

IT HAS BEEN SUGGESTED that Shakespeare's romances began not with *Pericles* or *Cymbeline* but with *King Lear*. Here as in later plays, writes one critic, we find the "spiritual wandering, the testing of patience, the opposition of court and country, brothers waging mortal combat against each other, and the separation and reunion of loved ones. By the time we reach Act V, this romance atmosphere has prepared us to accept the exciting denouement of turn and counterturn which also belongs to romance."[1] What makes *King Lear* antitragic rather than post-tragic, in other words, is largely its lack of a happy ending. In a sense, it is a romance where things go wrong. There is good reason for Bradley's suggestion[2] that Shakespeare, had he tackled the Lear theme at the time of *Cymbeline* and *The Winter's Tale*, would have saved Nahum Tate the trouble of writing his happy-ending adaptation for the Restoration audience.

But the affinities between *King Lear* and the romances are deeper than all this. The earlier play, as we have seen, is the result of a double transformation. Its basic source is a morality story of ingratitude in which the evil are punished and the good rewarded. Shakespeare, in killing off the protagonist and his good daughter, seems to transform this Job-like pattern into a tragedy. But in fact, he goes further still. Tragedy, in both its Greek and its Christian variants, implies a teleology of either progress-minded or eschatological orientation in which even suffering and evil in some way perform a meaningful function. Shakespeare consistently holds out promises of such meaningfulness in *King Lear*, but only in order to frustrate our expectations.

In a way, the entire play is a repeated *reductio ad absurdum* of teleology. At the same time, one can see how the same impulse drove the playwright, unwittingly perhaps but inevitably, to evolve a new dramatic mode which would portray life not teleologically but cyclically. The protagonist's rebirth from his madness may be neither final nor joyful. But otherwise it is not dissimilar to those of Pericles, Posthumus, Leontes, and Alonso, who are all cured of their particular kinds of madness. Thus Alonso in *The Tempest*, before he is reborn through his repentance, repeatedly imagines himself as sharing the grave where he thinks his son Ferdinand is buried forever. "I wish / Myself were mudded in that oozy bed / Where my son lies" (V.i; compare III.iii). Similar fantasies occur to Lear before he, at least temporarily, recovers his sanity after being reunited with his daughter:

> LEAR You do me wrong to take me out o'th'grave:
> Thou art a soul in bliss; but I am bound
> Upon a wheel of fire, that mine own tears
> Do scald like molten lead.   (IV.vii)

In radically transforming the source of *King Lear*, Shakespeare, one might say, stopped just short of post-tragedy. *The Winter's Tale* gives us an example in which Shakespeare, in a comparable situation, went all the way.

The Winter's Tale

What Shakespeare tried to achieve in this romance is most fully revealed by comparison with its primary source, Greene's *Pandosto*. Among Elizabethan novels this was one of the most enduringly popular.[3] *Pandosto* has something for everyone. Inconsistent as it may be, there is the psychological didacticism of showing how "Truth," as the subtitle proclaims, "is most manifestly revealed" by "Time in spight of fortune." There is the journeying through exotic countries and the retrieval of a lost child made popular by Greek romance. There is the world of pastoral. And finally there is tragedy. Pandosto, whose unjustified jealousy leads to the death of his queen and the exposure of his daughter, incurs an Oedipus-like destiny in the end. Unwittingly reunited with his daughter, he falls in love with her and tyrannically pursues her with his unwelcome desires. When finally made aware of his incestuous urges, "calling to mind how ... contrarie to the law of nature hee had lusted after his owne Daughter ... he fell into a melancholie fit, and to close up the Comedie with a Tragicall stratageme, he slewe himselfe."[4]

As in the case of *Lear* or *Troilus*, Shakespeare's adaptation of Greene's novel once again shows the playwright as the radical innovator, deliberately inverting the established literary patterns of his time in the pursuit of new ones. And again Shakespeare availed himself of his by-now well-developed strategy of anticlimactic audience manipulation. Some of the spectators watching the first performance probably remembered *Pandosto* sufficiently well to be surprised by the totally different ending of *The Winter's Tale*. For those who did not, there was equal surprise in the play itself.[5]

Leontes is far from the only one to remain ignorant of the fact that Hermione, thought dead for sixteen years, is still alive. It is the biggest secret

Shakespeare ever kept from an audience. In order to guarantee the surprise of his final scene, the playwright actually goes so far as to issue false information to his spectators. Paulina, whose forthright character appears to be the very guarantor of the truth, insists that Hermione is dead. The death of Mamillius seems to confirm Paulina's assertion. And for those spectators who, remembering Greene's novel, might still be in doubt, there is Antigonus, who, although ignorant of the queen's death, has Hermione's ghost appear to him in a dream. Leontes' "Prithee, bring me / To the dead bodies of my queen and son" (III.ii) seems to imply that the king may even have been taken to see his wife's corpse.

On the other hand, we are carefully prepared for the unexpected miracle of Hermione's resurrection that lies ahead. In rejecting his courtiers' suggestion that he marry again, Leontes invokes the possibility that Hermione, should he do otherwise,

> ... would make her sainted spirit
> Again possess her corpse, and on this stage,
> Where we offenders now appear, soul-vexed,
> And begin, "Why to me?" (V.i)[6]

Paulina, in eager response, tells Leontes how Hermione's ghost would make him murder his new wife. Not inappropriately, she slips herself into the role of that other-worldly visitor, imagining how her shrieks of "Remember mine" would rift Leontes' ears. The same role allows her to give Leontes and us a first hint of Hermione's possible revival. Leontes will only be allowed to remarry if Paulina herself has the right to choose the new queen:

> ... she shall not be so young
> As was your former, but she shall be such
> As, walked your first queen's ghost, it should take joy
> To see her in your arms. (V.i)

Hermione's resurrection in Paulina's chapel is merely the fulfilment of these ghostly forebodings.

The Winter's Tale, particularly on account of this final scene, has been claimed to bear out "the Christian view of the historical redemption of the human race" (J.A. Bryant)[7] or to corroborate, "without copying, the Christian revelation" (G. Wilson Knight).[8] Yet to read the play as a Christian "'resurrection' parable" in this way is almost as ill-informed as to describe as Catholic the philosophy of Giordano Bruno, whom the Inquisition burned for his heresies. Such an interpretation may appeal to today's Christian liberal eager to widen the scope of his creed, but it merely obfuscates the attempt to ascertain the mental attitude of a poet in an age as acutely aware of its spiritual dissensions as that of the aging Shakespeare. If the playwright had intended to make his play a parable of Christian resurrection, he surely would have given us the appropriate hints, which are conspicuous only by their absence. Instead, he associates the "resurrection" scene with the kind of Hermetic magic of which Bruno had been the major spokesman during his lifetime. As though remembering the punishment in store for those involved in black magic, Paulina sends away those that might suspect her of "unlawful business" before she orders the music that will "awake" Hermione's statue to life. But Leontes commands all to stay and, after Hermione has descended from her pedestal, exclaims:

> If this be magic, let it be an art
> Lawful as eating.

This may or may not be a direct allusion "to the famous god-making passage in the *Asclepius*."[9] But the notion, reported in the Hermetic text, of how the old Egyptian priests, frequently to the accompaniment of music, used to infuse their statues of the gods with life, was widely enough known to be recognized by at least some members of Shakespeare's audience. To all others the question of the lawfulness of Paulina's magic simply served as a reminder of what had already been talked about in the same scene. "There's magic in thy majesty," exclaims Leontes when he sees Perdita standing as if petrified before the statue of her mother. To be suspected of aid by "wicked powers" is what Paulina fears in offering to "make the statue move indeed."

For all that, Shakespeare shows little interest in Hermetic magic for its own sake. Instead, he mainly uses it for its symbolic implications. A simple way of deciphering the deeper meaning of the romances is to underline their key words. In the last scene, this method shows how frequently Shakespeare repeats words such as "life" and "death." He also misses no opportunity to evoke "summer" and "winter" or to stress how Hermione may have been "stol'n from the dead." At the same time we are reminded that this symbolism refers to a rebirth in this life, not in a beyond. While surprised to see how closely the statue resembles his former wife, Leontes notes that "Hermione was not so much wrinkled, nothing / So agèd as this seems." And immediately after Hermione's supposed resurrection, Paulina once again assures the king that her magic is lawful, but also that the queen might die again as quickly as she was reborn:

> Start not; her actions shall be as holy as
> You hear my spell is lawful. Do not shun her
> Until you see her die again, for then
> You kill her double.

This symbolism surrounding Hermione's magical revival in the last scene is carefully prepared in a consistent chain of images evoking both "things dying" and "things new-born" throughout the play. While Shakespeare deliberately feeds us misleading information in order to safeguard his final surprise, he is equally deliberate in making sure that the symbolic meaning of this revelation will not be lost on us. This double movement of straightforward and anticlimactic audience manipulation is apparent from the very beginning of *The Winter's Tale*.

The play's opening scene is in this sense unprecedented in Shakespeare's entire *oeuvre*. There is no action, and whatever thoughts about the future are exchanged between Camillo and Archidamus turn out to be misleading. The friendship between Leontes and Polixenes, which, Camillo thinks, "cannot choose but branch now," is to die in the very next scene. Mamillius, in Archidamus's eyes, "a gentleman of the greatest promise that ever came into [his] note," is to suffer real death shortly afterwards. And yet the two courtiers are made to utter truths on a level they are not even aware of. In evoking the coming summer, mentioning drinks that will put the senses to sleep, or talking about things rooted that are about to branch, they seem to weave the opening patterns of a finely knit symbolist tapestry traceable throughout the play. At the end of this opening scene, some of these death and rebirth images intersect to form the first of several nodal points of special symbolic density:

> CAMILLO I very well agree with you in the hopes of him. It is a gallant child; one that, indeed, physics the subject, makes old hearts fresh; they that went on crutches ere he was born desire yet their life to see him a man.
> ARCHIDAMUS Would they else be content to die?
> CAMILLO Yes, if there were no other excuse why they should desire to live.
> ARCHIDAMUS If the King had no son, they would desire to live on crutches till he had one.

Mamillius, the misleading embodiment of such hopes, is finally made to appear the oracle of his own death. At the same time he unwittingly weaves further configurations of the rebirth theme. This happens in a scene which also presents the theme in more concrete fashion. Hermione, pregnant with the future Perdita, has of late, as one of her ladies remarks, spread into "a goodly bulk" (II.i). Mamillius is adept at frightening his mother with his ghostly tales, and when Hermione asks him to tell a tale "As merry as [he] will," he characteristically proposes to deliver one of his specialties instead. "A sad tale's best for winter," he says; "I have one / Of sprites and goblins." But with the maniacally jealous Leontes storming into this wintry idyll, Mamillius never gets beyond his opening line, which, if read at its deeper symbolic level, forebodes his imminent death. "There was a man ... Dwelt by a churchyard – I will tell it softly, / Yond crickets shall not hear it."

In a play whose title derives from his last words, Mamillius will not speak again, and the winter's tale about the hope of a rebirth in spring, which the opening scene misleadingly invests in his person, will find its fulfilment in others. The irony here warns us against over-emphasizing the optimism of *The Winter's Tale* and of Shakespeare's romances generally. For though their final scenes may celebrate rebirth, their cyclical structure never lets us forget that, as surely as rebirth follows death, as inexorably will life be destroyed again.[10] Whereas an ultimate, teleological optimism is the essence of tragedy, a fatalistic acceptance of life in its endless cycles of death, rebirth, and further death characterizes post-tragedy. In play after play from *Pericles* to *The Two Noble Kinsmen*, Shakespeare, while elaborating upon the rebirth theme, puts increasing emphasis on the continuance of death and suffering.

The Tempest

Taken to its limits, the notion of a cyclical return of all life finally leads to what Borges calls a "vertiginous *regressus ad infinitum*."[11] Dream and reality become interchangeable, the absolute a paradox, and life a labyrinth without exit. Shakespeare's portrayal of such a world as adumbrated in *Cymbeline* was brought to perfection not in the almost contemporaneous *Winter's Tale*, but in *The Tempest*. In structural terms, this play resembles a hall of mirrors designed to produce the effect of infinite regression Borges speaks of.[12] The play's starting point, repeatedly recalled in Prospero's and Ariel's words, is the story of how Antonio, the protagonist's brother, "From Milan did supplant good Prospero" (III.iii) in conspiracy with Alonso, king of Naples, and Alonso's brother Sebastian. The stage action contains two replicas of this incident. In a kinship parallelogram, Sebastian is incited by Prospero's brother to murder and supplant his own. A second, sub-plot version of the same theme develops when Stephano, in conspiracy with Caliban and Trinculo, decides to murder Prospero in order to become king of the island.

As though such multiplication of events were not enough to produce the effect of infinite reduction, there are several further variants of the usurpation theme in the play. Prospero falsely accuses Ferdinand of usurping his father's title as king of Naples, of being a spy, and of trying to win the island from Prospero, "the lord on't" (I.ii). The protagonist himself is portrayed as the usurper of a realm formerly occupied by Caliban and his mother Sycorax, who in turn had enslaved Ariel as Prospero did Caliban. "I am subject to a tyrant / A sorcerer, that by his cunning hath / Cheated me of the island" (III.ii), Caliban complains to Stephano. Just as once, before Prospero enslaved him, he had shown the magician "all the qualities o'th'isle" (I.ii), so he now proposes to show his new master "every fertile inch o'th'island" (II.ii). A *sub specie aeternitatis* view of life, it seems, is revealed to us in the infinite reduplications of the same phenomenon.

The resultant sense of unreality is most powerfully conveyed in the scene in which Sebastian, incited by Antonio, is about to repeat the latter's usurpation of Prospero's realm by murdering the sleeping Alonso. "What? Are you waking?" he asks Antonio, who in his imagination has seen "a crown / Dropping upon [his] head."

> It is a sleepy language, and thou speak'st
> Out of thy sleep. What is it thou didst say?
> This is a strange repose, to be asleep
> With eyes wide open; standing, speaking, moving,
> And yet so fast asleep.   (II.i)

This turns into a word game in which Sebastian, not Antonio, becomes the one to be woken up to his potential expectations. But there is deeper meaning than either Antonio or Sebastian is aware of. The passions driving the two conspirators are like an evil nightmare whose setting, appropriately enough, is a play within a play staged by Ariel.

In part, this scene derives its suggestiveness from its interconnections with a train of imagery in which, as in Caliban's beautiful speech about the sounds of the island, dream melts into reality and reality into dream:

> Sometimes a thousand twangling instruments
> Will hum about mine ears; and sometimes voices
> That, if I then had waked after long sleep,
> Will make me sleep again; and then, in dreaming,
> The clouds methought would open and show riches
> Ready to drop upon me, that, when I waked,
> I cried to dream again.   (III.iii)

Just as dream and waking here have become interchangeable realms of experience, so everything else in the play seems to be in constant change and flux. The main agent in all these transmutations, who conjures up masques, banquets, and tempests only to make them vanish again as quickly as they appeared, is Ariel. As such this tricksy spirit assumes diverse roles, from a "nymph o'th'sea" to a devouring harpy, while being all the more ominous for his invisible presence (I.ii; III.iii).

The rebirth theme, then, which in the earlier romances denoted a primarily human phenomenon, appears in its more cosmic dimensions in *The Tempest*. The gift of "a second life" (V.i) that Ferdinand receives through his bride, for instance, is only one of the many manifestations of nature's unending metamorphoses, for which Ariel's song contains the central metaphor:

> Full fathom five thy father lies;
>   Of his bones are coral made;

> Those are pearls that were his eyes;
>> Nothing of him that doth fade
> But doth suffer a sea change
> Into something rich and strange.   (I.ii)

With its Hermetic magus as protagonist, *The Tempest*, in thus emphasizing universal metamorphosis, might be said to dramatize one of the central assumptions of the *Corpus Hermeticum*. Here the life-energy animating the "great and perfect Animal the World" also is the cause behind the death of every living thing. At the same time, it is immortal: "Not one thing neither hath become, nor is, nor shall be in the World, dead," despite the endless cycles of "making" and "unmaking":

And every generation of animated flesh, and of the fruit of seed, and of all art energy; those which are diminished, shall be renewed by necessity, and by renewal of Gods, and by course of periodical circle of Nature. For Divine is the whole cosmical composition renovated by Nature.[13]

The Tempest, like the *Corpus Hermeticum*, treats the divine as only a part of nature's unending cycles. While in reach of Prospero's conjuring powers and called from their confines "to enact / [His] present fancies" (IV.i), the mythological creatures of his wedding masque for Miranda and Ferdinand display a distinct will and life of their own once they have been invoked. Watching Juno and Ceres, the magician notices to his surprise how they have begun to "whisper seriously" (IV.i). Appearing like a dream, they are neither more nor less dreamlike than reality itself, an insight summed up in Prospero's well-known speech after they have vanished:

> Our revels now are ended. These our actors,
> As I foretold you, were all spirits and
> Are melted into air, into thin air;
> And, like the baseless fabric of this vision,
> The cloud-capped towers, the gorgeous palaces,
> The solemn temples, the great globe itself,
> Yea, all which it inherit, shall dissolve,
> And, like this insubstantial pageant faded,
> Leave not a rack behind. We are such stuff
> As dreams are made on, and our little life
> Is rounded with a sleep.   (IV.i)

But life, although it may appear to be a dream, is none the less real.[14] Thus Prospero's well-rounded rhetoric suddenly breaks off in an agonized exclamation:

Sir, I am vexed.
Bear with my weakness; my old brain is troubled.

The Tempest, like most of Shakespeare's romances, concludes on a happy note. But there is something almost cynical about it. Sebastian's and Antonio's attempt on the life of Alonso, just as Stephano's on the protagonist, has been foiled by Prospero's magic, but we have every reason to assume that, once back in Italy, Antonio and Sebastian will persevere in their evil schemes. Even within the play itself, they show an unabated determination to renew their onslaught: "The next advantage / Will we take throughly" (III.iii). Sebastian, unlike Alonso, shows few signs of remorse before he is forgiven by Prospero. "The devil speaks in him" (V.i) is his only comment, muttered in an aside, when Prospero decides not to reveal his and Antonio's attempt on Alonso's life. Even more sinister is Antonio's behaviour. In response to Prospero's forgiveness, he withdraws into an Iago-like silence in which, except for a snide remark about Caliban ("a plain fish and no doubt marketable" V.i), he persists to the end of the play. In turn, Prospero's own plans for his return to Milan bode no better for his future than his incorrigible blindness towards such evil. Having lost his dukedom for "being transported / And rapt in secret studies" (I.ii), he now plans to "retire me to my Milan, where / Every third thought shall be my grave" (V.i). *Plus ça change, plus ça reste la même chose.* Yet whenever he is a mere observer without having to take action, Prospero can be sardonically insightful about this rather depressing way of the world. His response to his daughter's enthusiasm when, for the first time, she sees a crowd of human beings points to the grim realities behind the happy endings of Shakespearean post-tragedy:

> MIRANDA O, wonder!
> How many goodly creatures are there here!
> How beauteous mankind is! O brave new world
> That has such people in't!
> PROSPERO 'Tis new to thee. (V.i)

Pericles, it is true, ends on an altogether happy note darkened only by the fact that the rebirths, which so many dramatis personae have come to enjoy in the course of the play, have not eliminated death. Instead of offering such hopes, rebirth has inured those reborn to the ineluctable rounds of life *and* death. The consolations of teleology, where even suffering and evil can be meaningful, ennobling, or at least uplifting, have given way to a more fatalistic appreciation of life. In the face of nature's unending cycles of creation and destruction, the happy ending even of *Pericles*, then, has the gratuitousness of a "Why Not?" As the play makes only too clear, all could just as well have ended in disaster. In an ultimate sense, Perdita's or Pericles' stoical patience and the very capacity to experience a spiritual rebirth are the only refuge in a world of random events, incidental disasters, and fatal errors.

In Shakespeare's later post-tragedies, this fatalistic vision is further darkened by several degrees. Leontes may show repentance,[15] but Polixenes, from whom we would least expect it, displays a despotism in act IV which, at least potentially, is equal to his friend's in act I. As we have seen, *Cymbeline* and *The Tempest* paint an even grimmer picture of the prospects beyond their happy endings. But happy endings they are, something Shakespeare was led to change in the last of his romances, written in collaboration with Fletcher.

The Two Noble Kinsmen

There is reason to agree with Theodore Spencer that Shakespeare's contributions to this play are the work of a man "no longer fully interested in what he was doing."[16] But rather than in a biographical sense, this may be true of the playwright's attitude towards a genre which he had created, brought to perfection, and somehow exhausted. What more indeed, after *The Winter's Tale* and *The Tempest*, could be said about the issues dealt with in these two plays, even by a Shakespeare? As so often in his career, then, the playwright, instead of adding to the obvious, is trying out new directions. Devices which in his own hands had already turned somewhat stereotypic are reduced *ad absurdum* and dismantled. This was made all the easier by his collaboration with John Fletcher, who, together with Francis Beaumont, had for some years been evolving his own brand of romance. In a way, the play reads like a new start. Why then did Shakespeare, at still under fifty years of age, cease to write for the stage? The question is all the more tantalizing in light of *The Two Noble Kinsmen*.

From the start, and in scenes which by scholarly consensus are Shakespeare's, the playwright inverts his own romance pattern. A wedding masque (held in honour of Theseus's marriage to Hippolyta) is something we have been conditioned to expect towards the end of a romance, not at its beginning. And nothing in *The Knight's Tale*, the play's major source, seems to have suggested it. To be sure, there is little more to the masque than elaborate stage directions. These involve Hymen and his nymphs as well as a four-stanza wedding song whose elaborate rebirth symbolism no doubt was the principal reason for introducing it:

> Primrose, first-born child of Ver,
> Merry spring-time's harbinger,
> With harebells dim;
> Oxlips, in their cradles growing,
> Marigolds, on death-beds blowing,
> Lark's-heels trim;

All dear Nature's children sweet
Lie 'fore bride and bridegroom's feet.   (I.i)[17]

The masque amounts to another of Shakespeare's deliberate manoeuvres in anticlimactic audience manipulation. It is suddenly cut short by the arrival of "three Queens in black." As in Chaucer, they ask Theseus's assistance against Creon, who refuses burial to their dead husbands lying before Thebes. But there was little in *The Knight's Tale* to suggest the elaborate brutality of language with which Shakespeare makes their speeches clash with the previous wedding song. Here is the Second Queen addressing Hippolyta:

Lend us a knee;
But touch the ground for us no longer time
Than a dove's motion when the head's plucked off;
Tell him if he i'th'blood-sized field lay swoll'n,
Showing the sun his teeth, grinning at the moon,
What you would do.   (I.i)

Also added to *The Knight's Tale* is another episode which Shakespeare uses in order to introduce the conflict between chance versus human planning. Before Palamon and Arcite, the play's heroes, are as in Chaucer found "Nat fully quike, ne fully dede"[18] from the battle, the playwright gives them an entire scene in which, disgusted with Creon's corruption, they are about to leave the court of Thebes. But Theseus's threat of war against their city makes them adopt an attitude which, ironically, is not too dissimilar to that of Creon, who in Palamon's disapproving words "deifies alone / Voluble chance" (I.ii). Faced with the conflict of having either to serve a tyrant or to betray their country, they leave the decision to circumstance. "Let th'event, / That never erring arbitrator, tell us," Arcite advises, "When we know all ourselves, and let us follow / The becking of our chance" (I.ii).

After Creon has been defeated by Theseus, the first act, in appropriate counterpoint to the wedding which opens it, concludes with a burial. Similar scenes are found in other of Shakespeare's romances. But those being buried here are not to be reborn like Imogen. And nothing in the imagery suggests the kind of natural rebirth associated with Lychorida's and Perdita's tombs in *Pericles*. In the Third Queen's words concluding act I, this world is no more than "a city full of straying streets, / And death's the market place where each one meets" (I.v).

In Fletcher's part of the play about the kinsmen's ill-fated rivalry for the hand of Emilia, we find a change from *The Knight's Tale* which may well have been suggested by Shakespeare. Chaucer's Theseus makes sure that nobody in the tournament between Palamon and Arcite suffers lethal harm. By contrast, his namesake in the play sentences the loser and his retainers to death.

Shakespeare, in his concluding scenes, exploits the resultant suspense to the utter limit. During the single combat, victory at first is repeatedly on Palamon's side. But finally Arcite wins, leaving Palamon and his men to the executioner. Emilia's off-scene comments underscore the thematic implications of these reversals. At first she concludes that Palamon has "the best boding chance." But as quickly as chance itself she reverses her verdict after Arcite's victory:

> I did think
> Good Palamon would miscarry, yet I knew not
> Why I did think so: our reasons are not prophets
> When oft our fancies are.   (V.iii)

Theseus is even more adept at adjusting his pronouncements on life to ever-changing circumstance. "The gods by their divine arbitrament / Have given you this knight" (V.iii), he tells Emilia upon Arcite's victory, while ordering Palamon's instant execution. But never before in Shakespeare's *oeuvre* did Fortune, in the playwright's own words, "play a subtler game" (V.iv). Just as Palamon places his head on the executioner's block, there is "*A great noise within, crying 'Run! Save! Hold!'*" before someone brings news that Arcite has been mortally wounded by falling off his horse. Thus Palamon, like Arcite in the duel, is in a sense reborn into life after narrowly escaping death. But this rebirth is paralleled by a scene in which Arcite, moments later, expires on the stage. "So the deities / Have showed due justice" (V.iv), concludes Theseus, who never misses an opportunity to interpret the most unexpected events as divinely ordained:

> Never Fortune
> Did play a subtler game. The conquered triumphs,
> The victor has the loss; yet in the passage
> The gods have been most equal.   (V.iv)

This metaphysical opportunism is all the more apparent because the quarrel between Mars and Venus, which motivates all these events in Chaucer, has been eliminated. As in *The Knight's Tale*, the divinities are invoked in Palamon's and Arcite's elaborate prayers for help, but their response, which Chaucer dwells on in Homeric detail, is silence. In an ultimate sense, the gods' function in *The Two Noble Kinsmen* is simply to enact nature's duality of creation and destruction. This is most directly stated when Arcite invokes Mars as the "great corrector of enormous times... that heal[s] with blood / The earth when it is sick, and cure[s] the world / O'th'plurisy of people" (V.i). But even Venus, as Palamon goes on enumerating instances of her power, is increasingly associated with death and decay. A seventy-year-old dotard who, "to the scorn of his hoarse throat," warbles love songs offers one instance of how Venus "from eleven to ninety" reigns "In mortal bosoms." Another is provided by the following account of "a man / Of eighty winters" making love to his fourteen-year-old bride:

> 'Twas thy power
> To put life into dust: the aged cramp
> Had screwed his square foot round,
> The gout had knit his fingers into knots,
> Torturing convulsions from his globy eyes
> Had almost drawn their spheres, that what was life
> In him seemed torture. This anatomy
> Had by his young fair fere a boy.   (V.i)

Did Shakespeare, in lines like these as in the play in general, attempt a parody of the rebirth theme? In other words, is *The Two Noble Kinsmen*, as Philip Edwards thinks, Shakespeare's "most cynical assessment of the progress of life since the writing of *Troilus and Cressida*?"[19] If such we choose to call it, then this cynicism merely spells out somewhat more brutally and overtly what is already implied in the earlier post-tragedies. When one person is reborn, another has to die. Where we like to discern the workings of the gods, nature simply follows her inexorable rotations of creation and destruction. Where man strives towards an imagined future, it were better for him simply to accept what is given him by chance. All these conclusions are hinted at in *Pericles*, *Cymbeline*, *The Winter's Tale*, and *The Tempest*, which yet emphasize the positive aspect of the rebirth theme. *The Two Noble Kinsmen*, by contrast, presents the same theme from an almost Schopenhauerian perspective. Appropriately enough, Theseus, metaphysical opportunist and political pragmatist, concludes the play with a final statement about life and destiny. The cynicism here is unlike that of a Pandarus at the end of *Troilus and Cressida*. Instead, it reflects the incisiveness of a poet who did not shy away from spelling out in the most uncompromising terms what he had come to believe before he ceased to write:

> O you heavenly charmers,
> What things you make of us! For what we lack,
> We laugh; for what we have, are sorry; still
> Are children in some kind. Let us be thankful
> For that which is, and with you leave dispute
> That are above our question. Let's go off,
> And bear us like the time.

In sum, the romances probably represent the post-tragic impulse at its most highly developed in Western literature to date. Shakespeare, however, was probably not the first thus to transcend tragedy since Euripides. Nor was he by any means the last to do so before Goethe. A reader of this study, while it was still a manuscript, suggested French classical drama. The author himself felt tempted to include a chapter on Jacobean anti-tragedy in general. But my aim, again, was to give examples, not to write a history of the recurrent transcendence of tragedy in Western literature. At the same time, one might venture to say that wherever this transcendence can be observed, we are dealing by and large with isolated instances rather than with coherent developments.

But why these disconnected outbreaks of a repeated discontent with the tragic, rather than a steady maturing of the impulse from Euripides through, say, Shakespeare and Goethe towards the twentieth century? Part of the answer to this question is an easy one. Shakespeare simply did not know Euripides well enough to take him as a model when, after *Romeo and Juliet*, he started to question the patterns derived from the "tragedies" known to him in his time. It is somewhat different with Goethe. His *Faust*, whose tragic first part evolved, after a lifetime's effort, towards the post-tragic resolution of the second part, owes as much to the model of Shakespeare as to the newly discovered masterpiece of Sanskrit drama, Kālidāsa's *Sacontalá*. But *Faust II*, in turn, remained without major impact upon subsequent literature. This is partly due to misapprehensions about the work, which Goethe feared and which have persisted into our own century.

Goethe's Transcendence of Tragedy

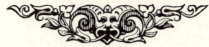

IN "Goethe and the Avoidance of Tragedy," Erich Heller has argued that Faust's tragedy is "that he is incapable of tragedy." There is "no catharsis, only metamorphosis." The protagonist, instead of being "purified in a tragic sense" or "raised above [his] guilt through atonement," simply follows a "never-ending journey of self-exploration." For ultimately, Goethe lacked what tragedy presupposes:

the belief in an external order of things which is ... incomplete without the conformity of the human soul, but would still be more defective without the soul's freedom to violate it.[1]

A belief in "an external order of things," in which even suffering can assume a meaningful role, has indeed been the condition *sine qua non* of our tragic understanding of life ever since the *Oresteia*, Job, and the *Poetics*. In Aeschylus tragic suffering is shown to lead to man's progress in history. In the Book of Job it is presented so as to strengthen our belief in God's ultimate justice. In Aristotle it is extolled for exerting a cathartic effect on the audience. And if the greatest modern theoretician of tragedy had lived to see *Faust II*, he too would presumably have criticized the play for lacking a truly tragic dimension. For Hegel, in synthesizing its classical and Judaeo-Christian components, described the tragic as a mode which, by its very presentation of human suffering, hints at the "vision of eternal justice" to be reached in the providential dialectics of world history.[2]

Goethe's *Faust*, of course, inverts and negates rather than follows such ideas. But are we entitled simply to attribute this fact to the poet's intellectual confusion and the "inevitable contradiction of the undedicated mind and heart"?[3] It is evident in Shakespeare and Euripides that the avoidance of the tragic can be a more dedicated pursuit than the often blind adherence to its compelling matrix, and Goethe left ample testimony to a similar endeavour. The whole question of tragedy, he wrote in a letter of 31 October 1831, is a delicate point:

I was not born to be a tragic poet, as my nature is conciliatory. Consequently the pure tragic case, which really must be fundamentally irreconcilable, cannot interest me, and in this after all so utterly trivial world, the irreconcilable seems to me quite absurd.[4]

The statement, made five months before Goethe's death, reads like a retrospective comment on the gradual evolution of *Faust*.

The legend of Doctor Faustus, Goethe's main source for the play, is tragic in the Christian punitive sense. As such it gives us the retributive counterpart to God's benevolent justice as displayed in the Book of Job. Doctor Faustus, a Renaissance magus whose occult and philosophical pursuits have led him to rebel against the Christian faith, forms a pact with the Devil and is damned. Goethe reinforces the biblical analogy by prefacing his play with a "Prologue in Heaven," whose heavenly courtroom scenario was directly inspired by the opening of Job. Exposed to the temptations of the Devil, Faust will be given a single lifetime to prove himself right or wrong. Goethe's Faust, of course, does neither, and the fusion of the stories of Job and Doctor Faustus results in a transcendence of the world-view implicit in both. Unlike Job, Faust is never vindicated by the Lord, who does not return to the play after his brief appearance in the prologue. Unlike the Doctor Faustus of the *Volksbuch* and the puppet plays, Faust is not damned but raised to heaven, although he never repents his sins. It seems deliberately ironic that Goethe, in the scene in which angels fight with devils for the possession of Faust's soul, has Mephisto incur the fate which the prologue has led us to expect for the protagonist. The hunter has become the hunted, and Mephisto, not Faust, is about to become a second Job: "What's happening to me! – I'm like Job, / All covered in boils, shuddering at myself" (11809–10).

The Discovery of Kālidāsa's *Sacontalá*

It is difficult to think of any major work of Western literature, including *Oedipus at Colonnus*, which could have served Goethe as a model for this transformation of the Job-Faustus myths. By contrast, an Indian drama by Kālidāsa seems to have played that very role in the gradual evolution of the drama. Goethe first read *Sacontalá* in Forster's 1791 German translation from the English version by Sir William Jones (1789). In an immediate outburst of enthusiasm, Goethe wrote to Jacobi:

If I wish to invoke the blossoms of Spring, the fruits of Autumn,
And all that charms and delights, that satisfies and nourishes;

> If I wish to invoke heaven and earth in one word,
> I name thee Sacontalá – and that says it all.[5]

We have Goethe's repeated testimony that *Sacontalá* overwhelmed him in an irresistible way, that it exerted "the greatest influence ... on his entire life," that he came to know it more or less by heart, and that it determined a whole epoch in his development. "When I first became aware of it," he wrote on 9 October 1830,

> it aroused in me such enthusiasm, attracted me so much, that I could not leave off studying it, and even felt myself driven to the impossible venture of appropriating it – be it only in part – for the German stage. Through these efforts, although fruitless, I have become so precisely familiar with the most estimable work, it has marked such an epoch in the course of my life, it has so much become a part of me, that not in thirty years have I ever again looked at either the English or the German version.[6]

Although Goethe failed to adapt *Sacontalá* to the stage, he successfully integrated its general theme, its overall structure, and many of its details into the second part of *Faust*. Here the cosmological test situation of the closed, legalistically determined universe found in Goethe's immediate sources gradually yields to a concept of life as quest and self-purification, both continuing beyond death. Like King Dushmanta in *Sacontalá*, Faust in the first part acts like a sex-obsessed egocentric who gets his beloved with child and then abandons her. Yet subsequently he learns self-detachment and compassion. This is achieved in pursuit of the beloved who, preceding the protagonist, is raised to heaven. But before the quest is fulfilled and the lovers reunited, Faust (like Dushmanta) must expose himself to the forces of the underworld and prove himself in action. Goethe's own short summary of *Sacontalá* alludes to many of these resemblances between the two plays:

> Feminine purity, guiltless yielding, a man's forgetfulness, a mother's isolation, a father and mother united through the son; the most natural of circumstances, yet here poetically elevated to the realms of wonders, that hover like fecund clouds between heaven and earth, and an altogether common drama of nature performed by gods and by the children of gods.[7]

"Feminine Purity," "guiltless yielding," and "a mother's isolation" are as appropriate to *Sacontalá* as they are to *Faust*. Equally applicable to both is "a man's forgetfulness": King Dushmanta forgets his beloved under the spell of a curse, as Faust forgets Gretchen under the phantasmagorical spells of Mephisto's *Walpurgisnacht*. Or consider the scene in which Faust and Helena rejoice about their union achieved through Euphorion's birth (9699ff). Here, although in a different context and with consequences other than in Kālidāsa's play, we have a second version of the motif, "a father and mother united through the son." And what more appropriate summing-up could one give of the general atmosphere of *Faust II* than that provided by the remainder of Goethe's *Sacontalá* interpretation, particularly regarding the play's last scene? To this one might add Goethe's characterization of Kālidāsa, most of which again could apply to the author of *Faust*:

Here the poet appears to us in his highest capacity, as the representative of the most natural condition, of the most cultivated way of life, of the purest ethical striving, of the most worthy majesty, and of the most earnest contemplation of God. But at the same time he remains so much lord and master of his creation that he can risk vulgar and absurd contrasts, which must nevertheless be regarded as necessary connecting parts of the whole structure.[8]

Aristotelian versus Sanskrit Poetics

As in the case of *Faust*, this "structure" of Kālidāsa's play may, of course, be disappointing to readers looking for the logical motivation and unity which Western critics since Aristotle tend to consider the prime attribute of drama or of literature in general. Neither *Faust* nor *Sacontalá* can boast "one action, a complete whole, with its several incidents so closely connected that the transposal or withdrawal of any one of them will disjoin and dislocate the whole." At best their plots might be called "episodic," which in Aristotle's vocabulary characterizes the "worst" kind of action.[9] Matthew Arnold, in saying that *Faust* "judged as a whole [is] defective,"[10] echoes the discontent felt by many readers, while A.B. Keith, author of a standard work on Sanskrit drama, criticizes his subject for similar deficiencies.[11]

Here, however, the poets themselves differ from their critics. Goethe emphatically agreed with Eckermann that the several sections of *Faust* all represent "autonomous little microcosms, which, closed up in themselves, do influence each other, yet have little common concern."[12] Thus the plot of *Faust*, and of part II in particular, which may have been influenced by another Oriental "source," *The Thousand and One Nights*,[13] seems to be completely at odds with Aristotelian precepts. As Goethe concluded in speaking of his great work, "the more incommensurable a poetic work and the more incomprehensible to reason, the better."[14]

Although we lack comparable statements by Kālidāsa, we know that, like other Sanskrit playwrights, he subscribed to the poetics of Bharata's *Nātya-śāstra* or *The Art of the Play* (circa first century BC). Bharata had no need to take his stand against anything like an Aristotelian critical tradition; hence, his statements lack the anti-rationalist vehemence of Goethe's. Bharata discusses various types of action and devices of plot structure. But instead of the unity of action, he emphasizes the unity of spirit and tone (*rasa*)[15] and defines drama in the most general terms, not as the "imitation of ... one action, a complete whole"[16] but as the "representation of conditions and situations."[17] The range of situations he prescribes seems to preclude the arrangement of the story in the neat causal chains of Aristotle's anthropocentric universe.

In the drama, Bharata writes, "there is no exclusive representation of you or of the gods: for the drama is a representation of the States (*bhāvānukīrtana*) of the three worlds." The same emphasis is evident in Bharata's discussion of the various psychological states (*bhāvas*) and sentiments (arising from the former). These, rather than plot structure and character portrayal, the highest criteria by Western standards, are the most crucial single elements of Sanskrit drama. Most of them – the "erotic sentiment," for instance, with its "two bases: union and separation," the basic theme of *Sacontalá* – can be presented in the framework of a rationally coherent plot. Others, however, such as "fainting," "paralysis," "insanity," "epilepsy," "sleeping," and "dreaming,"[18] some of which again appear in Kālidāsa's play, do, if portrayed in the manner of Sanskrit drama (or of Goethe's *Faust*), disrupt the simplistic psychological motivation required by such coherence.

Sanskrit drama generally, and *Sacontalá* in particular, rarely tries to rationalize the irrational. When it does, it more often than not defeats its own ends by the glaring illogicality of its premises. When King Dushmanta enters a hermitage during a hunt and spies the young Sacontalá, his immediate response, like Faust's when he first sees Gretchen, is sexual infatuation. Kālidāsa, although implying some approval of the king, depicts these opening scenes with obvious zest and gusto. Even before she meets Dushmanta, Sacontalá, her maturing figure bursting through her girlish dress, is associated with the phallic imagery which is ubiquitous in the play. Here is one of the jokes her playmates like to make at her expense:

> PRIYAMVADÁ O my Sacontalá, let us remain some time in this shade.
> SACONTALÁ Why here particularly?
> PRIYAMVADÁ Because the Amra tree seems wedded to you, who are graceful as the blooming creeper which twines round it.

The king, who shortly afterwards emerges from his hiding place behind a tree, seems to express the author's own bemused attitude in sexual matters when he hears that Sacontalá is the daughter of a sage who had been successfully seduced by a nymph:

> ANUSÚYÁ ... In the bloom of the vernal season, Causica [the sage], beholding the beauty of the celestial nymph, and wafted by the gale of desire – [She stops and looks modest.]
> DUSHMANTA I now see the whole.[19]

Yet *Sacontalá* is no mere pastoral romance. Before long, the king and his beloved find themselves helpless prey to a passion which threatens to rob them of sleep, health, and reason. The ensuing action – a hasty marriage, the king's departure, and Sacontalá's pregnancy – seems to prepare the ground for tragedy. Distracted by grief, Sacontalá neglects the law of hospitality and incurs a hermit's curse that Dushmanta will forget her. It is only because of Priyamvadá's last-minute intervention that the insulted hermit mitigates his curse: Dushmanta will recover his memory of Sacontalá once he sees the ring he gave her before his departure.

All this, of course, would not meet even the Aristotelian standard of a "likely impossibility."[20] Rather, it is full of those improbable incidents which, according to the *Poetics*, should have no place in a dramatic plot. On her way to the royal court, Sacontalá loses the ring in the Ganges. As a result, Dushmanta fails to remember her. Yet before the ring is retrieved from the belly of a fish to restore the king's memory, Sacontalá is raised into the sky by a "body of light, in a female shape."[21] Celestial powers must intervene again in order to save the king from the distraction caused by the loss of his beloved. Indra's charioteer Mátali challenges Dushmanta to fight the demons in the God's flying chariot; after the king has successfully performed his mission, he is escorted into the heavenly hermitage on Mount Hémacúta. Here, where the Lord of Creation does penance with his consort in the company of human hermits, Dushmanta is finally reunited with his beloved.

Kālidāsa's Influence on Goethe

The similarities between the opening scenes of *Sacontalá* and *Faust I*, much of which was completed before Goethe discovered Kālidāsa in 1791, are of course merely coincidental. Moreover, Kālidāsa's actual influence, unlike the enthusiasm Goethe felt for the Indian poet, was far from instantaneous. Instead it paralleled and reinforced a gradual process of self-liberation from "the old, crude folk-tale"[22] of Doctor Faustus which had held Goethe spellbound for several decades. Characteristically, he had been attracted to the Doctor Faustus legend because he had come to see the Renaissance magus as an alter ego of his youthful self, dabbling in "mystico-cabbalistic alchemy."[23] From the very beginning, Goethe's *Faust* testifies to the poet's endeavours to transcend the fatal implications of a mythic destiny he had come to recognize as his own. Prompted by the decapitation of a child murderess in Frankfurt, Goethe, in the *Urfaust*, transferred the tragic fate from the protagonist to his beloved. Yet even in this adapted form the ending seemed unacceptable to him. Suppressing the gruesome dungeon scene of the *Urfaust*, Goethe concluded *Faust: A Fragment* (1790) well before Gretchen's execution was fully in sight.

Faust: A Fragment is the abortive product of a spiritual deadlock, and it took Goethe nearly a decade "to make the old coagulated material melt again."[24]

Yet even then he found himself unable to eliminate its tragic conception, which threatened his own existence more than ever. On 9 December 1797, Goethe wrote to Schiller,

Indeed I don't understand myself sufficiently to know whether I could write a real tragedy; but I am frightened simply at the undertaking, and am almost convinced that I could destroy myself in the mere attempt.[25]

"Several tragic scenes ... in prose," in particular the scene of Gretchen in the dungeon, now appeared to Goethe "totally unbearable." Hence part of his work towards the publication of *Faust I* (1808) was to mitigate their impact by rewriting them in verse. Moreover, Goethe already anticipated that, despite Gretchen's tragic death, the end of the play was not to be tragic. Whatever he added to the *Fragment* was subordinated to what, paralleling the Sanskrit concept of *rasa*, he called the "spirit and tone of the whole," which in itself he saw as open-ended. All three of the "Epilogue Poems" (written sometime between 1797 and 1800) emphasize the same notion by referring either to the dreamlike process of creativity which inspired the play or to the open-endedness of life itself. "Adieu," the last of them, describes the same openness as "the way to clarity" out of the tragic impasse. In a "Schematic Survey of the Whole Poem," dated 11 April 1800, Goethe translated this metaphysical rejection of a closed and tragic concept of life into a poetics which anticipates that of many twentieth-century poets.[26] Form to him is no longer an ideational principle to be imposed on matter by way of filling out "the deficiencies of Nature" (Aristotle)[27] but a by-product of content ("Gehalt bringt die Form mit")[28] or, in Charles Olson's more recent formula, "never more than an extension of content."[29]

Goethe must have had similar intentions when, probably around 1800, he wrote the "Prologue in Heaven," which sets the Biblical stage for Faust's un-Christian salvation. The poet uses no lesser figure than God himself to predict this untragic end of the play:

> Even though he serves me now but confusedly,
> I shall soon lead him into the light.
> ...
> In his dark impulses a good man
> Is well aware of the right path.   (308–9, 328–9)

Along this way into the light, Mephistopheles himself will be a major help to the protagonist.[30] Unlike the "repulsive monster" of the *Urfaust*, Mephisto gradually assumes the function of preventing man from falling into lethargy in his search for self-perfection (332–43). Given the premises of Faust's subsequent wager with the Devil, this makes the latter's impotence complete: in order to win his bet, Mephisto would have to reduce the protagonist to the very state of lethargy he is there to prevent (1692–3). Goethe was fully aware that he had manoeuvred Mephisto into an inescapable impasse, or that Faust, as he puts it, "imposes a condition on the Devil from which everything ensues."[31]

Although *Sacontalá* may have been a major impulse behind all this, the play's impact on the creation of *Faust* was not to become fully obvious before the publication of its second part in 1832. At some time between 1795 and 1798, however, Goethe composed the "Prelude in the Theatre," which was directly inspired by *Sacontalá*. Whereas Kālidāsa's total influence on *Faust* has never been investigated, the fact that Goethe drew on *Sacontalá* for his prelude is one of the ubiquitous, though for the most part unverified commonplaces ·of Goethe scholarship.[32] It is no wonder that the influence has also been denied. In turn, Alwin Binder, in his book-length study of the prelude,[33] seems to reflect the attitude of most critics in acknowledging the possibility of such influence without bothering to argue the case in detail. Binder recognizes that the prelude points not so much to *Faust I* (1808), in which it first appeared, as to the play's second part. Yet he pays little heed to the possibility that the crucial lines thus projecting into the future were directly inspired by the following lines from *Sacontalá*:

Water was the first work of the Creator; and Fire receives the oblations ordained by law; the Sacrifice is performed with solemnity; the Two Lights of heaven distinguish time; the subtle Ether, which is the vehicle of sound, pervades the universe; the Earth is the natural parent of all increase; and by Air all things breathing are animated: may I'SA, the God of Nature, apparent in these eight forms, bless and sustain you![34]

Preparing the audience for an uncommon cosmological spectacle, Goethe, like Kālidāsa before him, quickly reviews the whole of creation, naming the four elements and invoking the sun, the moon, and the stars:

> Avail yourselves of the great and little lights of heaven,
> With the stars you may be lavish;
> There is no shortage of beasts and birds,
> Of water, fire, or walls of rock.
> So on this tiny boarded stage
> You may traverse the whole ring of creation,
> And make your way with leisurely speed
> From heaven through the world to hell.   (235–42)

Other similarities between the two preludes are equally obvious. In both there is a discussion of the relationship between audience and spectacle, while a director emphasizes the need to please the audience, urging the participants to get on with the action.

There are other themes which, in partial indebtedness to Kālidāsa, link the prelude with the epilogue poems. In rejecting tragedy and banishing the Devil, Goethe in "Adieu," his eyes directed towards the East ("Nach Osten sei der lichte Blick gewandt!"),[35] proposes a life of open-ended self-realization through "love and friendship" and an art which encourages man in this pursuit. Similarly, the poet in the prelude remembers the time when in full responsiveness to nature he yearned for a life of godlike "love and friendship." His words here read like another thematic précis of *Sacontalá* or a preview of *Faust II* as it was then beginning to evolve under Kālidāsa's influence:

> Nay, lead me to the quiet strait of heaven,
> Where pure joy blossoms for the poet alone;
> Where Love and Friendship create and nurture
> With godlike hands our heart's blessing.   (63-6)

How much of *Faust II* had been planned or written down when Goethe composed the prelude and the epilogue poems? The latter clearly presuppose a second part, which Goethe first discussed *expressis verbis* in his "Schematic Survey of the Whole Poem" of 11 April 1800. Shortly afterwards he composed "Helena in the Middle Ages," which was later integrated into the third act of part II. Records of a conversation on 3 August 1815 also show that Goethe, as early as 1800, may already have been drafting parts of the play's last act. Declaring that "much [of *Faust II*] was already completed," the poet, when questioned about the ending, replied: "That I am not saying, may not say, but it too is already finished, and very good and grandiose it has turned out: of my best period." When asked about the meaning of "the Mothers," Goethe, commenting on the final plan for his drama, simply referred to "my secret."[36] It may well be that part of that secret was Kālidāsa's *Sacontalá*, which the poet, so far as we know, never mentioned in connection with *Faust*.

Its solution *in nuce* is contained in the famous lines proclaiming Faust's salvation:

> Saved from evil
> Is this noble member of the spirit world.
> "He who strives and ever strives,
> Him we can redeem."
> And if Love from on high
> Has also taken his part,
> The blessed host will meet him
> With a warm welcome.   (11934-41)

These lines, Goethe said in 1831, "contain the key to Faust's salvation." Yet his attempts to relate them to the Christian concept of grace or to point out the "clearly delineated Christian and ecclesiastical figures and concepts" which supposedly give the last scene a "pleasurably limiting form and solidity" are misleading rather than elucidating. They seem prompted by the same defensiveness towards his readers which on other occasions could provoke Goethe to react more angrily yet also more truthfully. Such an instance was provided by F. Förster's conjecture that Mephisto would ultimately be made to confess that a good human being is well aware of the right path in his heart's impulses. In reply, Goethe shook his head, protesting: "No, that would be pure Enlightenment. Faust ends up an old man, and in old age we become mystics."[37]

Goethe noted that, in contrast to *Faust I*, that "barbaric composition" based on the "old, crude folk-tale," everything in the second part was raised to a "higher and nobler level," the whole taking place in "higher regions" approaching "the ideal." The poet's view of *Sacontalá* as a spectacle enacted in "realms of wonders, that hover like fecund clouds between heaven and earth," suggests the model for such elevation. It is true that Goethe did not completely eliminate the Judaeo-Christian framework from *Faust* and that, instead of the Indian myths with which he was familiar, he availed himself of Greek mythology in order to exorcise the "monkish barbarism" of his sources. Still, the ideational sequence in which he displayed his "perceptions and impressions"[38] finds an analogue in *Sacontalá* rather than in works of classical or Judaeo-Christian origin.

Sophocles' Oedipus, whose ultimate apotheosis is probably the closest parallel to Faust's salvation within Western drama, is the obvious case in point. As Goethe himself pointed out, Oedipus is not apotheosized because he has purified himself in action, but despite his "demonic constitution" and the "sinister vehemence of his existence."[39] By contrast, Faust has earned his apotheosis by turning from his sex-obsessed egocentricity to the service of others. Nor does his development tally with any of the diverse Christian doctrines concerning divine grace versus good works. Whether these declare man unable to do good (Rom 7:18) without the free gift of divine grace (St Augustine's *gratia gratis data*) or capable, at least in part, of earning God's grace through good works, they all share a general moralistic framework for judging man in terms of good and evil. By contrast, Faust's development is primarily psychological and takes place largely in a realm beyond good and evil.

This, in particular, has attracted the disapproval of Erich Heller, for whom Faust, as we saw, is "not raised above [his] guilt through atonement, but [enters], as it were, a biologically, not morally, new phase of life, healed by oblivion and restored to strength through the sleep of the just."[40] It would be more appropriate to say, in Aldous Huxley's terms, that Goethe, like Homer before him, "refused to treat [his] theme tragically" and instead "preferred to tell the Whole Truth."[41] For what more devastating, almost sardonic vision of the ever-implicit evil in human action could there be than that provided by the last act of *Faust II*? It is customary to quote Lynkeus's famous lines as Goethe's own credo:

> You fortunate eyes,
> All you ever saw,
> Whatever it may be
> Was yet so beautiful! (11300–3)

Far less often is it remembered that immediately afterwards the same eyes are made to see a hell of Faust's own creation. Philemon and Baucis, the good-natured old couple, are burned to death in their hut by Faust's henchmen because they refuse to surrender their little chapel to the colonizer's capitalist greed. Such evil is equalled only by the futility implicit in Faust's last endeavours. The blind old hero experiences his life's fulfilment at the sound of shovels which, he believes, are performing the work of colonization but which are, in fact, digging his grave.

Goethe was no doubt as aware of the deep-seated irony in these scenes as of the callousness with which his protagonist pursues his goal despite worry and guilt. Of the four allegorical old women, Guilt (like Want and Distress) does not even gain access to Faust's palace. Care, although she robs the hero of his eyesight, only heightens the colonizer's enthusiasm. As Heller notes, the opening scene of *Faust II*, where the hero relieves himself of his guilt-ridden conscience in sleep, sets this new tone of anti-tragic ruthlessness, yet hardly in the escapist and confused spirit which Heller attributes to the poet.

Goethe's universe resembles neither the courtroom cosmology of Job nor the *zoon politicon* congregation of rational citizens for whom Aristotle wrote his *Poetics*. Analogously, his general conception of drama has little in common with the shock-treatment display of passion and violence through which tragedy should purge spectators of such irrationalities. Goethe, commenting on Aristotle's *Poetics*, denies that art can teach and redefines catharsis in a way which seems closer to the Sanskrit concept of *śānta* than to the Aristotelian principle. What Indian aesthetics characterizes as "a sense of wholeness,"[42] inducing a state of serenity in the spectator, becomes a "reconciliating rounding off" to Goethe.[43]

Moreover, Goethe finds it difficult to see nature and fate in the anthropomorphic terms ascribed to them by the tragic humanism of Greek and biblical origin. As he explained to Eckermann, there is nobody in the opening scene of *Faust II* to sit in judgment on the hero, and "the question as to whether or not he was deserving [of his fate] is not raised, as it might be perhaps by human judges."[44] Nature, as embodied in Ariel and his elves, is indifferent to human right or wrong. Out of the infinite compassion of her regenerative force she brings the hero back to life: "Be he saintly or evil, / They pity the luckless man" (4617–20).

From the very beginning of *Faust II*, Goethe avoids the tragic falsification of life by turning the tragic destiny of the original Doctor Faustus into a quest involving the hero's death and rebirth. Considering the agonies Faust had suffered on account of Gretchen, Goethe could, as he pointed out later, "help himself in no other way" than to consider the protagonist as destroyed "and to rekindle a new life from this apparent death."[45] As elsewhere in the play, this healing journey takes its course through dream and the unconscious. After Faust has fainted at the sudden disappearance of Helena, for instance, he is made to undergo a similar shamanistic initiation of "stirb und werde." Here his dreams, in which the Eternal Feminine appears to him in the shape of Leda, beloved of Zeus and mother of Helen, are described by the newly born Homunculus who stands beside the sleeping hero (6903ff).

Both of these scenes seem to draw on similar ones in *Sacontalá*. Like Faust, King Dushmanta is paralysed by grief at the loss of his beloved and, like Faust at the disappearance of Helena, falls into a swoon. If imagined in the setting of a Greek play, the king, who is distracted to the point of madness, could well be expected to mutilate himself, like a second Oedipus. But Sanskrit drama avoids the grand gestures of tragic defiance. Although temporarily disturbed by worry and guilt, Dushmanta continues his search for peace (*sānta*), which, paralleling its equivalent in Indian aesthetics or Goethe's "reconciliating rounding off,"[46] also constitutes the ultimate effect the play should exert on the audience.

And whoever searches can be saved. It is in this sense, not in terms of either good works or divine *gratia gratis data*, that a number of elfin and mythological creatures come to the king's assistance; it is through this never-ceasing pursuit of self-enlightenment, not because of divine providence, that Faust's salvation, like Dushmanta's, is preordained:

> In his dark impulses a good man
> Is well aware of the right path.   (318–19)

> He who strives and ever strives,
> Him we can redeem.   (11936–7)

In both *Faust II* and *Sacontalá*, guardian spirits herald such salvation. Like Ariel hovering around the unconscious Faust, Misracési assures the audience that Dushmanta "will speedily be roused – I heard the nymph Dévajanani consoling Sacontalá in these words: 'As the gods delight in their portion of sacrifices, thus wilt thou soon be delighted by the love of thy husband.' "[47]

Misracési is only one of many spirits from Kālidāsa's colourful supernatural world, which, along with Shakespeare's, must have exerted a powerful influence on Goethe. While Kālidāsa's hero repeatedly fights the demons, Goethe's descends into the underworld or exposes himself to Mephisto's phantasmagoria. As the elves take pity on Faust, so "even the trees ... and the birds sympathize" with Dushmanta. The wood-nymphs show similar concern for Sacontalá when she is about to begin her journey in search of her lost husband:

CHORUS *of invisible* WOODNYMPHS May her way be attended with prosperity! May propitious breezes sprinkle, for her delight, the odoriferous dust of rich blossoms! May pools of clear water, green with the leaves of the lotos, refresh her as she walks! and may shady branches be her defence from the scorching sunbeams! [*All listen with admiration.*][48]

As in *Faust*, nature's life-giving forces are a central theme in *Sacontalá*; in both plays it is through love that man becomes an integral part of them. The phallic imagery of the creeper clinging to the tree emphasizes Sacontalá's and Dushmanta's sexual infatuation; an earlier mention of "the nuptials even of plants" seems to bestow nature's blessing upon their union in advance. And Sancontalá matures into marriage by her ever-growing love of nature. Priyamvadá predicts the heroine's nuptials from the fact that her "nurture of these plants has prospered," while the sage Canna, anticipating Sacontalá's reunion with the king, decides to stage a ritual ceremony in which he will marry Sacontalá's "favourite plant to the bridegroom Amra, who sheds fragrance near her."[49] Similarly, Faust's search for the regenerative forces of nature takes its impulse from distinctly sexual yearnings for the feminine principle, even before he meets Gretchen.

Faust's Quest for the Eternal Feminine

Steeped in Hermetic lore, Faust knows that it is his rational mind, not his unconscious, which is closed ("Die Geisterwelt ist nicht verschlossen; / Dein Sinn ist zu, dein Herz ist tot!" 443–4). But his self-questioning already suggests the right answer:

> Where can I grasp hold of you, infinite Nature?
> You breasts, where? You springs of all life,
> At which hang the heaven and the earth. (455–7)

These verses and the yearnings they express were, of course, conceived long before Goethe read *Sacontalá*. But it was only after he had done so that he devised the story of their fulfilment. Thus Faust's love quest for Helena and Gretchen closely follows Dushmanta's search for Sacontalá. Contemplating an image of his beloved, who, like Gretchen, has been raised into heaven by a "body of light, in a female shape," Dushmanta, "stark mad with love and affliction," begins to resemble a traveller thirsting "for a false appearance of water on the sandy desert."[50] In a similar scene, which prefigures the conclusion of the entire drama, Faust believes he recognizes Gretchen in a delicate, bright wisp of cloud (10055) rising into the sky:

> Like the beauty of the soul the charming image intensifies,
> Does not disperse. It rises into the higher air
> And draws away with it the best of my inner self.   (10064-6)

Unlike Kālidāsa, Goethe introduces this figure, beckoning the hero to follow him into heaven, as the last of many who, in a long and meandering search for the "springs of all life," become the guides of the quester. Almost all of these are female; an exception like Chiron completely fails to understand the hero's quest, attributing to craziness what Manto, the nymph who finally leads Faust into the underworld, celebrates with the highest praise: "Him I love, who covets the impossible" (7488; compare 1447). Thus the transformation of tragedy into a shamanistic quest for the Eternal Feminine goes hand in hand with the gradual disappearance of the masculine pantheon of Christian mythology, as presented in the "Prologue in Heaven."

To an Indian poet and his audience, the Eternal Feminine was a traditionally accepted concept. Kālidāsa therefore finds it sufficient to show how the king enters a new spiritual life through his love for a single woman. A passing reference to the "father of the immortals" and his divine consort on Mount Hémacúta,[51] the scene of the play's last act, is sufficient to remind the audience of the wider mythological implications of this love story. Lacking any such beliefs or mythologems in his immediate cultural heritage, Goethe would have met with little understanding if he had replaced Western with Indian mythology. Instead he causes Faust to undergo a long and painful process of reinitiation into the world of the Mothers. In his quest Faust is led by a series of mythological figures inhabiting a "fairyland" which he enters in a dream and which, as Homunculus puts it, will restore him to life (7054-5): among these are Helen's mother Leda, whom Faust sees in the dream described by Homunculus; the Sphinxes, imperturbably enthroned above war and peace; and Manto, the daughter of Tiresias, who "inwardly dreaming" stays in place while time circles around her (6906ff, 7245ff, 7471, 7481).

Although Goethe never finished (or included) the scene in which Faust as a "second Orpheus"[52] visits the realm of Persephone, the ultimate aim of this descent is clearly prefigured by Faust's previous quest for the Mothers. In these, creation seems only one step removed from what mystics throughout the world have described as the "void of inexhaustible contents"[53] or as "the Cause of all things [which] yet Itself is nothing"[54]:

> Mothers, who enthroned
> In the illimitable, dwell in eternal solitude,

And yet companionably. Around your heads hover
The images of life, active, yet lifeless.
What once existed in all its shining brilliance
Is there astir; for it seeks eternal being.
And you it is who divide it up, almighty powers,
Assigning some to the tent of day, the rest to the vault of
night. (6427–34)

Even in terms of Indian philosophy, this concept of *śūnyatā* or the "void of inexhaustible contents" is given a near-perfect formulation when Faust, in response to Mephisto's horror tales concerning the unutterably frightening nothingness of the Mothers' realm, expresses the hope of finding the All in this nothingness ("In deinem Nichts hoff' ich das All zu finden" 6256).

Throughout *Faust* the notion of a feminine source of creation close to the ultimate nothingness is reinforced by allusions to the "breasts [or] springs of all life," "Mother Night," "Mother Earth," the "miracle womb of the depth," or to Rhea, "high mother of all the gods" (456, 1351, 7621, 8665, 8969–70). The latter, along with Plutarch's mention of certain mother goddesses in the city of Engyion,[55] probably provided Goethe with the immediate model for this concept. Its fusion with the notion of an ultimate "void of inexhaustible contents," however, was inspired by different sources. One such source may have been the Sanskrit concept of *śūnyatā*, which in terms of Goethe's development came to reinforce similar notions such as the Cabbalistic Ensoph or "Orphic night."[56] As early as 1770, Goethe, engrossed in the study of the occult, had formulated a Latin pantheistic credo affirming the ultimate oneness of God and nature. This belief was probably confirmed by the ideas of the influential Hermeticist Sincerus Renatus, who had described the same notion in such terms as "the great center of the compass of time and eternity" or simply as "nothingness."[57]

Compared with Dushmanta's pursuit of Sacontalá, Faust's quest is a meandering odyssey involving several guides and digressions. In some of these, other dramatis personae simultaneously undergo the protagonist's destiny. While Faust descends to the world of the Mothers, for instance, Homunculus tries to find self-realization in pursuit of Galatea. This quest culminates in his transfiguration in act II, which seems to presage Faust's own ascent into celestial regions. As Homunculus precedes the protagonist by becoming one with the fiery world of Eros, so Euphorion, Faust's own son, parallels the protagonist's quest by entering the dark realm of Persephone in act III. Moreover, acts II and III prefigure the last by concluding in paeans of love, life, and, more specifically, everlasting Nature, the Dionysian mysteries, and Eros, "who began everything" (10031, 10089, 8479).

Kālidāsa's influence, clearly apparent in the general thematic structure of *Faust* though less so in its episodic digressions, again becomes explicit at these crucial links. As already pointed out, the director's evocation of heaven, earth, and the four elements in "Prelude in the Theatre" was probably prompted by the prelude to *Sacontalá*. The four elements are again evoked at the end of act II by the Chorus "All-Alle" ("Hochgefeiert seid allhier, / Element' ihr alle vier!" 8486-7) and more concretely though indirectly at the end of act III. Here the Chorus describes a scene of thunder, rivers, animals, humans, and divinities, precisely prefiguring the final scene of *Faust*.

Just as the careers of Homunculus and Euphorion provide reinforcing parallels to Faust's, so a third dramatis persona offers a kind of comical sub-plot version of the protagonist's search for the Eternal Feminine. In the course of *Faust II*, Mephisto has turned into an ever-more vitriolic misogynist. In one of the funniest scenes of the entire drama, he is distracted from his pursuit of Faust's soul by his homoerotic longings for the rescuing angels. Despite these inclinations, however, he is forced to embrace the feminine principle and, what is worse, to assume its negative elementary character by donning the shape of one of the monsters called Phorkyads. While the comical effect pro-vided by this poetic justice is more than obvious, Mephisto's enforced quest is not without more serious analogues to Faust's. According to a statement Goethe made in angry reaction to the incomprehension of his readers, Mephisto was even meant to find eventual "forgiveness and mercy" before the Lord.

In the play, Mephisto's celestial ascent stops short when he feels the pangs of love. Yet even within this limited scope, his development provides colourful contrasts and parallels to Faust's. Thus, in "Classical Walpurgis Night" he at first reacts with fear and confusion before the monsters which fill the protago-nist with admiration and wonder. Guided by the Dryad, however, he learns to approach the Phorkyads with the same feelings of awe (7967ff) with which the protagonist approached the Mothers (6264ff). Mephisto's sudden change of attitude and his subsequent delight at the sight of the Phorkyads (7993) contain apparently deliberate echoes of the earlier scenes in which Faust stands in respectful wonder before the Sphinxes (7181-2) or, about to descend to the Mothers, describes this "awe" as the best part of man (6272). Little wonder, then, that the Phorkyads, as they are gradually revealed to Mephistopheles, share certain characteristics with Faust's Mothers. In Mephisto's view they resemble Ops and Rhea (7989), while in their own they are

> Sunk in solitude and deepest night
> ...
> Born in night, kin of the nocturnal,
> Quite unknown to all, and almost to ourselves. (8000, 8010-11)

In learning to accept what he previously feared, Mephisto manages to free himself from the hellish superstitions of "monkish barbarism"[58] which falsified his true ancestry. By becoming a Phorkyad himself, he recognizes that, instead of being the evil antipode to God, he is the "much beloved son of Chaos" (8027) and as such an integral part of creation.

By expanding the thematic pursuit of the Eternal Feminine to include its negative elementary character – as in Helen, the Sphinxes, Lamies, Sirens, Phorkyads, and, in a semi-comical way, in Mephistopheles-Phorkyad – Goethe again went beyond *Sacontalá*. He was well aware that Kālidāsa would only have added to the obvious in trying to show that the creative principle as embodied in God's wife, or on a lower level in Sacontalá, does not appear in a benign aspect alone. As frequently as he defended the horrific as an integral part of the Faustian world,[59] he invoked the inclusiveness of Indian mythology and literature, which, he felt, best resolved the conflict between the "most abstruse philosophy on the one hand and the most monstrous religion on the other."[60]

We find such monstrosity in the description of the god Vishnu in the celebrated eleventh chapter of the *Bhagavad Gītā* (first translated in 1785 by G. Wilkins), or in the goddess who is to this day (to quote Heinrich Zimmer) "the most cherished and widespread of the personalizations of Indian cult." Innumerable images of Black Kālī, better known as Parvati, Siva's wife, depict the "wholly negative aspect of the Universal Mother." One shows her as "an emaciated, gruesome hag of bony fingers, protruding teeth, unquenchable hunger [feeding] upon the entrails of her victim," another "adorned with the blood-dripping hands and heads of her victims, treading on the prostrate, corpselike body" of her own husband.[61] Such mythologems express what Goethe, following Shakespeare, believed to be the true nature of evil. "What we call evil," he wrote, "is only the other side of good."[62]

Outside of the work of the English playwright, little in the Western cultural heritage could have helped Goethe to incorporate this belief in his poetry. The poet, of course, pointed to the Greek god-mother, who, though lacking the chameleon talents of Parvati, shares her ominous role as the destroyer of her husband. But to the consciousness of his time, Hesiod's *Theogony* would have been little closer than the recently discovered myths of India. In an effort to parallel the latter, Goethe therefore had to create a series of female mythological figures who would expose Faust to the full duality of nature's life-force and destructiveness.

This fearful duality marks the Faustian world even in the highest regions of the protagonist's quest. In the service of others, Faust, like Dushmanta, learns to rid himself of his sexual egocentricity, or in Rilkean terms, to release the beloved. Yet his actions still entail evil, and to the last moments of his life Faust uses the help of the Devil or destroys such innocents as Philemon and Baucis. Even Heavenly Love, which comes to meet the quester half-way in his ascent, has little of the one-sided Christian purity which Goethe attributed to it in his famous comment to Eckermann.[63]

Mater Gloriosa, its highest embodiment, seems closer to Parvati than to the Virgin Mary in her orthodox conception. As mother, queen, and highest empress of the world she is "equal to the Gods" (12012), a distinction which, in the very same words, Faust had earlier attributed to the demonic Helena (7440). As such, she is able to arouse emotions quite unlike those which Dante's Virgin Mary, for instance, inspires in St Bernard (*Paradiso* XXXIII). Doctor Marianus's prayer, which has been compared with St Bernard's, is full of the sexual fervour that gives wings to Faust's own invocations of the Eternal Feminine (12001–4). And what images could be more violent and destructive than those in which Pater Ecstaticus expresses his love of God?

> Seething heartache,
> Foaming devotion to God.
> Arrows, pierce me through,
> Lances, overpower me,
> Cudgels, crush me,
> Lightnings, strike through me! (11856–61)

In the following speech, Pater Profundus expounds how this fiercely dualistic principle of "almighty love which forms and cherishes everything" (11872–3) is nature's hallmark even in paradise. Lightning and waterfalls, evoked in a similar context in the first scene of *Faust II* (4716ff), provide him with examples:

> Around me there is a wild roaring,
> As though the woods and rocks were heaving;
> And yet, lovingly rushing,
> The torrent plunges into the gorge,
> Called to water the valley directly.
> And the lightning struck in flames
> To clear the atmosphere,
> Heavy with fumes and mist;
>
> They are Love's envoys, who proclaim
> What seethes around us in eternal creativity. (11874–81)

Yet here we are in the presence of Mary, a realm which in Dante's *Divina Commedia*, for instance, is the abstract core of a disembodied world of light-suffused crystalline spheres:

> Intellectual light, full of love;
> love of the truly good, full of joy,
> joy which transcends all delight.[64]

What could be further removed from Goethe's earthly paradise of lightning-ridden clouds, rocks, and thundering waterfalls? Yet what is closer to it than *Sacontalá*? The last scene of *Faust II*, headed "*Mountain-gorges, Forest, Cliffs, Wilderness. Holy Anchorites, scattered in the Mountain-sides, dwelling in the clefts of the rocks*" (11843), seems to be closely modelled on the conclusion of *Sacontalá*:

> The forest sways towards us,
> The crags weighing heavy,
> The roots clutching,
> Trunk hard upon trunk.
> Wave splashes upon wave,
> The deepest cavern gives cover.
> Lions creep around us,
> Silent yet genial,
> And honor the hallowed spot,
> The sacred shrine of Love.   (11844-53)

Kālidāsa's scenery, too, is a mountainous landscape of rivers, trees, and hermitages, where humans and divine beings live in perfect harmony with nature.[65] Lions, which as in *Faust* are part of that scenery, are cherished by men "as if they were [their] own off-spring." And how closely Kālidāsa's art of capturing the dynamic life of nature resembles Goethe's! As Dushmanta exclaims, this mountain wilderness

is more delightful than paradise itself ... clouds pregnant with showers ... the horses of Indra sparkle with lightning ... the low lands appear confounded with the high mountain tops; the trees erect their branchy shoulders ... the rivers look like bright lines, but their waters vanish; and, at this instant, the globe of earth seems thrown upwards by some stupendous power.[66]

This is what Goethe called "the realms of wonders that hover like fecund clouds between heaven and earth."[67] Here the poet can risk "vulgar and absurd contrasts, which must nevertheless be regarded as necessary connecting parts of the whole structure."[68]

Goethe followed *Sacontalá* equally closely in ending his *Faust* as an "altogether common drama of nature performed by gods and by the children of gods."[69] Like Dushmanta, Faust is raised to heaven to be reunited with the beloved, who in both dramas is described as a penitent practising her austerities in the presence of the divine: Sacontalá as a person in "*mourning apparel*," her "celestial face ... emaciated by the performance of austere duties,"[70] eager to rejoin her lost husband; Gretchen as "Una POENITENTIUM" (12068), who, in lines echoing and inverting her prayer to the Virgin Mary towards the end of *Faust I* (3587ff), pleads for her lover (12069-75). Each protagonist is forgiven not only by his beloved but by the gods.

As late as about 1825 Goethe had planned to set this final scene, headed "Judgment on Faust," in a celestial courtroom presided over by "Christ, the Virgin Mother, Evangelists and all Saints."[71] But the model of Kālidāsa's "drama of nature, performed by gods and by the children of gods" must have been stronger. As the Lord of the "Prologue in Heaven" was replaced by Mater Gloriosa, so judgment was replaced by exhortation. The Glorious Mother's final verdict is addressed to Gretchen: "Come! lift yourself up to higher spheres! / When he senses your presence, he will follow you" (12094-5). Here and in the final lines – "The Eternal Feminine / Draws us on high" – the central theme of *Faust II*, which finds a direct parallel in *Sacontalá*, is once more summed up. The closed world of tragedy, of guilt and punishment, sacrifice and redemption, has yielded to an open-ended quest for self-perfection in pursuit of the Great Mothers.

Goethe's paradise, like Kālidāsa's, is not a transcendent stellar universe of disembodied perfection but a world in which we try to perfect and purify ourselves. Both plays suggest this by emphasizing the notion of teaching and learning. Just as Dushmanta listens to a sage teaching a woman in the divine Ashram, so Gretchen pleads with Mater Gloriosa to let her teach her beloved (12092). Faust will instruct the "blessed boys" (12083) who are still aghast at the waterfall (11914ff) and must learn the lesson that life has taught the protagonist. The quest for self-perfection does not imply an escape from life but a deeper immersion in it. It means learning to accept life in its fearsome duality of creation and destruction without trying to subsume it under any teleological, moral, anthropomorphic, redemptive, or tragic scheme.

The basic pattern of this process, as in Shakespeare's romances, is that of death and rebirth. Kālidāsa, with his well-defined Vedantic belief in *karma*, reincarnation, and final salvation from rebirth, is somewhat more explicit here than Goethe. After being reunited with his wife and son, the king returns to rule as the better man he has become through his quest. Although in all his future endeavours the final aim will be the *nirvāna* invoked in the play's last line, this goal, as we see from the god Casyapa's blessing upon the king's departure, is still remote:

CASYAPA Henceforth may the god of the atmosphere with copious rain give abundance to thy affectionate subjects; and mayst thou with frequent sacrifices maintain the Thunderer's friendship! By numberless interchanges of good offices between you both, may benefits reciprocally be conferred on the inhabitants of the two worlds...
DUSHMANTA ... and may Siva... eternally potent and self-existing, avert from me the pain of another birth in this perishable world.[72]

Arising from a world of tragedy, the ending of *Faust* is less undeviatingly happy than this one, and there is no explicit statement that Faust, like Dushmanta, will travel through endless reincarnations toward *nirvāna*. Gretchen has killed

Faust's child, and both she and the protagonist have suffered real death. But in the earthly paradise they have reached, Faust will be the teacher of the "blessed boys" and Gretchen, about to observe Faust's coming back to life (12084ff), anticipates her happiness at being reunited with her lover.

The author of *Faust II* expected little understanding for his great work from his contemporaries. And he was far from wrong in his apprehensions. Probably the first to recognize fully the radicalness of Goethe's vision was Nietzsche, whose *Birth of Tragedy*, not surprisingly, also marks a major turning-point towards the avant-garde theatre of recent years. An earlier section of this study tried to explain this paradox by showing that Nietzsche's account, while prophetic of things to come, erred in heralding a rebirth of tragedy in his time. Wagner's operas, which were to bring about this renascence, failed to live up to the philosopher's own expectations. In turn, Nietzschean Dionysiac tragedy is to be associated not with traditional tragedy but with its anti- and post-tragic counterparts, particularly in the guise in which they have evolved in our century. Nietzsche thus anticipated major concepts of both the anti-tragic theatre of the absurd and the post-tragic theatre of cruelty, both of which have attracted major public and critical interest over recent decades.

But before we survey these connections in more detail, it bears remembering that tragedy proper is far from dead today. Psychological tragedy in particular has enjoyed a popularity in our age perhaps no less than that of traditional tragedy by, say, Shakespeare or Aeschylus in theirs. The reasons for this can be documented at deeper levels than those of mere poetic theory. Freudian psychoanalysis by no means prompted plays like *Death of a Salesman* or *Six Characters in Search of an Author*. Both Pirandello and Miller were largely unaware of Freud's theories when they wrote their plays. It is only the more revealing, therefore, that such modern tragedies and psychology share basic concepts such as "traumatic scene" and "case history," which, though derived from Freud, are equally applicable to much of modern tragic literature. Such affinities, in turn, are traceable to a common basis in the tragic tradition of predominantly Aristotelian persuasion. Thus one might venture to say that Freud's impact on twentieth-century thought is due less to the innovativeness of his theories than to the fact that he translated into a new terminology what constitutes one of the most tenacious traditions of our literary and philosophical heritage. No wonder, then, that this tradition also managed to survive in the tragedies of our time.

Tragedy and Psychology

ACCORDING TO ARISTOTLE, Sophocles' *Oedipus Rex* is a great play precisely because one need not perform it; a simple reading will reveal its full artistic impact.[1] The position of most recent avant-garde theatre is precisely the opposite of Aristotle's. To Jerzy Grotowski, for instance, the primary medium for the actor ought to be his body. "Everything must come from and through the body. First and foremost, there must be a physical reaction to everything that affects us. Before reacting with the voice, you must first react with the body. If you think, you must think with the body."[2] Grotowski's mentor Artaud had earlier demanded a similar primacy of the spectacle over the the spoken word. In following "the very automatism of the liberated unconscious," this theatre of cruelty should avoid the "cheap imitations of reality" of Aristotelian persuasion. While emphasizing the psychotherapeutic bias of his own efforts, Artaud at the same time inveighs against "a purely descriptive and narrative theater – story-telling psychology" as well as psychology in general. Just like the Aristotelian dramatic matrix, psychology, he seems to imply,

works relentlessly to reduce the unknown to the known, to the quotidian and the ordinary, [and] is the cause of the theater's abasement and its fearful loss of energy.[3]

All this calls for an explanation which Artaud himself or his various followers have so far denied us. What connections, if any, exist between Aristotelian poetics and the contemporary psychological theatre, as well as psychoanalysis itself? And to what degree can the efforts of an Artaud or Grotowski to evolve a new theatre of the body rather than the spoken word be seen as an alternative to this traditional nexus?

Oedipus Rex, *Six Characters in Search of an Author*, and *Death of a Salesman*

For lack of examples listed by Artaud himself, Pirandello's *Six Characters in Search of an Author* and Miller's *Death of a Salesman* may serve to illustrate our twentieth-century theatre of simultaneously Aristotelian and psychoanalytic persuasion. *Prima facie* the two plays have little in common except that their authors thought of them, in one way or another, as tragedies. Pirandello, while giving his play the subtitle *A Comedy in the Making*, felt that *Six Characters* dramatized "the inherent tragic conflict between life (which is always moving and changing) and form (which fixes it, immutable)."[4] Miller thought of his play as the tragedy of a man who "gave his life, or sold it, in order to justify the waste of it."[5] Yet even these concepts of tragedy are conspicuous for their differences rather than their affinities. What relates the two plays to each other and, in fact, makes them two of the most forceful manifestations of the tragic in our century remained a secret even to their authors.

The genesis of *Six Characters* is well known from the playwright's 1930 preface to the play. The story of the father who, possessed by the demon of experiment, sends his wife to live with another man and almost ends up sleeping with his "stepdaughter" by the surrogate husband had captivated Pirandello's imagination. But it somehow seemed to lack a central focus or form. For real poets, in the playwright's Aristotelian conviction, "admit only figures, affairs, landscapes which have been soaked, so to speak, in a particular sense of life and acquire from it a universal value." Pirandello eventually found this deeper significance in the conflict "between life-in-movement and form," which crystallized in two scenes of an "outrageous unalterable fixity."[6]

The characters' search for an author, the whole impromptu stunt of staging their melodramatic entanglements before the surprised manager, is little else than the search for these two crucial moments. The first occurs when the Father, about to sleep with a prostitute, realizes that she is his Step-Daughter; the second, a tragic result of the first, when the young Son out of the substitute marriage shoots himself with a revolver. The Step-Daughter, like the Father, is "dying to live" her scene in the belief that it caused all her present misery. In turn, the Father calls it his "eternal moment":

She [*indicating the* Step-Daughter] is here to catch me, fix me, and hold me eternally in the stocks for that one fleeting and shameful moment of my life.[7]

The eagerness with which Father and Step-Daughter want to re-enact this traumatic encounter finds its repressive counterpart in the twenty-two-year-old Son, who is made to relive the second scene. The Father's claim to have fathomed "the meaning of it all" is a matter of mere scorn and revulsion to him; such things, in his opinion, "ought to have remained hidden." But though he preaches repression, he is unable to escape the thrall of his two traumatic memories, one the suicide of the Boy, the other the death by drowning of the four-year-old Child. "There was no scene," he protests. "I went away, that's all! I don't care for scenes!" His final reliving of this traumatic moment is all the more authentic for being so involuntary:

I ran over to her; I was jumping in to drag her out when I saw something that froze my blood ... the boy standing stock still, with eyes like a madman's, watching his little drowned sister, in the fountain! [*The* Step-Daughter *bends over the fountain to hide the* Child. *She sobs.*] Then ... [*A revolver shot rings out behind the trees where the* Boy *is hidden.*][8]

Pirandello, in fusing pretence and reality, has actual death and suicide "re-enacted" on the stage here. This seems to imply that the repressed traumatic events become more powerful than reality once they are released. The playwright himself, of course, fails to speak of his play in these psychoanalytic terms. Instead of pointing out what from a post-Freudian perspective appears to be its case-history–like plot, Pirandello discusses the play in the traditional vocabulary of Aristotle. To him, as we recall, the most important aspect of a play is how the author transforms the random events of life into "one action, a complete whole, with its several incidents so closely connected that the transposal or withdrawal of any one of them will disjoin and dislocate the whole."[9] Similarly, the content of *Six Characters*, in the author's view, may well be chaotic, but its presentation is "the reverse of confused." After all, audiences around the world had recognized the clarity of the intrigue and the way in which the whole was finally "quite simple, clear, and orderly."[10]

We find Miller making similar claims for *Death of a Salesman*. The playwright's general sense of form, he confessed in an interview, "comes from a positive need to organize life":

The very impulse to write, I think, springs from an inner chaos crying for order, for meaning, and that meaning must be discovered ... or the work lies dead as it is finished.[11]

This search for significant form crystallized in a specific scene which, as in Pirandello's *Six Characters*, holds everything in its "outrageous unalterable fixity."[12] There is similarity even of content. Just as Pirandello's Father making love to his Step-Daughter–prostitute is discovered by the Mother, his former wife, so Miller's Willy Loman and his mistress are surprised by his son Biff in a Boston hotel room.

The two plays differ mainly in the way in which their "internal logic" (to use Miller's phrase)[13] is arranged around these focal scenes. Speaking in psychoanalytic terms. Pirandello's protagonist plays the role of his own analyst in explaining (and enacting) the cause of his misery. "I'm crying aloud the reason of my sufferings," he exclaims. His endless perorations on how a single encounter has forever crippled his life remind the manager of Pirandello, an author he heartily detests.[14]

The Father, in other words, assumes the role of the playwright in expounding what the author of, for instance, Aristotle's model tragedy *Oedipus Rex* reveals in the gradual unfolding of his play. In a brilliant detective-story pursuit in which the investigator searches out his own crime, Oedipus uncovers the cause of his misery, whereas the Father simply wants to demonstrate his and, what is more, theorize about it. For man, he explains, "never reasons so much and becomes so introspective as when he suffers; since he is anxious to get at the cause of his sufferings, to learn who has produced them, and whether it is just or unjust that he should have to bear them."[15]

Arthur Miller's relationship to his protagonist, then, resembles not so much Pirandello's towards the Father but Sophocles' towards Oedipus: the internal logic of each play gradually renders both audience and hero aware of his hidden guilt. In *Oedipus Rex*, this takes the form of an investigation into objective facts, while *Death of a Salesman* gives us a psychoanalytic variant of the same process. Willy Loman's half-demented forays into his past proceed with the random unpredictability with which a neurotic patient might talk to his analyst. But the *form* of this involuntary confession, as manifest in the play's structure, finally amounts to a coherent case history of the protagonist's dilemma. Significantly, the original version of the play was entitled *The Inside of His Head*.

Death of a Salesman, as Miller points out, is the tragedy of a man who unwittingly ruins his son, recognizes his guilt, and is forgiven by his victim. More than half-way through the play, Willy Loman, talking to Bernard, one of his son's former schoolmates, still wonders why Biff at age seventeen suddenly turned from a high-school football hero into a hopeless good-for-nothing. Surely, Biff's failure on a math course is not enough to explain this transformation. To both Bernard and Willy the matter is a total enigma:

WILLY Why? Why! Bernard, that question has been trailing me like a ghost for the last fifteen years. He flunked the subject, and laid down and died like a hammer hit him![16]

When Bernard suggests that it happened after Biff went to see his father in Boston, Willy, wavering between half-recognition and aggressiveness, reacts like Oedipus when Jocasta tells him the circumstances of Laius's murder at the crossroads.[17] To the spectator there is little surprise in all this, for throughout the first half of the play we have been made to watch Willy with the eyes of an analyst listening to his neurotic patient. What we witness now is what Freud calls a final outburst of "resistance due to repression."[18] Very soon the protagonist's embattled ego will yield its defences to the forces of a repressed traumatic experience as it invades from the unconscious. Willy Loman, in the playwright's own words, is "the kind of man you see muttering to himself on a subway ... he can no longer restrain the power of his experience from disrupting the superficial sociality of his behaviour."[19] And as we see his day-dream fantasies enacted in front of our eyes, one single event stands out with particular obtrusiveness.

At one point, his wife Linda tells the protagonist that he is "the handsomest man in the world." This, in Willy's guilt-ridden mind, evokes a scene in which his former mistress called him "a wonderful man" and thanked him for some stockings he had given her. There is a second association when Willy wakes up from his reverie, sees Linda mending stockings, and angrily screams: "Now throw them out!" All this, we are made to understand, is somehow connected with Biff's failure in the math course, for following the hotel-room scene, there is another flashback disrupted by the mistress's laughter and Willy's "Shut up!" In the same scene, young Bernard warns the Lomans that their son is about to flunk math. But at this point we are still asking ourselves how the two incidents interconnect.[20]

Willy's overflowing unconscious, however, does not withhold the answer for much longer. His conversation with the adult Bernard has stirred up the crucial link in his own mind. Willy is at a restaurant with his two sons and their pick-ups. When Biff refuses to tell about his interview with his former boss Oliver, Willy suddenly, to the confusion of everybody, bursts out: "No, no! You had to go and flunk math!" Now his wandering mind returns to the scene in which young Bernard reported Biff's failure. But the scene has undergone a significant change. Only Linda and young Bernard are present, while Biff has already left for Boston. Meanwhile, in the restaurant, Biff asks himself why he ever went to see Oliver. In Willy's mind this question is promptly answered by the laughter of his former mistress, which is enough to finally break down his remaining conscious defences. Abandoned by his two sons, he relives the traumatic scene which, long repressed, contains the solution to the riddle that has plagued him for so long. Biff, thinking that his father might intercede for him with his math teacher, found Willy in the company of the half-naked woman.[21]

Freud and Aristotle

As much as they point back to Aristotle's *Poetics* and Sophocles' *Oedipus Rex*, the plot structures of both *Death of a Salesman* and *Six Characters in Search of an Author*, then, show an equal affinity with twentieth-century psychoanalysis. This is all the more striking as both Pirandello and Miller seem to have been practically ignorant of Freud's specific theories when they wrote their plays in 1921 and

1947.[22] It also suggests that both Freudian psychoanalysis and contemporary psychological drama, each through independent channels, have common roots in the Aristotelian tragic matrix as derived largely from Sophocles' *Oedipus Rex*. It remains to be seen what connections there are between psychoanalysis proper and this time-honoured tradition.

Such links can be found even for more recent psychoanalytic methods which might at first seem to offer radical alternatives to Freud's rationalist methods. What, for instance, could be further removed from strictly discursive psychoanalysis than primal-scream therapy? But rereading Arthur Janov one quickly realizes that screaming here is only a means to the end of uncovering the unbroken chain of neatly interconnected events or "scenes" often leading back to the "major scene" which caused the neurosis. To quote from Janov's examples:

A patient who had no memory before the age of ten began to relive experiences at the age of fourteen and worked her way down the age ladder until she relived a terrible event that caused the final split at the age of ten ... Some patients are able to go directly to the major scene in which they felt the split; others take months to get there.[23]

A similar picture emerges from bioenergetics. Its main exponent, Alexander Lowen, proposes to "help a person get back together with his body and to help him enjoy to the fullest degree possible the life of the body." To this end, Lowen designed a number of ingenious physical exercises combined with primal therapy. But these are subservient to a kind of torture-chamber psychoanalysis in which the patient reveals his past in a state of exhaustion or emotional turmoil induced by screaming and physical exercise. In Lowen's own words:

One of the purposes of the analysis is to create that map in the patient's mind. It is a map of words, made up of memories, and is therefore the full history of the person's life. When it all comes together like the pieces in a jigsaw puzzle, it finally makes sense, and the person sees who he is and how he is in the world, as well as knows the why of his character.[24]

Lowen's and Janov's obvious indebtedness here of course is to Freud, who throughout talks about his patients' repressed experiences in terms of highly specific, dramatic, and traumatic "scenes." The analyst, like Theseus in the labyrinth of the unconscious, has to "get hold of a piece of the logical thread" that will lead him to a logically coherent case history. Not before all the pieces of the puzzle are assembled should he reveal the patient's true life-history to its protagonist, who will then be "overborne by the force of logic":

It is only towards the end of the treatment that we have before us an intelligible, consistent, and unbroken case history. Whereas the practical aim of the treatment is to remove all possible symptoms and to replace them by conscious thoughts, we may regard it as a second and theoretical aim to repair all the damages to the patient's memory. These two aims are coincident. When one is reached, so is the other; and the same path leads to them both.[25]

Alternatively, one might argue that Janov's and Lowen's indebtedness to Freud reaches far beyond the father of psychoanalysis; or, if viewed from a different angle, that Freud's impact on his disciples and on twentieth-century thought generally to a large extent stems from the fact that his own theories form part of a tradition of Western thought over two thousand years old.

Freud was partly aware of these roots. Even before the birth of psychoanalysis proper, Aristotle's concept of the purging of certain detrimental emotions (fear and pity), reached by witnessing someone else's calamities, provided Freud and Breuer with the label for their cathartic method. Here the psychical process which caused the neurosis "must be repeated as vividly as possible; it must be brought back to its *status nascendi* and then given verbal utterance." Even though the patient, to describe him in Aristotelian terms, becomes his own spectacle, the analogy holds, for most of the repressed material he is made to relive will strike him as an alien experience. Freud before long abandoned this more dramatic method for one in which the patient rids himself of his neurosis by learning to see it as a part of his intelligible case history. But even as late as 1924 he still admitted that "the cathartic method was the immediate precursor of psychoanalysis, and, in spite of every extension of experience and of every modification of theory, is still contained within it as its nucleus."[26]

Freud's indebtedness to the traditional tragic matrix is equally apparent regarding the complex which to him constitutes "the nucleus of all neuroses" as well as the beginning point of all "religion, morals, society and art."[27] From its earliest mention in the letters fo Fliess,[28] Freud named the complex after *Oedipus Rex*. The discovery, he wrote in *The Interpretation of Dreams* (1900),

is confirmed by a legend ... whose profound and universal power to move can only be understood if the hypothesis I have put forward in regard to the psychology of children has an equally universal validity. What I have in mind is the legend of King Oedipus and Sophocles' drama which bears his name.[29]

One question to be raised at this point is whether Freud, without his model, would ever have "discovered" the complex. Another concerns the supposedly "universal validity" of the legend. Freud may question the interpretation of *Oedipus Rex* as a "tragedy of destiny," but only by reinterpreting the notion of destiny. Destiny to him is not one man's specific fate according to the will of the gods, but "the fate of all of us." Oedipus's "destiny moves us only because it might have been ours – because the oracle laid the same curse upon us before our birth as upon him ... King Oedipus, who slew his father Laïus and married his mother Jocasta, merely shows us the fulfilment of our own childhood wishes."[30]

Yet recent investigations into the history of the myth come to the opposite conclusion. As Thalia P. Feldman points out, Oedipus, in the extant literature up to Aeschylus, was not treated as an offender who needed punishment. "It is the Aeschylean Oedipus who first blinds himself, an unprecedented individual action which signifies that the offender is loading himself with the enormous burden of shame and horror which he feels at his involvement, even though he and everyone else knows that he is not guilty."[31] This throws serious doubts on Freud's view that the killing of the primal father, the formation of the Oedipus complex, and the birth of tragedy all happened at the dawn of human history. What seems to be closer to the truth is that both tragedy and the Oedipus legend represent relatively recent phenomena in a specific culture which as such bequeathed its limitations to Freud's discoveries regarding neuroses and the discontents of civilization.

Freud's third major debt to the traditional tragic matrix is reflected in his general preference, shared with Aristotle, for *Oedipus Rex* as a play whose action "consists in nothing other than the process of revealing, with cunning delays and ever-mounting excitement ... that Oedipus himself is the murderer of Laius."[32] Sophocles' tragedy, if it is not an actual precursor of the modern detective story, can certainly be termed an early example of what Edgar Allan Poe called a "tale of ratiocination."[33] Particularly ingenious here, as we have seen, is the use of suspense, reversal, and final recognition. What Freud calls "the process of revealing, with cunning delays and evermounting excitement," is what Aristotle describes as an example of peripeteia and anagnorisis combined, a fusion made even more powerful by the fact that both arise "out of the structure of the plot." Thus, the two devices add the final touch of perfection to a plot whose several incidents are "so closely connected that the transposal or withdrawal of any one of them will disjoin and dislocate the whole."[34]

No wonder that Freud, in calling the action of *Oedipus Rex* a mere "process of revealing, with cunning delays and ever-mounting excitement," was reminded of similar revelations in which he was involved almost daily. The process, he writes, "can be likened to the work of a psycho-analysis." This, in turn, leads to the equivalent of Aristotle's plot, an "intelligible, consistent and unbroken case history."[35] One might add that the analogy has a causal dimension, in that the Aristotelian tragic matrix played midwife at the very birth of psychoanalysis.

Both tragedy and psychoanalysis deal with and, in a way, try to resolve human suffering. Ironically, Aristotle here was far more optimistic than Freud, who from the beginning purported to do no more than to transform "your hysterical misery into common unhappiness."[36] For implicit in the concept of catharsis, as we have seen, is Aristotle's conviction that fear and pity, as aroused by the deed of horror, can be purged by making the spectators understand as a logical train of events what at first surprised them. The concept, in short, seems to cover the whole spectrum of the Freudian doctrine – from the early "cathartic method" of acting out repressed experiences to psychoanalysis proper, which tries to cure the patient by making him understand these experiences as part of his intelligible and causally coherent case history.

What also links Aristotelian catharsis with Freudian psychotherapy is an almost total reliance on discursive language. Just as Freud restricts analysis to the patient's verbal articulation of his erratic life-story, developing towards the logically consistent discourse of his case history, so Aristotle prefers to have the cathartic impact of tragedy depend on the spoken word, to the exclusion of a spectacle:

> The Plot in fact should be so framed that, even without seeing the things take place, he who simply hears the account of them shall be filled with horror and pity at the incidents; which is just the effect that the mere recital of the story in *Oedipus* would have on one.[37]

Towards a Twentieth-Century Post-tragic Theatre

Whoever remembers the Happenings of the sixties and seventies will know that Artaud by no means offered the most radical reaction against this Aristotelian position. While Michael Kirby hailed *The Theatre of Cruelty* as "almost a text for Happenings,"[38] Artaud himself was far from advocating a total abolition of language in drama. But he was equally removed from Freud's or Aristotle's belief that language can resolve the contingency of experience in its discursive order. On the contrary, language, he felt, has simply been ossified by such assumptions: before it can be used in the theatre, it must be cleansed of its abstract encrustations. For hidden underneath these is the old dynamic potential, which Artaud concluded can be reclaimed from the respiratory sources of language:

> let words be joined again to the physical motions that gave them birth, and let the discursive, logical aspect of speech disappear beneath its affective, physical side, i.e., let words be heard in their sonority rather than be exclusively taken for what they mean grammatically.[39]

Artaud had his own ideas about how the theatre of cruelty would benefit the spectators. This goal can be realized neither by letting them see the randomness of events in their deeper causal coherence nor by making them understand life as a logically consistent case history. No amount of explaining or understanding will do away with the basic cruelty of life – "that life is always someone's death."[40] Man, rather than delude himself that suffering might be eliminated, should simply learn to confront it.

The new theatre, then, "far from copying life, puts itself whenever possible in communication with pure forces." It should immerse the spectator in the irrational rather than strive to purge it out of him. The actor is to provide him with a model in this pursuit. To Artaud, "every emotion has organic bases," so that the soul, for instance, is no more than a "skein of vibrations." Yin and yang, Chinese acupuncture and the Cabbala are invoked in discussing possible new acting techniques that will provide the alternative to the Aristotelian mimetic theatre and its twentieth-century variant, story-telling psychology. As an "athlete of the heart," the actor should explore the different modes of respiration in his acting. Thus, joining "the passions by means of their forces, instead of regarding them as pure abstractions," will confer a "mastery upon the actor which makes him equal to a true healer."[41]

Artaud's alternative to the psychological theatre was to a large extent inspired by non-Western sources. A Balinese dance group that he saw at a colonial exhibition in Paris brought his diffuse ideas about "The Theater and the Plague" or "The Alchemical Theater" to a concrete focus. It also led him to define his goals in analogy to "the Oriental theater of metaphysical tendency" as opposed to "the Occidental theater of psychological tendency." These Balinese productions, he wrote, "take shape at the very heart of matter, life, reality. There is in them something of the ceremonial quality of a religious rite, in the sense that they extirpate from the mind of the onlooker all idea of pretense, of cheap imitations of reality." In turn, Hindu cosmology helped him to describe how cruelty is the central law of the universe. Unlike the Judaeo-Christian God, Brahma suffers his own creation, "with a suffering that yields joyous harmonics perhaps, but which at the ultimate extremity of the curve can only be expressed by a terrible crushing and grinding."[42] The passage serves to remind us that Artaud was the first neither in opposing the Aristotelian tragic matrix nor in deriving his alternatives from non-Western sources. It also recalls the one-sided distortions which characterize this tradition, now nearly two hundred years old, stemming from Schopenhauer's pessimistic reception of Eastern thought. For the latter considered in its own right is neither pessimistic nor optimistic, but perhaps what we would call fatalistic.

In depicting the supreme divinity as a monster of destruction, the *Bhagavad Gītā* clearly admits to the natural cruelty of life. At the same time it exhorts us to act, even if such action involves someone else's suffering or death. Neither teleological laws inherent in life nor rational orders that man might impose upon it will eliminate this dilemma; all man can do in trying to face it is to develop the appropriate kind of self-detachment through meditation. Analogously, Sanskrit drama has little concern with implicit teleological schemes, coherent plots showing things "as they ought to be," or the purging of fear and pity with the aim of producing more rational citizens. Bharata's *Nāṭyaśāstra*, the Sanskrit equivalent of Aristotle's *Poetics*, defines drama not as the "imitation of ... one action, a complete whole,"[43] but as the "representation of conditions and situations."[44] Rather than fear and pity, it tries to induce a state of appreciative serenity analogous to the life-affirming self-detachment reached through meditation.

Arthur Schopenhauer, the first Western philosopher-aesthetician to make such ideas his own, misinterpreted the Eastern acceptance of suffering as a denunciation of life, and the attempt to come to terms with it as resignation. Lacking all sense of the psychophysiological core of Eastern mysticism, he consistently advocated a repression ("Unterdrückung") and negation of all life-impulses. Hence, tragedy to him was simply a powerful artistic medium to the same end. In portraying the "horrific side of life" ("die schreckliche Seite des Lebens")[45] and in showing how all the misery of life results from the blind workings of the Will, it induces a state of quietism in the spectator:

The power of transport peculiar to tragedy may be seen to arise from our sudden recognition that life fails to provide any true satisfactions and hence does not deserve our loyalty. Tragedy guides us to the final goal, which is resignation.[46]

Schopenhauer's words from *The World as Will and Idea* are quoted in Nietzsche's 1886 "Critical Glance Backward" on *The Birth of Tragedy* (1872), which inverts the Schopenhauerian position by way of anticipating the more recent theatre of cruelty. Reacting against all previous teleological and rationalist make-believe, Nietzsche, like his teacher, sees tragedy as dealing with the "natural cruelty of things" ("natürliche Grausamkeit der Dinge")[47]; and he makes light of critics who "never tire of telling us about the hero's struggle with destiny, about the triumph of the moral order, and about the purging of the emotions." Facing "the Heraclitean double motion" of Apollonian creativity and Dionysiac destructiveness, the tragedian focuses on "the eternal wound of being." He shows how, again and again in life, the Apollonian illusion, or "veil of Maya," is torn apart until nothing remains but "shreds floating before the vision of mystical Oneness." But as "an augury of eventual reintegration," the Dionysiac spirit, "which playfully shatters and rebuilds the teeming world of individuals," induces the very opposite of Schopenhauerian resignation in the spectator:

Tragedy cries, "We believe that life is eternal!" ... It makes us realize that everything that is generated must be prepared to face its painful dissolution ... Pity and terror notwithstanding, we realize our great good fortune in having life not as individuals, but as part of the life force with whose procreative lust we have become one.[48]

In advocating this untragic celebration of life despite the "horror of individual existence,"[49] Nietzsche anticipates Artaud to the point of proposing Messianic schemes, while failing to investigate the practical possibilities of the new theatre. There is little even in *Le théâtre et son double* that enables us to imagine how, as the potential audience of such spectacles, we would be made to join in such *amor fati* rejoicing. All it amounts to, as Jerzy Grotowski concludes, is "a very fertile aesthetic proposition. It is not a technique."[50] Artaud, like Nietzsche before him, evolved a theoretical alternative to the Aristotelian tragic matrix and its psychoanalytic derivations. Neither of them, however, explored the ways in which their theory could be turned into practice, a task more recently tackled by Brook, Grotowski, and others.

The primary aim of Grotowski's poor theatre, for instance, is "a form of social psycho-therapy." The spectator is meant to share the actor's psycho-physiological self-penetration towards some "inner harmony and peace of mind." This is achieved neither by an Aristotelian portrayal of characters for the sake of their actions nor by a psychoanalytic dissection of emotions for the sake of establishing tragic case histories. Acting to Grotowski is the very opposite of imitating an action or emotion: "An actor should not use his organism to illustrate a 'movement of the soul,' he should accomplish this movement with his organism."[51] Instead of enacting the words codified in a literary text, he ought to use his body in order to find a language of signs.

Words to Grotowski "are always pretexts." More often than not they even disguise the impulse that tries to reveal itself in them. To make words the guidelines for acting is as ill-advised, therefore, as, say, to try to suggest boredom by letting the actor act in a "bored" manner. For a bored man, as he desperately tries to find something that will end his boredom, is far more active than usual. Before all else, the theatre's medium is the body of the actor: "Before reacting with the voice, you must first react with the body. If you think, you must think with your body."[52]

In this regard, Grotowski's poor theatre differs not only from its Aristotelian and Freudian counterparts but also from more recent process psychotherapy. *Towards a Poor Theater*, with its handbook-like lists of physical exercises and its psychoanalytic vocabulary, sometimes sounds distinctly like Lowen's *Bioenergetics*. Living, Grotowski writes,

is not being contracted, nor is it being relaxed: it is a process. But if the actor is always too contracted, the cause blocking the natural respiratory process – almost always of a psychical or psychological nature – must be discovered. We must determine which is his natural type of respiration. I observe the actor, while suggesting exercises that compel him into total psycho-physical mobilisation.

But to Grotowski, the process of "total psycho-physical mobilisation,"[53] including primal-scream techniques, no longer serves as a means towards the end of establishing consistent case histories within the overall framework of a psychoanalytically discursive logic. Its truer counterparts perhaps are treatises like the Sanskrit *Nāṭyaśāstra* or the Japanese *Kwadensho*. Such treatises at least show that an actor's training that resembles a process psychotherapy devoid of rationalist systematization is more than a recent fad of the West. It has been known in Indian and Japanese drama for many centuries, and may well become common practice in ours.

Conclusion

BUT OTHER THAN THAT, one should probably refrain from further prophecies. Too much speculation of a similar kind has encouraged the rather simplistic notion that tragedy, alive for some two thousand years, has gradually died in our time. What we have found instead is that tragedy in its modern psychological variant is as vital today as it was at the time of Euripides, Shakespeare, and Goethe. Also, what might be said to have succeeded tragedy – such as the theatre of the absurd and of cruelty – is characterized by negating and / or going beyond the tragic rather than by its autonomous nature. What's more, this anti- and post-tragic transcendence of tragedy is by no means restricted to the immediate past. Only a few decades after the genre was created, Euripides recognized and went beyond the limitations of its visions. Shakespeare and Goethe, each in his own way, took similar though even more radical steps. They, too, negated and transcended the notion, associated with tragedy from its beginnings, that human suffering can be shown to have a purposive, ennobling, or otherwise meaningful function in an overall order of things. And no doubt there are other playwrights who could be discussed in the same context.

But my endeavour has been to provide examples of a so-far neglected aspect of our literary heritage, not the more formidable attempt, perhaps to be tackled by others, of giving a complete account of it. In turn, what has been said about the present is meant to give only a few traces of the more complete picture that one might draw; even another book-length study might not be sufficient to complete this task. For what in Shakespeare, Goethe, and Euripides can be described, in each case, within the range of a single creative lifespan, has now split into diverse movements and trends, each with its followers and opponents. And who would feel certain in trying to assess what might result from all of this, even if it were looked at from the wider perspective offered in the preceding pages? Ionesco, for instance, charges the existentialists with failing to find a formal correlative for their absurdist vision of life. But has he managed to do so himself? Practitioners of the theatre of cruelty would probably answer in the negative. But what more is such dissent than a failure perhaps to recognize the whole spectrum? How, on the other hand, could modern art and thinking stay alive without the energy generated by such differences?

To quote one further example, Robbe-Grillet, taking his cue from Roland Barthes, criticizes Sartre and Camus for merely providing us with new variants – "l'absurde et la nausée" – of the age-old tragic complicity between man and the unalterably hostile universe. In this way, his essay, "Nature, humanisme, tragédie" offers an insightful though partisan analysis of what this present study calls the anti-tragic. Yet Robbe-Grillet errs, I think, in claiming that Beckett's plays or his own writings represent the step beyond in presenting things in their pure "être là," devoid of morality, metaphysics, and psychology.[1] After all, both Camus and Sartre affirmed the validity of the tragic, Camus in "an attempt to create a modern tragedy"[2] out of what he calls "la victoire absurde,"[3] Sartre by returning to Hegel and the Greeks in his search for a "theatre of situations."[4] To claim that their concept of the absurd is related to the tragic is to tell them something that they would have been the first to admit themselves.

However, to argue that Vladimir's and Estragon's waiting for Godot is Beckett's way of demonstrating a pure case of "being there" amounts to misreading the text by abstracting it from its historical – that is, tragic – context. Robbe-Grillet argues that the only thing the two tramps are not free to do is to depart, to cease being there: "La seule chose qu'ils ne sont pas libres de faire, c'est de s'en aller, de cesser d'être là."[5] But what makes *Waiting for Godot* stop short just this side of a post-tragic "être là" is precisely the fact that Vladimir and Estragon feel somehow condemned to wait. Communications breakdown, the failure of language, the loss of identity, these and other supposedly disillusioning insights implied by the play are harmless enough when seen in the light of modern philosophy or, perhaps, a Buddhist approach to the same issues. Waiting for Godot and the paralysing effect it has on the two tramps, however, has an altogether more sinister dimension. It cripples not only their lives but their every impulse to help others:

> POZZO Help!
> ESTRAGON Let's go.
> VLADIMIR We can't.
> ESTRAGON Why not?
> VLADIMIR We're waiting for Godot.
> ESTRAGON Ah! [*Despairing.*] What'll we do, what'll we do![6]

If *Waiting for Godot* points beyond the absurd towards the post-tragic, it does so not in demonstrating a desensitized "être là" *à la* Robbe-Grillet, but in a powerfully stated symbol of rebirth:

VLADIMIR Look at it.
[*They look at the tree.*]
ESTRAGON I see nothing.
VLADIMIR But yesterday evening it was all black and bare. And now it's covered with leaves.

Once again, towards the very end of the play, Beckett makes sure that this little glimpse of hope, now put in jarring juxtaposition with its opposite – man paralysed by his Kafkaesque fear of an empty transcendence – will not be lost on the audience:

ESTRAGON Oh, yes, let's go far away from here.
VLADIMIR We can't.
ESTRAGON Why not?
VLADIMIR We have to come back to-morrow.
ESTRAGON What for?
VLADIMIR To wait for Godot.
ESTRAGON Ah! [*Silence.*] He didn't come?
VLADIMIR No.
ESTRAGON And now it's too late.
VLADIMIR Yes, and it's night.
ESTRAGON And if we dropped him? [*Pause.*] If we dropped him?
VLADIMIR He'd punish us. [*Silence. He looks at the tree.*] Everything's dead but the tree.[7]

But such hope is quickly darkened when the tree, which has begun to bloom, suggests to one of the tramps that they should, after all, hang themselves. None the less, the notion of something reborn amid this wasteland of death remains strongly fixed in the spectators' minds. If we can judge the play by its predecessors in the works of Goethe, Shakespeare, and Euripides, then it points the way beyond the tragic and anti-tragic towards a post-tragic vision of life. As it stands, today's theatre of cruelty seems to have gone the furthest in that direction. However, it has hardly progressed beyond the point where Euripides, by unearthing the predominantly destructive or "cruel" side of nature, left it in the *Bacchae*. Whether Goethe's and Shakespeare's more fully realized post-tragic visions of suffering anticipate the next stage can only be answered by the future.

Notes

IN THE HOPE THAT this study will reach the student and general reader, I have quoted Shakespeare and the Greek tragedians from the most widely used and easily available editions. Unless otherwise indicated, citations from Aeschylus, Sophocles, and Euripides are from the Chicago edition of *The Complete Greek Tragedies*, ed David Grene and Richmond Lattimore, 4 vols (Chicago: University of Chicago Press 1959). Quotations from Shakespeare are from the Signet editions of the New American Library, with variant readings from other editions (such as the Arden and Variorum) listed in the notes wherever relevant. Goethe's *Faust* is quoted from *Urfaust, Faust I und II, Paralipomena, Goethe über "Faust,"* ed W. Dietze (Berlin: Aufbau Verlag 1973), in my translation. As a rule, none of these citations from Goethe's *Faust*, the works of Shakespeare, and those of the Greek tragedians is listed in the notes. Otherwise, I have tried to limit annotations to the necessary minimum.

Introduction

1 *The Death of Tragedy* (New York: Farrar, Straus and Giroux 1963) p 353. The other title referred to above is that of a book by Erich Kahler (New York: Braziller 1968).

2 *Beyond the Tragic Vision: The Quest for Identity in the Nineteenth Century* (New York: George Braziller 1962) pp 368–9

3 *Notes and Counternotes* (New York: Grove Press 1964) p 27

4 *Essais critiques* (Paris: Editions du Seuil 1964) p 102

5 *Tragedy: Vision and Form* ed Robert W. Corrigan (San Francisco: Chandler Publishing Company 1965) p 151

6 Quoted by Martin Esslin in *The Theatre of the Absurd* (Harmondsworth: Penguin 1970) p 23

7 See, for instance, Walter Stein "Das Tragische und das Absurde" in *Tragik und Tragödie* ed Volkmar Sander (Darmstadt: Wissenschaftliche Buchgesellschaft 1971) pp

303–41; and Jan Kott *Shakespeare Our Contemporary* (New York: Norton 1974) pp 127–68.

8 See Gerald F. Else *The Origin and Early Form of Greek Tragedy* (New York: Norton 1972) p 97.

9 *Four Plays: The Bald Soprano. The Lesson. Jack or the Submission. The Chairs* trans Donald M. Allen (New York: Grove Press 1958) p 146

10 *Pour un nouveau roman* (Paris: Gallimard 1963) p 21

11 *The Essays* trans John Florio (Menston, Yorks: Scolar Press 1969) pp 628 (3:12), 46 (1:21)

12 See *Poetics* 1450 a 39ff, which here as in subsequent references is quoted in the translation of Ingram Bywater, *Rhetoric and Poetics* (New York: Random House 1954).

13 *Poetics* 1454 a 27–8, 1454 a 34–8

14 See Chang Chung-yuan *Creativity and Taoism. A Study of Chinese Philosophy, Art, and Poetry* (New York: Harper & Row 1970) pp 43–44.

15 *Poetics* 1453 b 20–2

16 *Selected Essays* (London: Faber and Faber 1966) p 258

17 *Bhagavad Gītā* trans Swami A.C. Bhaktivedanta (London: Collier-Macmillan 1969) pp 53 (1:26–9), 55 (1:32), 60 (1:45–6), 229–30 (11:32–3)

18 For more general discussions of our Western tragic sense of life by contrast with its Hindu counterpart, see G.K. Bhat *Tragedy and Sanskrit Drama* (Bombay: Popular Prakashan 1974) p 105; Minakshi L. Dalal *Conflict in Sanskrit Drama* (Bombay: Somaiya Publications 1973) pp 279ff; K.C. Pandey *Indian Aesthetics* Comparative Aesthetics vol I (Varanasi: Chowkhamba Sanskrit Series 1959) pp 30ff; and A.B. Keith *The Sanskrit Drama in Its Origin, Development, Theory and Practice* (London: Oxford University Press 1970) p 354.

19 *Bhagavad Gītā* p 228 (11:19, 25)

20 See, for instance, Gilbert Murray *Aeschylus: The Creator of Tragedy* (Oxford: Clarendon Press 1940) p 92.

21 See Willard Farnham *The Medieval Heritage of Elizabethan Tragedy* (Oxford: Basil Blackwell 1970) passim.

22 See page 9 above, as well as Zeami *La tradition secrète du Nô* trans René Sieffert (Paris: Gallimard 1960); and Peter D. Arnott *The Theatres of Japan* (London: Macmillan 1969) pp 109ff.

23 Cf Oscar Mandel, who in *A Definition of Tragedy* (New York: New York University Press 1961) suggests that such a definition "must be expansive enough to include as many as the hitherto proposed referends as possible" (p 8).

24 *Principles of Literary Criticism* (London: Kegan Paul 1924) p 246. See also Murray Krieger *The Classic Vision: The Retreat from Extremity in Modern Literature* (Baltimore and London: Johns Hopkins University Press 1971), where the tragic, along with the classic vision is described as "fearfully and maddeningly Manichean" (p 4).

25 *Tragedy Is Not Enough* (Boston: Beacon Press 1952) p 45

26 *Principles* p 247. George Steiner, while associating the death of tragedy with that of God, paradoxically holds a similarly pessimistic view of tragedy. Ignoring the mainstream understanding of the tragic since Aristotle, Steiner characterizes its mood as

"irreparable" and as presenting things "as they are, unrelenting and absurd." "When we say 'tragic drama,'" he claims, "we know what we are talking about... well enough to recognize the real thing" (*Death of Tragedy* pp 8, 9).

27 *Tragedy* ed Corrigan, pp 150–1

28 "Hegel's Theory of Tragedy" in *Hegel On Tragedy* ed Anne and Henry Paolucci (New York: Harper & Row 1975) pp 367–88, 367, 378

29 *Tragedy and Comedy* (New York: Simon and Schuster 1968) p 44. The book referred to by Kerr is John Jones *On Aristotle and Greek Tragedy* (New York: Oxford University Press 1962).

30 *Poetics* 1454 a 5–7, 1453 a 29–30

31 *Tragedy* p 54

32 See Albin Lesky *Greek Tragedy* (New York: Barnes & Noble 1967) p 5.

33 "Die Marxistische Auslegung des Tragischen" in *Tragik* ed Sander, pp 99–108. With regard to Marxism and tragedy see also Charles I. Glicksberg *The Tragic Vision in Twentieth-Century Literature* (Carbondale: Southern Illinois University Press 1968) pp 110ff.

34 *Schriften zum Theater* 7 vols (Frankfurt: Suhrkamp 1963–) 2:44

35 Karl Marx and Friedrich Engels *Werke* 39 vols (Berlin: Dietz Verlag 1969) 1:381

36 *Tragedy* pp 178, 325

37 Cf Peter Szondi "Zu Hegels Bestimmung des Tragischen" in *Tragik* ed Sander, pp 420–8.

38 *Karl Marx und Friedrich Engels als Literaturhistoriker* (Berlin: Aufbau Verlag 1948) p 42

39 For the preceding see Reinhold Grimm "Ideologische Tragödie und Tragödie der Ideologie. Versuch über ein Lehrstück von Brecht" in *Tragik* ed Sander, pp 237–78.

40 Cf *Totem and Taboo* trans James Strachey (London: Routledge & Kegan Paul 1975) pp 155, 156.

41 *The Pelican Freud Library* 15 vols, ed Angela Richards (Harmondsworth: Penguin 1973–) 8:47

42 *Totem and Taboo* p 95

43 *Poetics* 1451 a 32–3

44 *Three Plays: Amédée. The New Tenant. Victims of Duty* trans Donald Watson (New York: Grove Press 1958) pp 159, 119

45 Ibid, p 159

46 Quoted in Esslin *Theatre* p 23

47 *Notes* p 27

48 Quoted by Karl S. Guthke in *Modern Tragicomedy: An Investigation into the Nature of the Genre* (New York: Randon House 1966) p 131

49 See *Theatre* p 346.

50 *The Trial* (New York: Random House 1969) pp 7, 149, 152, 268, 268–9

51 Book of Job 23:3–4

52 *Trial* pp 149, 7

53 J.L. Borges's phrase in *Labyrinths: Selected Stories & Other Writings* ed D.A. Yates & J.E. Irby (New York: New Directions 1946) p 202

54 *Waiting for Godot: A Tragicomedy in Two Acts* (New York: Grove Press 1954) pp 13, 12, 51, 22, 56

55 *Four Plays* p 146

56 Cf Else *Origin* p 97.

57 *Four Plays* pp 147, 154, 158

58 *Tragedy* p 135

59 Quoted in Guthke *Tragicomedy* pp 102–3, 105, 106

60 Ibid, p 106

61 *Werke* 14 vols (Hamburg: Christian Wegner Verlag, 1957–60) 12:495, 497, 498, 688

62 *Elizabethan Critical Essays* ed G.G. Smith, 2 vols (New York: Oxford University Press 1937) 1:199

63 *Essays* pp 295 (2:12), 175(1:56). A comprehensive discussion of the literature concerning Montaigne's influence on Shakespeare is found in Robert Ellrodt "Self-consciousness in Montaigne and Shakespeare" *Shakespeare Survey* 18 (1975) 37–50.

64 *Essays* p 304 (2:12)

65 *Poetics* 1448 a 2, 1454 a 35–40, 1454 b 1

66 Ibid, 1456 a 24f

67 This, as Philip Vellacott points out in *Ironic Drama: A Study of Euripides' Method and Meaning* (Cambridge: Cambridge University Press 1975) p 14, is an error on Aristotle's part.

68 *Tragedy* p 135

69 *Poetics* 1461 b 21–2, 1460 b 33–5

The Birth of Tragedy

1 Else *Origin* p 83

2 See *The Birth of Tragedy and The Genealogy of Morals* trans Francis Golffing (Garden City, NY: Doubleday 1956) pp 67–8 and passim.

3 See Jones *Aristotle* p 65.

4 See, more recently, Mark Griffith *The Authenticity of "Prometheus Bound"* (Cambridge: Cambridge University Press 1977) pp 252f.

5 Quoted in Else *Origin* p 34

6 Here quoted from *Aeschylus* trans H.W. Smyth, 2 vols, Loeb Classical Library (Cambridge, Mass: Harvard University Press 1963) 1:339

7 Cf R.P. Winnington-Ingram, "Septem contra Thebas" *Yale Classical Studies* 25 (1977) 1–45, who interprets the play as dealing with the dialectical conflict (relevant to contemporary Athenian history) between an older, family-grounded and a new, city-oriented order of society.

8 Quoted in Lesky *Tragedy* p 70

9 Cf W.H. Roscher *Ausführliches Lexikon der griechischen und römischen Mythologie* 7 vols (Hildesheim: Georg Olms Verlagsbuchhandlung 1965–) 1:422–68.

10 *The Greeks and the Irrational* (Berkeley: University of California Press 1973) p 75; see

also Herbert Hunger *Lexikon der griechischen und römischen Mythologie* (Hamburg: Rowohlt 1974) p 49.

11 Hegel *Tragedy* pp 74, 68, 177

12 See, *inter alia, Vom Ursprung und Ende des Metaphysik* (München: Deutscher Taschenbuch Verlag 1972); and *Mythos, Philosophie, Politik. Zur Naturgeschichte der Illusion* (Freiburg im Breisgau: Verlag Rombach 1969).

13 Cf Dodds *Greeks* p 156.

14 *Tragedy* pp 177, 178

15 "Morals and Politics in the *Oresteia*" *The Ancient Concept of Progress and Other Essays on Greek Literature and Belief* (Oxford: Clarendon Press 1973) p 61

16 Cf W. Nicolai "Zur Theodizee des Aischylos (am Beispiel der *Orestie*)" *Zeitschrift für Religions- und Geistesgeschichte* 29 (1977) 18–28; and W.C. Greene *Moira: Fate, Good, and Evil in Greek Thought* (New York: Harper & Row 1944) pp 101, 109, 124, and passim.

17 John Ferguson's phrase in *A Companion to Greek Tragedy* (Austin: University of Texas Press 1972) p 106

18 See Hegel *Tragedy* p xii.

19 *History of the Peloponnesian War* trans Rex Warner (Harmondsworth: Penguin 1978) p 93

20 Cf Hunger *Lexikon* p 49.

21 Cf *Birth* pp 68, 106.

22 Quoted in Dodds *Greeks* p 180

23 *Birth* pp 102–3

24 Lattimore's phrase in the introduction to his translation of the *Oresteia* (Grene and Lattimore I. 31)

25 *Birth* pp 6, 5, 9

26 Cf ibid, p 77.

27 Ibid, p 81

28 G.S. Kirk and J.E. Raven *The Presocratic Philosophers: A Critical History with a Selection of Texts* (New York: Cambridge University Press 1977) p 168

29 *Tragedy* ed Corrigan, p 151

30 *Three Plays* p 119

31 Concerning the question as to whether or not Greek audiences knew the outcome of the Oedipus myth in advance, see John Moles "Notes on Aristotle, *Poetics* 13 and 14" *Classical Quarterly* ns 29 (1979) 77–94.

32 *Poetics* 1451 b 34–5, 1451 a 33–4

33 Ibid, 1455 a 17–18

34 Ibid, 1449 b 24–8

35 *The Works of Aristotle* ed J.A. Smith and W.D. Ross, vol 5 *Generation of Animals* (Oxford: Clarendon Press 1970) 788 b 28–9

36 *Poetics* 1448 b 16. See also Leon Golden, whose "The Clarification Theory of *Katharsis*," *Hermes* 104 (1976) 437–52, is the closest of all interpretations I am aware of to my own understanding of the concept. See especially p 445: "The essential point made about the nature of *mimesis* in this passage [1448 b 4–19] is that it represents a learning process that affords the pleasure of understanding ... and inference ... to all human

beings ... The source of our pleasure is our deepened understanding of the precise nature of the pitiable and fearful events represented." See also G.F. Else *Aristotle's Poetics: The Argument* (Cambridge, Mass: Harvard University Press 1963) p 449.

37 *On Generation and Corruption* (336 b 27) in *The Basic Works of Aristotle* ed Richard P. McKeon (New York: Random House 1941) p 527

38 *Politics* (1337 a 41) in *Basic Works* p 1305

39 *Physics* (199 a 16–17) in *Basic Works* p 250

40 Cf *Poetics* 1453 b 1f.

41 *Politics* (1334 b 14–21) in *Basic Works* p 1300

42 *Poetics* 1453 b 9–11, 1453 b 3–7, 1453 b 29–30, 1454 a 6–7. Concerning the contradictions between the last statement and another well-known Aristotelian position – "the change in the hero's fortunes must be not from misery to happiness, but on the contrary from happiness to misery" (1453 a 13–15) – see J. Moles *Classical Quarterly* ns 29 (1979) pp 82ff.

43 *Poetics* 1461 b 12–13, 1460 b 34–5

44 C.H. Whitman's phrasing in *Sophocles: A Study of Heroic Humanism* (Cambridge, Mass: Harvard University Press 1966) p 33. See also Else *Aristotle's Poetics* pp 378 ff.

45 *Poetics* 1454 b 8–14, 1460 b 37 to 1461 a 1

46 Ibid, 1460 b 37 to 1461 a 1

47 Cf L.R. Cresci "Il prologo dell' *Aiace*" *Maia* 26 (1974) 217–25, espec p 222.

48 *Sophocles* p 79

49 Ibid, p 216

50 Here quoted from E.F. Watling's translation, *Electra and Other Plays* (Harmondsworth: Penguin 1978) p 204

51 Cf Lesky *Tragedy* p 121. See also Charles Fuqua "Studies in the Use of Myth in Sophocles' 'Philoctetes' and the 'Orestes' of Euripides" *Traditio* 32 (1976) 29–95, espec pp 32ff.

52 *The Eating of the Gods: An Interpretation of Greek Tragedy* (New York: Random House 1973) p 178

53 Ferguson *Companion* p 224

54 Lesky *Tragedy* p 128

55 *Tragedy* p 10

Euripides: Towards Anti-tragedy

1 See Martin Heidegger *Sein und Zeit* 1 Hälfte (1927) and Rudolf Carnap *Scheinprobleme in der Philosophie* (1928), discussed in my *Offene Formen in der modernen Kunst und Literatur. Zur Entstehung einer neuen Ästhetik* (München: Goldmann 1975) p 86f.

2 Kirk and Raven *Presocratic Philosophers* pp 270, 273

3 *The Older Sophists* ed Rosamond K. Sprague (Columbia, SC: University of South Carolina Press 1972) p 42

4 *The Sophists* (Cambridge: Cambridge University Press 1971) pp 193–4

5 See Guthrie *Sophists* passim; Friedrich Solmsen *Intellectual Experiments of the Greek*

Enlightenment (Princeton, NJ: Princeton University Press 1975) pp 24ff and passim; see also Peter W. Rose's recent attempt to trace the connections between "Sophocles' *Philoctetes* and the Teachings of the Sophists" *Harvard Studies in Classical Philology* 80 (1976) 49–105.

6 Quoted in Guthrie *Sophists* p 232

7 Anecdote reported in Dodds *Progress* p 84

8 *The Laws* trans Trevor J. Saunders (Harmondsworth: Penguin 1978) p 445. See also Dodds *Greeks* pp 223f.

9 *Laws* p 310. See also *The Republic* trans Desmond Lee (Harmondsworth: Penguin 1979) pp 157 (398).

10 *Tragedy* p 68

11 *Catastrophe Survived: Euripides' Plays of Mixed Reversal* (Oxford: Clarendon Press 1971) p 222. Without employing the terms used here, A.P. Burnett's study is largely about Euripides' techniques of audience manipulation. See also C. Fuqua, who, in his essay on *Philoctetes* and *Orestes*, attempts "to show how Sophocles' and Euripides' use of myth goes beyond the immediate adaptation of a particular narrative to the stage and includes a manipulation of the audience's sentiments with regard to the figure as a whole" (*Traditio* 32 [1976] 94).

12 *Sophists* ed Sprague, pp 284, 285–6. For the following see also Charles O. McDonald *The Rhetoric of Tragedy: Form in Stuart Drama* (Boston: University of Massachusetts Press 1966) pp 9ff, 23–39 ("Euripidean Tragedy"); and more recently Joel B. Altman *The Tudor Play of Mind: Rhetorical Inquiry and the Development of Elizabethan Drama* (Berkeley: University of California Press 1978) passim.

13 The present writer remains unconvinced of attempts to date Euripides' *Electra* as prior to Sophocles'; among recent examples of such attempts see Brian Vickers *Towards Greek Tragedy: Drama, Myth, Society* (London: Longman 1973) p 587. In any case, the anteriority of Sophocles' *Electra* to Euripides' is not essential to our argument; Sophocles' *Antigone*, for instance, provided Euripides with a similar model.

14 *A History of Greek Literature* (New York: Columbia University Press 1950) p 95

15 *The Nature of Greek Myths* (Harmondsworth: Penguin 1978) p 103

16 In her introduction to *Electra* (Grene and Lattimore IV.392)

17 Here quoted from *Electra* trans Watling, p 98

18 Ibid, p 86

19 Cf Vickers *Tragedy* p 573, where the author describes Sophocles' *Electra* as following the playwright's "preferred story pattern of 'the solitary figure of heroic integrity refusing to compromise.'"

20 Here quoted from *Electra* trans Watling, pp 101, 102, 114

21 *Mornings in Mexico, Etruscan Places* (Harmondsworth: Penguin 1971) p 62

22 In her introduction to *Electra* (Grene and Lattimore IV.392). See, similarly, Vellacott *Ironic Drama* 20–2; and T. Guardi "La polemica antiapollinea di Euripide" *Pan* 3 (1976) 5–23.

23 In her introduction to *Electra* (Grene and Lattimore IV.392). Cf Charles Fuqua's discussion and partial refutation of the common tendency of "critics of Euripides in

general and the *Orestes* in particular [to feel] that the dramatist is sharply critical of the mythical paradigms he presents" ("The World of Myth in Euripides' *Orestes*" *Traditio* 34 [1978] 4).

24 *Birth* p 51

25 Cf Vickers *Tragedy* pp 174f.

26 Cf Hunger *Lexikon* p 49.

27 *Homeric Hymns* ed T.W. Allen, W.R. Halliday, and E.E. Sikes (London: Oxford University Press 1963) p 33 (ll 300f)

28 Philip E. Slater *The Glory of Hera: Greek Mythology and the Greek Family* (Boston: Beacon Press 1971) pp 139, 137

29 *Themis* (Cleveland: Meridian Books 1962) p 389

Euripides: Towards Post-tragedy

1 Quoted in William Arrowsmith's introduction to *Heracles* (Grene and Lattimore III.266, 267)

2 See Dodds *Greeks* pp 183f.

3 *Birth* p 81

4 *Greeks* p 186

5 *Hesiod and Theognis* trans Dorothea Wender (Harmondsworth: Penguin 1973) p 29, ll 181ff

6 Kirk and Raven *Presocratic Philosophers* p 168

7 Ibid, pp 372, 373

8 Aristophanes *The Wasps. The Poet and the Women. The Frogs* trans David Barrett (Harmondsworth: Penguin 1978) pp 140-1; ll 1102ff

9 *Catastrophe* p 191

10 *Tragedy* p 68

11 Cf Guthrie *Sophists* p 50.

12 *The Politics of Experience and The Bird of Paradise* (Harmondsworth: Penguin 1975) p 74

13 Cf Burnett *Catastrophe* p 204.

14 Kirk and Raven *Presocratic Philosophers* pp 211, 193

15 Cf William K. Wimsatt, Jr & Cleanth Brooks *Literary Criticism: A Short History* (New York: Random House 1957) p 22.

16 Kirk and Raven *Presocratic Philosophers* p 191

17 *Essays* p 351 (2:12)

18 See T.B.L. Webster *The Tragedies of Euripides* (London: Methuen 1967) p 26.

19 For the following I am partly indebted to E.R. Dodds's introduction to his edition of the *Bacchae* (Oxford: Clarendon Press 1944), pp ixff.

20 Cf *The Bacchae by Euripides* ed G.S. Kirk (Englewood Cliffs, NJ: Prentice Hall 1980) p 13.

21 Cf *Bacchae* ed Dodds, pp xxf, xxvf.

22 This is an attitude still held by several contemporary critics. See, for instance, Kott *Eating* pp 220ff; and Vickers *Tragedy* pp 317-18.

23 Ernest Schanzer *The Problem Plays of Shakespeare* (New York: Schocken 1965) p 6. Other than Ernest Schanzer, a considerable number of Shakespeare critics, such as A.C. Sprague, S.L. Bethell, A.P. Rossiter, William Rosen, and Maynard Mack, have analysed Shakespeare's techniques of audience manipulation. See more recently Harold Skulsky *Spirits Finely Touched: The Testing of Value and Integrity in Four Shakespearean Plays* (Athens, Ga: Georgia University Press 1976); E.A.J. Honigmann *Shakespeare: Seven Tragedies – The Dramatist's Manipulation of Response* (London: Macmillan 1976), espec pp 1 ff, 194; and R.L. Nochimson "The End Crowns All: Shakespeare's Deflation of Tragic Possibility in *Antony and Cleopatra*" *English* 26 (1977) 99-132.

24 *Essays* pp 308 (2:12), 298 (2:12), 305 (2:12), 337 (2:12)

Shakespeare: The Theoretical Background

1 See, for instance, G. Wilson Knight *Shakespeare and Religion* (New York: Simon and Schuster 1968) p 179; N. Frye *A Natural Perspective: The Development of Shakespearean Comedy and Romance* (New York: Harcourt, Brace & World 1965) pp 58f.

2 *Shakespeare and the Nature of Man* (New York: Macmillan 1971) p 187

3 *Essays* ed Smith, 2:27. See also J.W.H. Atkins *English Literary Criticism: The Renaissance* (London: Methuen 1947) pp 241f.

4 In *Medieval Heritage of Elizabethan Tragedy* passim

5 See, for instance, Stephen S. Hilliard "Stephen Gosson and the Elizabethan Distrust of the Effects of Drama" *English Literary Renaissance* 9 (1979) 225-39.

6 *Essays* ed Smith, 2:83

7 See Atkins *Criticism* pp 219, 235.

8 *Essays* ed Smith, 1:199

9 See, for instance, *Essays* ed Smith, 1:398-9, as well as E. Schanzer "Shakespeare and the Doctrine of the Unity of Time" *Shakespeare Survey* 28 (1975) 57-61.

10 For more recent interpretations of this famous speech, see K. Muir "Shakespeare's Poets" *Shakespeare the Professional and Related Studies* (London: Heinemann 1973) pp 25-7; S.K. Heninger, Jr *Touches of Sweet Harmony: Pythagorean Cosmology and Renaissance Poetics* (San Marino, Calif: Huntington Library 1974) pp 203f; and *A Midsummer Night's Dream* ed Harold F. Brooks, Arden edn (London: Methuen 1979) pp cxxxviiiff, 103-5, 163.

11 See G.A. Thompson *Elizabethan Criticism of Poetry* (Folcroft, Pa: Folcroft Press 1969) pp 67, 72; and *Essays* ed Smith, 1:71.

12 *Essays* ed Smith, 1:156, 386

13 *The Mirror and the Lamp: Romantic Theory and the Critical Tradition* (New York: Norton 1958) p 274. Abrams's view contrasts with that of C.S. Lewis, who (I think erroneously) describes Sidney's claim that "the poet is a second Creator producing a second Nature" as his "central doctrine" (*English Literature in the Sixteenth Century,*

Excluding Drama [Oxford: Clarendon Press 1962] p 343). See also D.H. Craig "A Hybrid Growth: Sidney's Theory of Poetry in *An Apology for Poetry" English Literary Renaissance"* 10 (1980) 183–201, espec pp 195ff.

14 *Essays* ed Smith,1:486

15 Ibid, 2:238; see also ibid, 2:276. Concerning the general Elizabethan distrust of the imagination, see also R.L. Anderson *Elizabethan Psychology and Shakespeare's Plays* (New York: Russell & Russell 1966) pp 132ff.

16 *Essays* ed Smith, 2:3, 20. See also W. Rossky "Imagination in the English Renaissance: Psychology and Poetic" *Studies in the Renaissance* 5–6 (1958–9) 49–73, espec pp 64ff.

17 *Literary Criticism of Seventeenth-Century England* ed E.W. Tayler (New York: Alfred A. Knopf 1967) p 84

18 *Essays* ed Smith, 2:389

19 *Literary Criticism* ed Tayler, p 101. See also Sara van den Berg " 'The Paths I Meant unto Thy Praise': Jonson's Poem for Shakespeare" *Shakespeare Studies* 11 (1978) 207–18, as well as Joan Rees's interesting attempt to assess Shakespeare's spontaneous creativity from the structure of his plays, *Shakespeare and the Story: Aspects of Creation* (London: Athlone Press 1978) passim.

20 The most complete survey to date is found in David Klein's *The Elizabethan Dramatists as Critics* (London: Peter Owen 1963) pp 243–306.

21 For a detailed interpretation of the Perdita-Polixenes exchange and its underlying dramatic ironies, see E.W. Tayler *Nature and Art in Renaissance Literature* (New York: Columbia University Press 1966) pp 121–41.

22 A claim made by Tayler in *Nature and Art* pp 135–6

23 Cf Erwin Panofsky *Idea: A Concept in Art Theory* (New York: Harper & Row 1968) pp 3ff

24 See Abrams *Mirror* p 122. For a similar, more recent, interpretation of Polixenes' speech see Atkins *Criticism* p 248: "In other words he maintains that the distinction between Nature and art was in itself artificial."

25 *Fables of Identity: Studies in Poetic Mythology* (New York: Harcourt Brace Jovanovich 1963) p 115. Puttenham, it is true, states that the poet, in a certain sense, is "even as nature her selfe working by her owne peculiar vertue and proper instinct and not by example or meditation or exercise as all other artificers do" (*Essays* ed Smith, 2: 191–2). But such creative autonomy has little to do with what Frye misinterprets as the poet's "greatest moments" (*Fables* p 115). Instead, it is only one of the elements of the creative process – "as first to devise his plat or subject, then to fashion his poeme, thirdly to use his metricall proportions" (*Essays* ed Smith, 2:191) – which in every other sense is guided by the conscious craftsmanship of the artist.

26 *Essays* ed Smith, 2:188

27 *Pericles* V. prol. 7

28 *Essays* p 525 (3:5)

29 Cf R. Ellrodt *Shakespeare Survey* 28 (1975) 37.

30 *Essays* pp 101–2 (1:30)

31 Ibid, pp 596 (3:9), 595 (3:9), 126 (1:39), 202 (2:202)

32 Charles Olson *Selected Writings* ed R. Creeley (New York: New Directions 1966) p 16

33 *Essays* pp 596 (3:9), 115 (1:36). See also John Florio's "To the Reader."

34 *Essays* pp 90 (1:27), 15 (1:8). See also I.D. McFarlane "Montaigne and the Concept of the Imagination" *The French Renaissance and Its Heritage, Essays Presented to Alan M. Boase* ed D.R. Haggis et al (London: Methuen 1968) pp 117–37, espec p 133.

35 Cf P. Harvey *The Oxford Companion to English Literature* 3rd edn (Oxford: Clarendon 1953) p 684; Abrams *Mirror* p 266.

36 *Works* ed R.L. Ellis, J. Spedding, and D.D. Heath, 7 vols (London: Longman 1887–92) 3:343. Concerning Bacon's theory of the imagination see Karl R. Wallace *Francis Bacon on the Nature of Man* (Urbana: University of Illinois Press 1967) pp 69–95, espec pp 82ff. Critics widely misrepresent Bacon's theory of poetry and the imagination by failing to see it in the context of Bacon's philosophy in general. See for instance, L.C. Knights, *Explorations* (New York: New York University Press 1964) p 120, who blames Bacon for initiating the dissociation of sensibility, a view challenged by Jeanne Andrewes "Bacon and Dissociation of Sensibility" *Notes and Queries* 199 (1954) 484–6, 530–2. See also J.L. Harrison "Bacon's View of Rhetoric, Poetry, and the Imagination" *Huntington Library Quarterly* 20 (1957) 107–25; James Stephens *Francis Bacon and the Style of Science* (Chicago: University of Chicago Press 1975) p 61; and D.G. James *The Dream of Learning: An Essay on "The Advancement of Learning"* (Oxford: Clarendon 1951) pp 29ff.

37 Cf M.W. Bundy *The Theory of Imagination in Classical and Medieval Thought* (Urbana: University of Illinois Press 1927) pp 242–64; " 'Invention' and 'Imagination' in the Renaissance" *Journal of English and Germanic Philology* 29 (1930) 535–45; and more recently, Frances A. Yates *The Art of Memory* (Harmondsworth: Penguin 1978) pp 45ff; M. Schofield "Aristotle on the Imagination" *Aristotle on Mind and the Senses* ed G.E.R. Lloyd and G.E.L. Owen (Cambridge: Cambridge University Press 1978) pp 99–130.

38 *Works* 3:343

39 *Works* 3:382. Of similar interest with regard to Shakespeare's poetics is Francis Bacon's "elimination of any absolute distinction between that which is natural and that which is artificial," noted by J.A. Mazzeo in *Renaissance and Revolution: The Remaking of European Thought* (New York: Random House 1965) p 192, as well as Bacon's early theorizing about myth. As Paolo Rossi points out, Francis Bacon, in suggesting that the fable preceded the interpretation, anticipated Vico's reassessment of myth as "a form of metaphysics, not rational and abstract like the metaphysics of the learned, but instinctive and imaginative" (Paolo Rossi *Francis Bacon: From Magic to Science* [London: Routledge & Kegan Paul 1968] pp 77, 95).

40 Quoted by Frances A. Yates in *Giordano Bruno and the Hermetic Tradition* (New York: Random House 1969) p 266

41 *De Occulta Philosophia* ed K.A. Nowotny (Graz: Akademische Druck- u Verlagsanstalt 1967) p 328 (3:49). Agrippa's words are borrowed from the *Asclepius*, in *Hermetica* ed Walter Scott, 4 vols (London: Dawsons of Pall Mall 1968) 1:295. See also Yates *Bruno* p 282.

42 See, for instance, Thompson *Elizabethan Criticism* p 83 and passim.

43 *Elizabethan and Metaphysical Imagery* (Chicago: University of Chicago Press 1963) p 37 and passim. See also A.O. Lovejoy "'Nature' as Aesthetic Norm" *Essays in the History of Ideas* (New York: Putnam 1960) pp 69–77; H.S. Wilson "Some Meanings of 'Nature' in Renaissance Literary Theory" *Journal of the History of Ideas* 2 (1941) 430–48.

44 "An Hymn of Heavenly Beauty" *The Shepherd's Calendar and Other Poems* (New York: E.P. Dutton 1932) p 352

45 See Thompson *Elizabethan Criticism* p 83.

46 *Essays* ed Smith, 1:167, 159

47 *Essays* p 324 (2:12)

48 *Works* 3:395

49 *Essays* p 342 (2:12)

50 *Works* 3:395. For a later, more extensive discussion of the four idola than that found in *The Advancement of Learning*, see Bacon's *Novum Organum* (*Works* 4:53ff).

51 *Essays* p 342 (2:12)

52 Ibid, p 328 (2:12)

53 *Works* 3:396

54 *Essays* p 289 (2:12)

55 *Works* 3:396

56 *Essays* p 636 (3:13). For a recent discussion of Montaigne's concept of language with reference to Buchanan's tragedies, see Timothy J. Reiss *Tragedy and Truth: Studies in the Development of a Renaissance and Neoclassical Discourse* (New Haven: Yale University Press 1980) pp 40ff, and especially p 48. Margreta de Grazia, in an otherwise informative essay, "Shakespeare's View of Language: An Historical Perspective" *Shakespeare Quarterly* 29 (1978) 374–88, arrives at what are, in my view, erroneous conclusions concerning her topic by failing to account for Montaigne's deep-rooted scepticism of language as a precedent for Francis Bacon's Idols of the Market Place and a similar distrust of language as found in several of Shakespeare's works.

57 *Essays* p 311 (2:12)

58 *Works* 3:353, 355

59 *Essays* pp 313 (2:12), 596 (3:9)

60 *Works* 3:343, 346

61 Schanzer *Problem Plays* p 6

62 Ibid, pp 108–9

63 *Essays* pp 291 (2:12), 292 (2:12), 637 (3:13)

64 Ibid, pp 637 (3:13), 254 (2:12)

65 *The Anatomy of Melancholy* ed Holbrook Jackson (New York: Random House 1977) 2:60

66 *Essays* p 255 (2:12)

67 *Narrative and Dramatic Sources of Shakespeare* ed G. Bullough, 8 vols (New York: Columbia University Press 1966–75) 7:305. See also W.R. Elton *"King Lear" and the Gods* (San Marino, Calif: Huntington Library 1966) passim.

68 The Arden edition here has "vilde offenses" instead of "vile offenses" (ed Kenneth Muir [London: Methuen 1963] p 156).

69 *Essays* pp 219 (2:6); cf 381 (2:17), 385 (2:18).

70 Ibid, pp 201 (2:2), 195 (2:1), 483 (3:2), 195 (2:1)

71 *Shakespeare Survey* 28 (1975) 42

72 The main text of the Variorum edition here has "That cause sets vp, with, and against thy selfe / By foule authoritie: where reason can reuolt" (ed Harold N. Hillebrand [Philadelphia: J.B. Lippincott 1953] p 277).

73 See, for instance, P. Cruttwell *The Shakespearean Moment* (New York: Random House 1960) pp 24f.

74 *Shakespeare Survey* 28 (1975) 49, 43

75 For the original wording of this sonnet as published in *The Passionate Pilgrim* of 1599, see *The Poems* ed F.T. Prince, Arden edn (London: Methuen 1961) pp 154–5.

76 See *Politics* pp 49ff.

77 Introduction to *The Sonnets*, Signet edn (New York: New American Library 1964) p xxxiv

78 *Anatomy* 3:407, 406–7

From Tragic to Anti-tragic Closure

1 An added reason, though hardly the only one, for Shakespeare to have eliminated such references from his plays may have been an act passed in 1606 "to Restrain Abuses of Players" by prohibiting actors from using the names of God or Jesus either profanely or in jest. See Peter Milward *Shakespeare's Religious Background* (London: Sidgwick & Jackson 1973) p 213.

2 For a similar view of Shakespeare's development, see Spencer *Shakespeare* p 174 and passim.

3 This has been noted by a number of critics since A.C. Bradley (see introduction, p 12). See, for instance, I. Ribner *Patterns in Shakespearean Tragedy* (London: Methuen 1960) p 9: "Tragedy must impose upon the raw material of human experience a pattern in which the relation of human suffering to human joy becomes apparent, and out of this must come the feeling of reconciliation with which every one of Shakespeare's tragedies ends, and which critics of the most divergent views have recognized." Ribner's own bibliographical list includes S.L. Bethell, J.F. Danby, P.N. Siegel, H.S. Wilson, and J. Vyvyan among "Christian" and D.G. James, A. Sewell, and G. Bush among "secular" critics.

4 See, for instance, G. Wilson Knight "*King Lear* and the Comedy of the Grotesque" (1930) in *King Lear: A Casebook* ed Frank Kermode (London: Macmillan 1974) pp 118–36; and Kott *Shakespeare Our Contemporary* pp 127–68.

5 Quoted in *Lear: A Casebook* ed Kermode, pp 29,30, 36, 44

6 *Tragedy* p 135

7 Cf John Shaw "*King Lear*: The Final Lines" *Essays in Criticism* 16 (1966) 261–7.

8 For critical discussion of the time-honoured controversy as to whether Lear's last words signify redemption or despair, see, for instance, Judah Stampfer "The Catharsis of *King Lear*" *Shakespeare Survey* 13 (1960) 1–10; Nicholas Brooke "The Ending of *King*

Lear" *Shakespeare 1564–1964* ed E.A. Bloom (Providence: Brown University Press 1964) pp 71–87; and John Reibetanz *The Lear World: A Study of King Lear in Its Dramatic Context* (Toronto: University of Toronto Press 1977) pp 108ff.

9 *Majesty and Magic in Shakespeare's Last Plays: A New Approach to Cymbeline, Henry VIII, and The Tempest* (Boulder: Shambhala Publications 1978)

10 Quoted by Sylvan Barnet in the Signet edition of *Titus Andronicus* p xxiii

11 *Sources* ed Bullough, 1:274

12 Ibid, 1:284, 285, 299 (1 500), 308 (1 859), 320 (1 1328), 329 (1 1669), 326 (ll 1546–8)

13 Cf H.B. Charlton *Shakespearean Tragedy* (London: Cambridge University Press 1948) p 75, who, I think, underestimates the way in which Shakespeare changed Brooke's emphasis on Fortune into one on Fate. See also *Sources* ed Bullough, 1:277.

14 *Sources* ed Bullough, 1:310 (1 949)

15 *Poetics* 1461 b 11–12

16 Concerning the possible links between *Romeo and Juliet* and the post-Aristotelian concept of tragedy as evolved by G. Cinthio, see H.B. Charlton *Senecan Tradition in Renaissance Tragedy* (Folcroft, Pa: Folcroft Press 1969) pp lxxixff.

17 *Sources* ed Bullough, 1:297 (1 428); cf pp 301 (ll 608–10), 315 (1 1118), 326 (1 1562), 341 (1 2168), 361 (1 2929)

18 *Problem Plays* p 6. See also Honigmann *Shakespeare* pp 30ff.

19 Cf McDonald *Rhetoric* pp 122–37 ("The Rhetoric of *Hamlet*"). See also Sister Miriam Joseph *Shakespeare's Use of the Arts of Language* (New York: New York University Press 1949) pp 190ff.

20 *Essays* p 380 (2:17)

21 Quoted by F.E. Halliday *A Shakespeare Companion 1564–1964* (Harmondsworth: Penguin 1964) pp 501–3

22 *Notes* p 216

23 *Magiae Naturalis Libri* (Neapoli 1589)

24 *Shakespeare* pp 109–21

25 "*Troilus and Cressida* Reconsidered" *University of Toronto Quarterly* 32 (Jan 1963) 142–54; see also *Shakespeare: The Dark Comedies to the Last Plays: From Satire to Celebration* (Charlotteville: University Press of Virginia 1971) pp 43–62.

26 Cf R.A. Foakes *University of Toronto Quarterly* 32 (Jan 1963) 142f, whose conclusions from the textual evidence, however, differ from those presented here. See also Ralph Berry *The Shakespearean Metaphor: Studies in Language and Meaning* (London: Macmillan 1978) pp 85f.

27 The main text of the Variorum edition here has "Coole statues" instead of "Cold statues" (p 313).

28 Epistle in 1609 Quarto (2nd state), quoted by Halliday *Shakespeare Companion* p 502

29 *Shakespeare* p 121

30 *Sources* ed Bullough, 7:318–19

31 Ibid, 7:317, 389, 377, 384

32 Reibetanz *Lear World* pp 112–13

33 Quoted in *Lear: A Casebook* ed Kermode, pp 38, 36

34 Cf John Holloway *The Story of the Night: Studies in Shakespeare's Major Tragedies* (London: Routledge & Kegan Paul 1961) pp 85f.

35 The Arden edition here has "to out-storm" instead of "to outscorn" (p 102).

36 Cf *Essays* pp 260ff (2:12).

37 Quoted by Spencer *Shakespeare* p 38

38 *Sources* ed Bullough, 7:404, 406

39 Ribner *Patterns* p 66

40 S.L. Bethell *Shakespeare and the Popular Dramatic Tradition* (London: Staples Press 1944) p 145

Hamlet, or the Slave-Moralist Turned Ascetic Priest

1 Here as elsewhere in this chapter, the term "Hell" is meant to comprise both Hell and Purgatory.

2 The Arden edition here has "With tristful visage, as against the doom" (ed Edward Dowden [London: Methuen 1938] p 139).

3 Cf A. Alvarez *The Savage God: A Study of Suicide* (Harmondsworth: Penguin 1975) p 175.

4 *Pelican Freud Library* ed Richards, 4:366f

5 Avi Ehrlich *Hamlet's Absent Father* (Princeton NJ: Princeton University Press 1977) p 24

6 Cf Norman N. Holland *Psychoanalysis and Shakespeare* (New York: McGraw-Hill 1966) pp 166ff; and Theodore Lidz *Hamlet's Enemy: Madness and Myth in Hamlet* (New York: Basic Books 1975) pp 9ff.

7 *Pelican Freud Library* ed Richards, 4:367, 368. Ernest Jones, by way of trying to solve the same question, simply appeals to "Shakespeare's extraordinary powers of observation and penetration," which "granted him a degree of insight that it has taken the world three subsequent centuries to reach" (*Hamlet and Oedipus* [Garden City NY: Doubleday 1955] p 76).

8 *Selected Essays* pp 146, 143, 145

9 *Shakespearean Tragedy: Its Art and Its Christian Premises* (Bloomington: Indiana University Press 1969) pp 244ff

10 For a variant reading of "sullied" – ie, "solid" – see the Variorum edition, ed Horace Howard Furness (Philadelphia: J.B. Lippincott 1905) p 41. See also Arden edn, ed Dowden, p 21.

11 (New York: Da Capo Press 1969) p 129

12 See G. Bateson, D.D. Jackson, J. Haley, and J. Weakland "Toward a Theory of Schizophrenia" *Behavioral Science* 1 (1956) 251–64.

13 *La Divina Commedia* ed C.H. Grandgent, rev Charles S. Singleton (Cambridge Mass: Harvard University Press 1972) p 28

14 *De Spectaculis* trans T.R. Glover, Loeb Classical Library (Cambridge Mass: Harvard University Press 1960) p 299

15 Eleanor Prosser's results in investigating Shakespeare's use of Christian doctrine in *Hamlet* speak for themselves on this point: "In order to gain perspective, I turned to the medieval mystery cycles, and over a period of several years, worked up to 1610, reading every play that might be relevant. When I came to the revenge plays, I was thrust back into the Hamlet quandary. My survey revealed not one example of a noble revenger who sought the damnation of his victim, not one example of a play in which revenge was clearly portrayed as a moral duty" (*Hamlet and Revenge* 2nd edn [Stanford Calif: Stanford University Press 1971] pp xi–xii).

16 See also V.ii.48: "Why, even in that was heaven ordinant."

17 See W. Clemen *The Development of Shakespeare's Imagery* (London: Methuen 1966) pp 113ff.

18 Quoted in *Hamlet* ed C. Hoy (New York: Norton 1963) p 147

19 Cf L.C. Knights's comments on Hamlet's treatment of Ophelia in *An Approach to "Hamlet"* (London: Chatto & Windus 1960) p 64: "What he says to her in the 'get thee to a nunnery' scene and in the play scene can only be described in D.H. Lawrence's terms as 'doing dirt on sex.' "

20 For a detailed study of these themes see P.J. Aldus *Mousetrap: Structure and Meaning in Hamlet* (Toronto: University of Toronto Press 1977) pp 68–84, 148–75, and passim.

21 See also B.R. Pollin "Hamlet, a Successful Suicide" *Shakespeare Studies* 1 (1965) 240–60; and E. Jones *Hamlet and Oedipus* (Garden City NY: Doubleday 1955) p 100.

22 See *Gesta Danorum* I.31, discussed in H.R. Ellis Davidson *Gods and Myths of Northern Europe* (Harmondsworth: Penguin 1974) pp 149, 152.

23 Concerning Montaigne's influence on Shakespeare and its dating, see Max Deutschbein "Shakespeare's *Hamlet* und Montaigne" *Shakespeare-Jahrbuch* 80–1 (1944–5) 70–107; and R. Ellrodt "Self-consciousness in Montaigne and Shakespeare" *Shakespeare Survey* 28 (1975) 37–50.

24 *Essays* p 255 (2:12), 3 (1:2)

25 Concerning Nietzsche's interpretation of *Hamlet* in *The Birth of Tragedy*, section VII, see William R. Brashear "Nietzsche and Spengler on *Hamlet*: An Elaboration and Synthesis" *Comparative Drama* 5, no 2 (Summer 1971) 106–16.

26 *Totem and Taboo* pp 156–7

27 *Genealogy* pp 170, 226

28 *Hamlet and Revenge* p 137

29 *Genealogy* pp 183, 226

30 Ibid, p 226

31 Ibid, pp 165, 172, 299

32 Ibid, p 173

33 *The Will to Power* trans W. Kaufmann and R.J. Hollingdale (New York: Random House 1968) p 202

34 *Genealogy* p 172

35 Cf ibid, p 183.

36 *Twilight of the Idols and The Anti-Christ* trans R.J. Hollingdale (Harmondsworth: Penguin 1974) pp 132, 150

37 *Genealogy* p 263

38 *Will to Power* p 190

39 *Genealogy* p 186

40 *Beyond Good and Evil: Prelude to a Philosophy of the Future* trans Walter Kaufmann (New York: Random House 1966) p 75; see also ibid, pp 129, 221.

41 As shown by Nietzsche's casual and unspecific references to *Hamlet* in his later works; see, for instance, *Will To Power* p 468.

42 Concerning Dostoyevsky's borrowings from and interest in *Hamlet*, see Eleanor Rowe *Hamlet: A Window on Russia* (New York: New York University Press 1976) pp 83–93; Konstantin Mochulsky *Dostoyevsky: His Life and Work* trans Michael A. Minihan (Princeton NJ: Princeton University Press 1971) p 248; and Stanley Cooperman "Shakespeare's Anti-Hero: Hamlet and the Underground Man" *Shakespeare Studies* I (1965) 37–63.

43 Cf *Selected Letters* ed and trans Christopher Middleton (Chicago: University of Chicago Press 1969) p 261. Concerning Nietzsche's discovery of and relation to Dostoyevsky, see W. Kaufmann *Nietzsche: Philosopher, Psychologist, Antichrist* (Princeton, NJ: Princeton University Press 1974) pp 340–1.

44 *Twilight* p 99

45 *Will To Power* pp 248, 87–8

46 *Notes from Underground and The Double* trans Jessie Coulson (Harmondsworth: Penguin 1976) pp 25–6, 21, 55, 20

47 Ibid, pp 22, 100

48 Ibid, pp 23, 41

49 *Will To Power* p 166

50 *Notes* pp 18–19

51 *Genealogy* p 170

52 *Notes* pp 115, 115–16

53 *Genealogy* p 262

54 *Notes* p 91

55 Ibid, pp 90, 100, 101, 107

56 Ibid, p 20

57 Ibid

58 Ibid, p 21

59 *Genealogy* p 190

60 Ibid

61 *Notes* pp 21, 22, 119, 33

62 T.S. Eliot *Essays* p 143

63 See, for instance, G. Wilson Knight's and Northrop Frye's comments re Kālidāsa's *Sacontalá* and Shakespeare's romances mentioned in an annotation to page 76 above.

64 Cf Carol Gesner, *Shakespeare and Greek Romance* (Lexington: University of Kentucky Press 1970), who in chapter four, "The Critical Tradition," sums up critical attempts to describe the romances as providing us with a "vision beyond the scope of tragedy, a vision which accepts the tragic and evil elements in life, but refuses to admit them as

final, sees such negative elements as no more than a transient stage in the everlasting cycle of birth, death, and rebirth" (p 81).

The Post-tragic Vision of Romance

1 The rebirth imagery of the romances, although analysed by several critics, is widely misinterpreted as pointing towards the Christian resurrection. See, for instance, G. Wilson Knight *The Crown of Life* (London: Methuen 1961) passim; see also Northrop Frye: "But the only one of the four romances in which I suspect any explicit – which means allegorical – references to Christianity is *Cymbeline*. Cymbeline was king of Britain at the birth of Christ, and in such scenes as the Jailer's speculations about death and his wistful 'I would we were all of one mind, and that mind good,' there are hints that some far-reaching change in the human situation is taking place off-stage" (*Fables* p 112). While Frye fails to mention Polixenes' references to hereditary sin and to Jesus Christ in *The Winter's Tale* (I.ii.70ff, 420), his own examples from *Cymbeline* can hardly be said to amount to "explicit" references to Christianity.

2 This is even more obvious in comparison with Hero's epitaph in *Much Ado About Nothing* V.iii. which in Shakespeare's *oeuvre* before the romances provides the most striking precedent for the rebirth symbolism deployed around a person erroneously thought dead as well as for such symbolism in general: "Done to death by slanderous tongues / Was the Hero that here lies. / Death, in guerdon of her wrongs, / Gives her fame which never dies. / So the life that died with shame / Lives in death with glorious fame." See also *Sources* ed Bullough, 8:132.

3 *Essays* pp 39 (1:19), 262 (2:12), 625 (3:12), 619 (3:12), 631 (3:12)

4 Ibid, p 409 (2:30)

5 Similarly, Time, the chorus in *The Winter's Tale*, is clearly presented as the preserver and destroyer in one. He causes "both joy and terror," plants and overwhelms custom, etc. It seems wrong, therefore, to associate him with Spenser's *Mutability Cantos* with their distinctly Christian and teleological orientation, as does Frank Kermode in his introduction to the Signet edition (p xxvii).

6 *Essays* pp 351 (2:12), 46 (1:21)

7 See last chapter, "Tragedy and Psychology," below.

8 *Essays* p 628 (3:12)

9 Ibid, p 310 (2:12)

10 Ibid, pp 300 (2:12), 351 (2:12)

11 Thomas Aquinas's words are: "In cognitionem aeternitatis oportet nos venire per tempus"; quoted in K. Rahner *Zur Theologie der Zukunft* (München: Deutscher Taschenbuch Verlag 1971) p 69.

12 *Essays* p 351 (2:351)

13 We shall not here discuss the curious fact that acts III, IV, and V, as most critics agree, seem to be substantially Shakespeare's, while acts I and II are not. However, the consistent rebirth symbolism found throughout *Pericles* strongly suggests Shake-

speare's hand in all parts of the play. The playwright, on the other hand, may have been well content with letting acts I and II stand largely untouched for the sake of contrast, regardless of whether they derive from an earlier play or a collaborator. See my discussion below.

14 *Sources* ed Bullough, 6:399

15 Ibid, 6:421, 434, 472, 466, 458

16 Ibid, 6:467, 406, 454

17 Ibid, 6:417, 471

18 Cf ibid, 6:378, 428.

19 Ibid, 6:452

20 Ibid, 6:399, 447

21 See Yates *Majesty* p 91; *Bruno* p 39.

22 In the Arden edition this passage reads: "I heard of an Egyptian / That had nine hours lien dead, / Who was by good appliance recovered" (ed F.D. Hoeniger [London: Methuen 1963] pp 90–1). As Hoeniger notes, however, "most modern edd. agree that the passage is corrupt and that the original spoke of Egyptian physicians rather than of an Egyptian patient" (ibid). See also E. Schanzer's comments in his introduction to the Signet *Pericles*, p xxiii.

23 The Arden edition here has "All faults that name, nay, that hell knows" instead of "All faults that have a name, nay, that hell knows" (ed J.M. Nosworthy [London: Methuen 1964] p 76).

24 *Shakespeare's Comedies* (Oxford: Clarendon Press 1960) pp 217, 227. See also Barbara A. Mowat *The Dramaturgy of Shakespeare's Romances* (Athens: University of Georgia Press 1976) pp 78ff.

25 The main text of the Variorum edition here has "fourth rights" instead of "forthright's" (ed H.H. Furness [Philadelphia: J.B. Lippincott 1892] p 174).

From *King Lear* to *The Two Noble Kinsmen*

1 Reibetanz *Lear World* p 116. See also R.W. Uphaus "Shakespearean Tragedy and the Intimations of Romance" *The Centennial Review* 22 (1978) 299–318, espec p 307; and Leo Salingar "Romance in *King Lear*" *English* 27 (1978) 5–20.

2 *Shakespearean Tragedy* (London: Macmillan 1956) p 252.

3 See Stanley Wells "Shakespeare and Romance" *Stratford-upon-Avon Studies* 8 (London: Edward Arnold 1966) pp 49–79.

4 *Sources* ed Bullough, 8:156, 199

5 See B. Evans *Shakespeare's Comedies* pp 296ff; and also D.M. Bergeron "The Restoration of Hermione in *The Winter's Tale*" *Shakespeare's Romances Reconsidered* ed C.M. Kay and H.E. Jacobs (Lincoln: University of Nebraska Press 1978) pp 125–33.

6 The Arden edition here has "Again possess her corpse, and on this stage / (Were we offenders now) appear soul-vex'd, / And begin 'Why to me?'" (ed J.H.P. Pafford [London: Methuen 1963] p 138).

7 *Hippolyta's View: Some Christian Aspects of Shakespeare's Plays* (Lexington: University of Kentucky Press 1961) p 222

8 *Shakespeare and Religion* (New York: Simon and Schuster 1968) pp 235, 234; see also R.M. Frye *Shakespeare and Christian Doctrine* (Princeton NJ: Princeton University Press 1963) pp 37ff.

9 Yates *Majesty* p 90

10 For a similar view of the romances, see Clifford Leech "The Structure of the Last Plays" *Shakespeare Survey* 11 (1958) 19–30; and Mowat *Dramaturgy* pp 95–110.

11 *Labyrinths* p 207

12 Jan Kott (*Shakespeare Our Contemporary* p 337) speaks of the "law of repetition" determining the play's structure.

13 *Corpus Hermeticum: The Divine Pymander and other Writings of Hermes Trismegistus* trans John D. Chambers (New York: Samuel Weiser 1975) pp 69, 83, 29; for the original Greek text and English translation, see *Hermetica* ed Scott, I:208, 209, 232, 233, 148, 149.

14 Concerning this and other themes involving dichotomies (eg, art–nature, artistic illusion–reality), the romances seem to propose a both-and monism, or *coincidentia oppositorum* of paradox. See also Mowat *Dramaturgy* pp 111ff; and Righter *Idea of the Play* pp 172ff.

15 For the following see E. Schanzer "The Structural Pattern of *The Winter's Tale*" *A Review of English Literature* 5 (1964) 72–82; and Philip M. Weinstein "An Interpretation of Pastoral in *The Winter's Tale*" *Shakespeare Quarterly* 22 (1971) 97–109: "My point, of course, is not that *The Winter's Tale* is uniformly obsessed with death and the passage of time - in Act IV, scene iv, as well as elsewhere - but rather that the Pastoral Scene in no way avoids these matters, as critics tend to avoid them in their reading of the scene" (p 99).

16 "*The Two Noble Kinsmen*" *Modern Philology* 36 (1939) 276

17 A variant reading of this song has "With her bells dim" instead of "With harebells dim" (John Fletcher and William Shakespeare *The Two Noble Kinsmen* ed G.R. Proudfoot [London: Edward Arnold 1970] p 7).

18 *Complete Works* ed W.W. Skeat (London: Oxford University Press 1957) p 432

19 "On the Design of *The Two Noble Kinsmen*" *A Review of English Literature* 5 (1964) 105

Goethe's Transcendence of Tragedy

1 *Tragedy* ed Corrigan, p 390

2 *Tragedy* p 51

3 *Tragedy* ed Corrigan, p 78

4 *Briefe* Hamburger Ausgabe, 4 vols (Hamburg: Christian Wegner Verlag 1967) 4:458

5 Ibid, 2:140

6 Ibid, 4:401

7 *Werke* 4:401

8 Ibid

9 *Poetics* 1451 a 32-4, 1451 b 33

10 *The Poems* ed K. Allott (London: Longmans 1965) p 599

11 *Sanskrit Drama* pp 280ff

12 *Urfaust, Faust I und II, Paralipomena, Goethe über "Faust"* ed W. Dietze (Berlin: Aufbau Verlag 1973) p 584

13 Cf K. Mommsen *Goethe und 1001 Nacht* (Berlin: Akademie Verlag 1960) pp 186, 301.

14 *Urfaust* p 584

15 Cf Pandey *Indian Aesthetics* pp 30ff.

16 *Poetics* 1451 a 32-3

17 P. Lal's phrase in *Great Sanskrit Plays in Modern Translation* (New York: New Directions, nd) p xvii

18 *Nāṭyaśāstra* trans Manomohan Ghosh (Calcutta: Granthalaya 1967) pp 14, 109, 138-9, 146, 242

19 Kālidāsa *Sacontalá; or, The Fatal Ring: An Indian Drama by Calidás* trans Sir William Jones (London: Edwards of Pall Mall 1789) pp 8, 12

20 *Poetics* 1460 a 26-7

21 *Sacontalá* p 64

22 *Urfaust* p 464

23 *Werke* 9:414

24 *Urfaust* p 543

25 *Werke* 12:688

26 *Urfaust* pp 543, 541, 754, 431

27 *Politics* 1337 a 41; *Basic Works* p 1305

28 *Urfaust* p 439

29 *Selected Writings* p 116

30 *Urfaust* p 57

31 Ibid, p 548

32 Even K. Krishnamoorthy, although well aware of the impact Kālidāsa had on Goethe, comes to the conclusion that there "can be no likeness in detail between a German apostle of modern culture and an Indian poet who wrote at least fifteen centuries later" (*Kālidāsa* [New York: Twayne Publishers 1972] p 130).

33 *Das Vorspiel auf dem Theater* etc (Bonn: H. Bouvier 1969). See also O. Seidlin "Ist das 'Vorspiel auf dem Theater' ein Vorspiel zu 'Faust'?" *Euphorion: Zeitschrift für Literaturgeschichte* 46 (1952) 307-14, espec p 313.

34 *Sacontalá* p 1

35 *Urfaust* p 430

36 Ibid, p 548; cf p 638.

37 Ibid, pp 464, 589, 571

38 Ibid, pp 472, 542, 463, 561, 593, 566, 563

39 *Werke* 12:343-4

40 *Tragedy* ed Corrigan, p 78

41 "Tragedy and the Whole Truth" *Selected Essays* ed H. Raymond (London: Chatto and Windus 1967) p 118

42 See Lal *Sanskrit Plays* p xvii; and Pandey *Indian Aesthetics* pp 73, 95, and passim.

43 *Werke* 12:343

44 *Urfaust* p 556

45 Ibid

46 *Werke* 12:343

47 *Sacontala* p 80

48 Ibid, pp 29, 47

49 Ibid, pp 8, 9, 48

50 Ibid, pp 64, 77, 75

51 Ibid, p 87

52 *Urfaust* pp 471, 504

53 D.T. Suzuki *Mysticism: Christian and Buddhist* (Westport Conn: Greenwood Press 1975) p 28

54 Dionysius the Areopagite *The Divine Names and the Mystical Theology* trans C.E. Rolt (London: Lewis Reprints 1975) p 60

55 Cf *Urfaust* p 705.

56 See Yates *Bruno* pp 125, 177.

57 See R.C. Zimmermann *Das Weltbild des jungen Goethe: Studien zur hermetischen Tradition des 18. Jahrhunderts* (München: Fink Verlag 1969) pp 48, 108, 122.

58 *Urfaust* p 566

59 Cf ibid, pp 549, 572–4, etc.

60 *Werke* 12:301

61 *Myths and Symbols in Indian Art and Civilization* ed J. Campbell, Bollingen Series 6 (Princeton NJ: Princeton University Press 1972) pp 213, 215

62 *Werke* 12:227

63 *Urfaust* p 589

64 *Paradiso* 30:40–2, ed Mario Marcazzan, Lectura Dantis Scaligera (Florence: Felice le Monnier 1971) p 1094

65 The resemblances here are far more striking than those between *Faust* and the "fourteenth century frescos of the Camposanto in Pisa depicting the Triumph of Death, the Last Judgment, and Hell," which are widely acknowledged as the source of Goethe's heavenly scenario. See *Faust: A Tragedy* ed Cyrus Hamlin (New York: Norton 1976) pp 295, 615.

66 *Sacontala* pp 88, 86–87

67 *Werke* 12:301

68 *Briefe* 4:401–2

69 *Werke* 12:301

70 *Sacontala* pp 72, 92

71 *Urfaust* p 489

72 *Sacontala* pp 88, 98

Tragedy and Psychology

1 *Poetics* 1453 b 6–7. Cf Else *Aristotle's Poetics* p 441.

2 *Towards a Poor Theater* (New York: Simon and Schuster 1968) p 204

3 *The Theater and Its Double* (New York: Grove Press 1958) pp 54, 60, 76, 77

4 *Naked Masks: Five Plays* ed Eric Bentley (New York: E.P. Dutton 1952) p 367

5 *Death of a Salesman: Text and Criticism* ed G. Weales (New York: Viking Press 1967) p 150

6 *Naked Masks* pp 364–5, 371, 367

7 Ibid, pp 223, 260

8 Ibid, pp 239, 274, 276

9 *Poetics* 1451 a 32–4

10 *Naked Masks* p 374

11 *Death* ed Weales, pp 185, 171

12 *Naked Masks* pp 371, 367

13 *Death* ed Weales, p 149

14 *Naked Masks* p 267

15 Ibid

16 *Death* ed Weales, pp 167, 93

17 Cf *Death* ed Weales, p 94, with *Oedipus Rex* ll 711ff.

18 *An Outline of Psycho-Analysis* trans James Strachey (New York: Norton 1969) p 36

19 *Death* ed Weales, p 158

20 Ibid, pp 37, 38, 39, 40

21 Ibid, p 109

22 Miller maintains that he "was little better than ignorant of Freud's teachings when [he] wrote" *Death of a Salesman* (ibid, p 161).

23 *The Primal Scream* (New York: Dell 1974) p 97

24 *Bioenergetics* (Harmondsworth: Penguin 1975) pp 43, 327

25 *Pelican Freud Library* ed Richards, 3:380, 387; 8:47

26 Ibid, 3:57, 44

27 *Totem and Taboo* pp 156–7

28 Cf *The Origins of Psycho-Analysis: Letters to Wilhelm Fliess, Drafts and Notes: 1887–1902* ed Marie Bonaparte et al (New York: Basic Books 1954) p 223.

29 *Pelican Freud Library* ed Richards, 4:362–3. For a detailed analysis of Freud's *Oedipus* interpretation in *Die Traumdeutung*, see Cynthia Chase "Oedipal Textuality: Reading Freud's Reading of Oedipus" *Diacritics* 9 (1979) 54–68. The author, however, seems to me to derive erroneous conclusions from misinterpreting Oedipus's self-blinding as an act of repression (see p 57).

30 *Pelican Freud Library* ed Richards, 4:364

31 "Taboo in the Oedipus Theme" *Oedipus Tyrannus* trans and ed L. Berkowitz and T.F. Brunner (New York: Norton 1970) p 63

32 *Pelican Freud Library* ed Richards, 4:363

33 See *The New Columbia Encyclopedia* ed W.H. Harris and J.S. Levey (New York: Columbia University Press 1975) p 752.

34 *Poetics* 1452 a 18, 1451 a 33–4

35 *Pelican Freud Library* ed Richards, 4:363; 8:47; 3:393

36 Ibid, 3:393

37 *Poetics* 1453 b 3–7

38 *Happenings: An Illustrated Anthology* (New York: E.P. Dutton 1966) p 34

39 *Theater* p 119

40 Ibid, p 102

41 Ibid, pp 82, 140, 135, 133, 135

42 Ibid, pp 72, 60, 103

43 *Poetics* 1451 a 32–3

44 See Lal *Sanskrit Plays* p xvii. See also my *"Faust* and *Sacontala'" Comparative Literature* 31, no 4 (Fall 1979) 373.

45 *Werke. Zürcher Ausgabe* ed Arthur Hübscher, 10 vols (Zürich: Diogenes Verlag 1977) 2:472, 1:318–19

46 Nietzsche *Birth* p 12

47 *Werke. Kritische Gesamtausgabe* ed G. Colli and M. Montinari (Berlin: de Gruyter 1972) pt 3, vol 1, 115

48 *Birth* pp 133, 120, 108, 23, 67, 143

49 Ibid, p 102

50 *Poor Theatre* p 206

51 Ibid pp 46, 45, 123

52 Ibid, pp 235, 236, 204

53 Ibid, pp 208–9

Conclusion

1 *Roman* pp 70, 131

2 *Caligula & Three Other Plays* trans Stuart Gilbert (New York: Random House 1958) p vii

3 *Le mythe de Sisyphe* (Paris: Gallimard 1943) pp 166–7

4 "Forgers of Myths" *Playwrights on Playwriting* ed Toby Cole (New York: Hill and Wang 1961) p 119

5 *Roman* p 131

6 *Waiting* p 54

7 Ibid, pp 42, 59

Index